G U R

RELIGION

Gods, Priestly Powers, and Cosmic Truths

By Janet Naylor and Caroline Julian

**Additional material by Robert Gilson,
Scott D. Haring, and Virginia Nelson**

Edited by Susan Pinsonneault, with Loyd Blankenship
Cover by Pat Morrissey
Illustrated by Jean Elizabeth Martin
Additional illustrations by Laura Eisenhour and Jeff Koke

GURPS System Design: Steve Jackson
GURPS Line Editor: Sean Punch
GURPS Project Manager: Steven Marsh
Chief Executive Officer: Philip Reed
Chief Creative Officer: Sam Mitschke
Chief Operating Officer: Susan Bueno
Page Layout and Typography: Jeff Koke
Interior and Color Production: Jeff Koke
Prepress Assistance: Monica Stephens
Creative Direction: Phil Reed
GURPS FAQ Maintainer: Vicky "Molokh" Kolenko
Director of Sales: Ross Jepson

Playtesters: Philip Bardaville, Drew Bittner, Chris J. Burke, J.C. Connors, Debbie Denes, David Dotson, Shawn Fisher, Michael S. Fox, Richard Gilson, David Gross, David Haren, Andrew Hartsock, Glen Irwin, David Johnston, John Kullman, Don Lamb, Elizabeth McCoy, Larry Nutt, John C. Post, George Rickle, Tony Ridlon, Tim Robinson, David Q. Spitzley, David Summers, Daniel U. Thibault, Michael Wallace, and Tom Zunder

Softcover: stock # 01-6078 • ISBN 978-1-55634-921-8 • PDF: stock # 30-6510 • Version 4.0 – November 2020

STEVE JACKSON GAMES

CONTENTS

INTRODUCTION

About GURPS

Steve Jackson Games is committed to full support of ***GURPS*** players. We can be reached by email: **info@sjgames.com**. Our address is SJ Games, P.O. Box 18957, Austin, TX 78760. Resources include:

New supplements and adventures. ***GURPS*** continues to grow – see what's new at **gurps.sjgames.com**.

Warehouse 23. Our online store offers ***GURPS*** print items, plus PDFs of our books, supplements, adventures, play aids, and support . . . including exclusive material available only on Warehouse 23! Just head over to **warehouse23.com**.

Pyramid (**pyramid.sjgames.com**). For 10 years, our PDF magazine *Pyramid* included new rules and articles for ***GURPS***, plus systemless locations, adventures, and much more. The entire 122-issue library is available at Warehouse 23!

Internet. To discuss ***GURPS*** with our staff and your fellow gamers, visit our forums at **forums.sjgames.com**. You can also join us at **facebook.com/sjgames** or **twitter.com/sjgames**. Share your brief campaign teasers with #GURPShook on Twitter. Or explore that hashtag for ideas to add to your own game! The web page for ***GURPS Religion*** can be found at **gurps.sjgames.com/books/religion**.

Store Finder (**storefinder.sjgames.com**): Discover nearby places to buy ***GURPS*** items and other Steve Jackson Games products. Local shops are great places to play our games and meet fellow gamers!

Bibliographies. Bibliographies are a great resource for finding more of what you love! We've added them to many ***GURPS*** book web pages, with links to help you find the next perfect element for your game.

Errata. Everyone makes mistakes, including us – but we do our best to fix our errors. Errata pages for ***GURPS*** releases are at **sjgames.com/errata/gurps**.

Questions about who we are, where we come from, how the world works, and so on, are the source of myth. Stories about gods and heroes, monsters darker and more fearful than any that might crawl out of the night – myths fascinated, entertained and comforted our ancestors. These stories provided explanations for the workings of things, for each person's place in the world, and even for disasters and good fortune. Because myths offer explanations of the divine and the supernatural, they form the backbone of most religions. People gather to hear and retell myths, to pray in a set fashion, to act out mythical events in remembrance. Eventually traditions of worship develop. In time, the true meaning behind the ritual may be forgotten. New ways are often found to glorify and serve the divine and these are added to the growing repertoire of religious rites. Like people of the real world, people of game worlds will have their own beliefs, their own answers to the basic questions of life. And most likely they will have religion, be it based in mysticism and superstition, or rational science and fact.

Religion and its associated mythology can add depth to a campaign setting – a richer texture of potential conflicts and the source of fervently-held beliefs. Legends and myths can provide history, magical places and treasures and even hints to solving current problems. Churches can send their clerics and followers on particular quests and missions. And a strong basis of faith can strengthen any character concept, providing moral and ethical codes of behavior, and allowing for all sorts of interesting roleplaying potential.

This book is organized into three sections. The first section discusses the creation of religions – the formulation of the cosmos, myths, deities and religions themselves. The second deals directly with rules for clerical (or religious) characters, including three different systems for handling divinely-inspired magics. The last section presents a series of sample religions, drawing on the information in earlier chapters.

One need only consider history to see the importance of religion in this world. Detailed game worlds are no different. Whether the genre be fantasy, space, horror, historical or something else again, religion will play a part!

About the Authors

Caroline Julian

Caroline lives in Toronto, Ontario, where she works as the Games and Imports manager for the Silver Snail. She holds BSc honors from the University of Toronto in anthropology and archeology, and has worked for the Ministry of Citizenship and Culture on local salvage digs. She collects everything: fiction and reference books, alternative comics, games, ceramics, original art, miniature figures, mugs, Japanese animation, thimbles, tins, movies, art deco perfume bottles and housemates. She started GMing in 1980 and roleplays extensively.

Janet Naylor

Janet also lives in Toronto, Ontario, along with three dogs and a cat, in the very same house as Caroline, where she is presently engaged in a bitter battle for wall space. She is the co-author of ***GURPS Fantasy***, and a frequent victim of Caroline's GMing. She works as a software developer, and moonlights as a sysop on Compuserve's RPGames Forum. She has been roleplaying and GMing since 1980. A recent immigrant to Canada, she has recently discovered the joys of herb gardening.

Page References

Rules and statistics in this book are specifically for the ***GURPS Basic Set,*** *Third Edition*. Any page reference that begins with a B refers to the ***GURPS Basic Set*** – e.g., p. B102 means p. 102 of the ***GURPS Basic Set,*** *Third Edition*. Page references that begin with CI indicate ***GURPS Compendium I.*** Other references are M for ***GURPS Magic,*** *Second Edition*, and BB for ***GURPS Bunnies & Burrows.*** For a full list of abbreviations, see p. CI181 or the updated web list at **gurps.sjgames.com/abbrevs.html**.

GURPS Spirits

This book was first published in 1994. In 2001, SJ Games published ***GURPS Spirits,*** which approaches similar topics from a different direction. The fundamental distinction between the two is that this book discusses *gods,* and notes that mortals might classify some gods as "spirits," while ***Spirits*** discusses *spirits,* and notes that mortals might worship some spirits as "gods." Significantly, ***Spirits*** does not assume that every entity known as a "god" is ineffable – or even notably powerful.

A consequence of this is that ***Spirits*** does not attempt to hand-wave the abilities of gods. It assigns full game statistics to spirits – something that this book avoids. This contrast can be used to good effect in campaigns where the PCs are ascended spirits, demigods, and the like: use this book to handle either end of the "cosmic power spectrum" – cosmology at one end, the earthly belief systems of mortal worshippers at the other – and use ***Spirits*** for the power levels in between.

Another feature of ***Spirits*** is that magic-using priests are not assumed to be totally outclassed by and thus in awe of their gods. This opens up the possibility of bargaining or even coercion. The ritual magic system included in ***Spirits*** is built on this premise, and differs radically from the divine magic systems in Chapter 6. Again, the two can complement one another: the ***Spirits*** rules are ideal for shamans and priests of deities of limited potency (e.g., ancestor spirits or nature spirits), while the rules in this book work well for the traditional miracle-worker or fantasy cleric – and both can be used in the same campaign.

THE COSMOS

1

A cosmology is an attempt to explain the origin and structure of the universe, by creating a system of belief from the myriad of details known about the world. Each religion defines cosmology according to its worldview, drawing from everyday experience and divine revelation. (Even those which refuse to speculate are inferring that the cosmology of the world is beyond the hope of mortal understanding.) Often it is a need for a cohesive cosmology that draws people to religion, to help them answer questions they cannot deal with on their own.

Defining a cosmology is an important step in developing a religion. But before doing even that, a GM should decide *why* he needs to add a religion, myth or cosmology to his story line. The myth or religion can impart the morality system the GM intends to use, or provide a "map" of locations the PCs will need to visit. It can introduce powerful NPCs whom the characters will eventually meet, fight, help or ask for aid. It can describe some great wrong that the heroes will be called to right, or simply act as a parallel story highlighting the impact of moral choices.

It is important that the GM decide from the beginning if the gods truly exist. If they do, then the religions that develop will be influenced and molded by the gods' actions. The gods may tell worshipers precisely what to do by influencing prophets or instructing specially chosen priests. If gods do not exist – or if they do and for some reason remain silent – then the religions that develop are social constructs. People create myths to explain the puzzles and problems of the world. Both of these views are valid and might have a basis in "truth," but the religions that result will usually have different flavors.

The Real World

This book addresses the development of religions for imaginary worlds. However, it is difficult to discuss the concept of religion without using examples from the *real* world. Indeed, borrowing traditions and ideology from ancient religions, or even relatively current ones, can add a great deal of realism to a game world. But it is still a game world. When we speak of "true" belief, we mean the true belief of the character, not the player – an important distinction.

Creation Myths

Myths are stories – "historical" stories of the cosmological and supernatural traditions of a people. They define the belief system of a people – where the people came from, how they began, who their gods and heroes are, and what they believe is important. Myths define a worldview which is most often conveyed to the people through their religion.

Creation myths discuss beginnings – the beginnings of the universe, the beginnings of the gods, the beginnings of life. Such myths are the basis for everything which comes later. When defining a cosmology, they are the foundation, the obvious place to start.

Building a Creation Myth

The first thing the GM should consider in designing a creation myth is the scope and relative truth of the myth. Does the myth recall absolute truth, or is it filled with symbolic allegory? Is the myth common to every culture on the world (perhaps with minor variations) or does each culture group have a different version? Is there more than one set of gods involved, or are they the same gods with different names? If the GM is focusing the campaign on a small portion of the world, deciding that the myth is specific to one culture allows other myths to be developed later for other parts of the world.

The second thing the GM should consider is the type of culture he is dealing with. Some types of myths are more common to some cultures than to others – for instance, "awakening" myths (p. 11) are common in aboriginal cultures. If the society is advanced, the creation myth might be a remnant of an older, now forgotten culture. In this case some aspects of the myth might seem odd or out of place. A fertility goddess who reigned in an older culture might be relegated to a lesser position – perhaps as mother of the new gods – in a later one.

Combining Mythic Elements: Hopi Creation Myth

Many creation myths combine different elements. The creation myths of the Hopi include, among others, the creation themes of multiple and twinned creators, abortive attempts, awakening and emergence.

The First World

First there was the Creator *Taiowa*. He created *Sotuknang,* his nephew, whom he instructed to go out and put everything in order. From endless space Sotuknang gathered up the solids, the waters and the winds, and put them all in their proper places. Then he was sent to create life.

Sotuknang went to the first world, *Tokpela,* and out of it created his helper on the world, *Kokyangwuti,* the Spider Woman. When she awoke her first question was, "Why am I here?" and Sotuknang told her she was to create all that lived in Tokpela. So she made two beings out of earth and her spittle, and covered them with a cape made of creative wisdom, and sang the Creation Song over them. When she uncovered the twins, they asked, "Why are we here?" The Spider Woman named them *Poqanghoya* and *Palongawhoya* and sent them forth. Poqanghoya was sent to the north pole and Palongawhoya to the south pole; Poqanghoya was given power to hold the earth stable and Palongawhoya was given power to hold the winds in ordered motion. Then the Spider Woman created all manner of plants, birds and animals.

Then Taiowa said that it was time to create human life. Once more the Spider Woman gathered up earth, but this time it was of four colors; red, yellow, white and black. As before, she mixed earth with spittle and molded it, then covered the beings with her cape, and sang to them. These four were creatures in the shape of Sotuknang. Then she did the same thing with four more creatures, but these she made in her own shape. When she uncovered them, they came alive. This was in *Qoyangunuptu,* the age of dark purple light at the dawn of Creation. After a little while, they awoke and began to move. This was the time of yellow light, *Sikangnuqa,* the second phase of the dawn of Creation. The time of the red light, *Talawva,* soon followed and they faced their Creator – Father Sun – for the first time.

Continued on next page . . .

The next thing the GM should decide is what kinds of questions the creation myth will answer – or just as importantly, will not answer. If the myth asserts that people were specially created, it might give the people who believe in it a sense of divine purpose. Sometimes a myth will set dividing lines between the gods, explaining the reasons behind long-existing grudges and conflicts. If the gods have been fighting since the beginning of time, their people will not expect a cease-fire anytime soon. In any case, the GM can decide whether a question is one that adventurers might be able to find out the answer to, or one of the unanswerable mysteries of the universe.

Creation myths allow the worldbuilder to set the stage for many further developments, and can open the door for many roleplaying opportunities.

How *did* it all begin?

Deus Faber

The universe was built by a *deus faber,* a divine artisan or craftsman. It may have been crafted, as the Egyptian god Ptah of Memphis was said to have created the entire world and the other gods upon his potter's wheel. Or it may have been spun or woven, as the Greeks pictured the goddess Nemesis sitting at the center of the cosmos, with the world spinning about her womb like a spindle. Or the universe may have been forged out of some primordial chaos, as the Lithuanians believed Teljavelik forged the sun and placed it in the heavens.

Deus faber myths require active deities with needs and desires. Most often these deities are anthropomorphic and are limited in what they can and cannot do. Though they might shape the cosmos, even they are governed by the laws of nature. Their religion may glorify craftsmen, considering them closest to the gods of all humans.

Sexual Myths

The universe and/or the gods were born of a sexual act. The parties involved in the reproduction usually have mysterious origins, or no origins at all. The Mayans of Yucatán describe the sudden appearance of Puma-snake and Jaguar-snake who took human form, united sexually and created the world. Other myths involve the widespread concepts of Father Sky and Mother Earth. Such myths usually ignore the question of where the couple came from, and concentrate on what happened afterward. Some myths do not require a sexual union at all: one Egyptian cosmology holds an example in which the god creates four other gods and the world through masturbation!

Deities who beget the world often have many other offspring. They are often pantheistic in nature and quite anthropomorphic. Followers of sexual mythologies tend to view the actions of the gods in terms of human motivations, thereby reducing the psychological distance between people and deities. Birth and birth motifs will always be important to them, as well as ties of family.

Creation as Byproduct

The act of creation is a byproduct of a greater occurrence. When Cronus, the Greek Titan, castrated his father Uranus, the blood that fell upon Mother Gaea created the Furies, the giants and the Meliae nymphs. When the primordial goddess of the Aztecs, Tzipactli, was torn apart by two rival serpent-gods, her lower body fell through chaos to form the earth, while her upper body rose to form the heavens. The Father Raven of Eskimo lore pushed a seed he found into the ground, and was most surprised when a man stepped forth from a pod of the resultant plant. When the Chinese deity P'an Ku died, his remains fell apart and formed the mountains of China.

Byproduct creations provide a chance for the worldbuilder to make mythic legends of the gods, which can spawn heroic quests or prophecies to seed future adventures.

First Victim

Creation arises from the sacrifice of some proto-divinity. For example, an Indian myth tells how the primeval giant Purusha was cut up, each part of him then transforming into a specific part of the universe: his head becoming the sky, his navel the air, his feet the earth and so on. The underlying theme here is that the act of creation balances an act of destruction, personified by the death of a single individual.

Or it may simply be the demise of an earlier order. The Mesopotamian dragon mother-goddess Tiamat was killed by her son Marduk, the hero of the newer gods. Half of her body became the dome of heaven, the other half the wall which contained the waters. Similarly, when the Norse gods Odin, Vili and Ve slew the giant Ymir, the world was formed from his flesh, the hills from his bones, the trees from his hair and the sphere of heaven from his skull.

Religions based on a first-victim cosmology will tend to carry a strong underlying theme of sacrifice in their teachings, whether it be in terms of personal sacrifice for personal gain or in actual offerings to appease the deities.

Combining Mythic Elements (Continued)

Spider Woman told them they must remember the phases of their creation and the time of the three lights; the dark purple of mystery, the yellow of life and the red of love. But they could not reply, for they had no voices. So the Spider Woman called Sotuknang and he gave them speech – a different language for each color – and the wisdom and ability to reproduce themselves. Only one thing he asked: that they respect their Creator at all times and live in wisdom and harmony. So they went off in different directions, and began to multiply.

In the beginning the First People lived in peace, and although they had different languages, they all understood each other; so did all the animals. In time they forgot the commands of Sotuknang and the Spider Woman. The animals grew frightened of people; in the same way all the people grew frightened of one another. But a few people remembered, and Sotuknang came to them. He told them that the first world would be destroyed and that a new world would be created for them to start again. He took them to the Ant People, who opened up the anthill at his command. All the people went down into the Ant *kiva*. When they were safe, *Tokpela* was destroyed by fire.

Continued on next page . . .

Multiple Creators

The cosmos is created by the combined efforts of several entities.

Division

The universe is created by the division of a single entity into separate, distinct parts. In many Native American cosmologies, the first couple, such as Father Sky and Mother Earth, existed in a continuous embrace, so close that nothing else might be created. Creation occurred when the divine couple was separated, allowing the creation of light and darkness and the establishment of time. Often this separation of heaven and earth reveals what had previously been hidden, such as plants, animals and people.

Multiple divisions are sometimes linked with the concept of direction. Sioux lore tells of the creation of four men, who are in reality the four winds and the god's main helpers. Another four brothers are sent to the four poles of the universe, to support humanity.

Twin Creators/Opposing Forces

The act of creation is a combined effort of two creators. They may be completely opposite in nature, one evil and one good, for example. Or they may simply bear each other enmity. The positive creator of the Iroquois was Maple Sprout, who created and taught humanity, and brought maize and other good plants into being. He was in constant battle with his twin Tawiskaron, who could only bring forth crocodiles, mosquitoes and other horrible animals.

In other cases, the two creators have few differences. Perhaps one is a bit more dexterous, the other more inventive. In this case, often the second creator either elaborates upon the efforts of the first, or fails to participate and then later attempts to destroy the creation. Both Coyote and Silver Fox were formed from cloud and mist and cooperated in forming a boat in which they could live upon the endless waters. But after Silver Fox created the earth out of Coyote's hair while he slept, Coyote awoke and, out of pique, immediately gobbled up all the fruits and crickets within reach.

The act of creation might also be nothing more that a contest of one-upmanship between the two different creative forces. This may result in religions and beliefs based on dual (and often opposing) principles.

Triples

A trio of deities creates the cosmos. In South American cosmologies it is a trio of gods who created the world. Triple-aspect deities such as Ishvara (Brahma, Vishnu and Shiva) abound in Vedic mythologies. Sometimes each member of the trio is responsible for a particular phase of creation; other times they act in concert. For example, Ishvara's three aspects, Brahma, Vishnu and Shiva, are responsible for creating new things, maintaining things created, and destroying to make way for new creation, respectively!

Abortive Attempts

The current cosmology is the latest in a series of aborted attempts. The creation myth of the Hopi (sidebar, pp. 8-10) is a good example of this. Sometimes even the divine does not get it right the first time. Such motifs tend to focus upon the creation of humanity as opposed to the creation of a cosmos. The creating force may simply abandon its failures, or may attempt to destroy them. If they still remain, these previous attempts can develop into powerful or twisted

Combining Mythic Elements (Continued)

The Second World

When the first world had cooled off, Sotuknang purified it and created *Tokpa,* the second world. Then he thanked the Ant People and called the others out of the earth. Again he warned them to remember to respect the Creator. They multiplied rapidly, and while this world was not as beautiful as the first, it was still a wonderful place. But now the animals were wild and did not talk to them. So they bartered and traded with other people and then the trouble began. They wanted more than they needed and they began to forget the Creator. So once more Sotuknang spoke to those few who remembered, and asked the Ant People to open up their underground world. When they were all safe, he commanded the twins to leave the poles. The earth teetered off balance and spun around crazily. It froze into solid ice. So ended Tokpa.

The Third World

For many years those who remembered were safe in the underground world. In time, Sotuknang sent the twins back to their posts. The world began to melt and life awoke again. Sotuknang put everything in order and then called the people out again, into the third world, *Kuskurza.* Again they were warned to remember, and again some forgot. Those who remembered lived and sang praises to the Creator from the hilltops; those who forgot made big cities, and soon the third world was full of corruption and war. This time Sotuknang went to the Spider Woman and said the world would be destroyed by water. So she took the people who remembered and sealed them up in hollow reeds. When the floods and rushing waters came, the reeds floated on top. Then the people looked for land; it took them a long time, but at last they found *Tuwaqachi,* the fourth world.

The Fourth World

Once more Sotuknang spoke to the people. This world was not all beautiful and easy to live on like the others. There were hot parts and cold parts, ugly parts and nice parts. Sotuknang told the people to separate, each group following their own star until it stopped. He promised to send them good spirits, and warned them to remember. And that is how the present world, the fourth world, came to be.

entities which then plague the newly-created beings. Occasionally the god creates something that is a little *too* good before a happy medium is struck and humanity results. But in most cases the previous creations of the god are still seen as possessing some hidden or supernatural power.

According to the Edda, before the gods there were the giants. The gods created the innumerable dwarves before finally deciding to create the first people.

Abortive myths are an excellent way to explain widely differing races in a world. Centaurs, elves, twisted gnomes, all might be earlier creations of the gods.

Awakening

There is no act of creation – the world simply exists, as it always has. One day the gods awoke, unaware of what may have created them, or any reason for their existence. There may even be no gods, just a world that exists without direction or purpose, continued survival being the highest law. Or the divine might be insubstantial and undefined, considered beyond the ken of mere mortals. The first life may have come through a cave or a hole in the ground. This rationale is especially common in tribal cultures with strong shamanistic traditions. Religions based on awakenings may be highly philosophical, seeing themselves as cogs in a greater machine.

Common Motifs

Motifs are common threads that run through creation myths, symbolizing various aspects of the creation.

The Cosmic Egg

One of the most common motifs used to represent the cosmos is that of the egg. This view involves both transformation and division, and is usually associated with light and sunrise.

In some cosmologies, the divine is an eternal force; in others it dwells within the egg itself. Usually this egg is not the ultimate origin of the cosmos, but the material from which it is created. Both Phoenician and Egyptian cosmologies use this symbolism. Chusoros ("the opener") broke the egg apart, creating the heaven and earth of the Phoenicians. Predominant in Egyptian belief was the belief in the creative spirit personified by the god Thoth. From him came four godly couples who represented the eight divine principles. Then creation began with the manufacture of a great egg, from which sprang the sun god Ra.

Transformation is the important element of this motif, incorporating the idea that what now is may not always be. There may even be a further stage of which this world is simply a precursor.

Chains and Patterns

In some myths, creation is a long chain of small steps, each following from the one before, covering the span from the divine to the mundane. This is particularly apparent in cosmologies where the gods diminish in power and glory to walk upon the earth. Semi-divine or divine ancestors are commonly cited in royal lineages. The *Enuma Elish,* the creation epic of Babylon and Assyria, ends with a long list of primordial kings. This type of creation myth forms an excellent basis for "the divine right of kings," where the society is led by those with a true calling or gift for ruling.

From Beginning to End

Some myths tell not only how the world was made – they tell how (and sometimes when) it will end. This can have a strong effect on the culture, giving people a sense of where they are going as well as how they came to be. Such a sense of purpose can become a driving force in both the individual and cultural sense. Such myths continue ancient conflicts until a final battle – and sometime even beyond, to a new cycle of creation. Norse myth is a classic example.

The Beginning . . .

In the beginning was the vast abyss, Ginnungagap. To think on its vastness would overwhelm the mind, sending it spiraling down into the depth of terror. There was no light, no darkness, not a single sound, twig or even grain of sand. Yet despite all this, Ginnungagap was not truly empty, although only the gods knew this secret.

Continued on next page . . .

In other cosmologies, these chains and patterns define the order of creation in minute detail, listing each small plant and animal by name. In Hawaiian cosmology, from the Night came the Abyss and Darkness, then were born the worms in crawling swarms, then the mites, the smaller worms, then the eggs which live in the sea, then specific sea eggs and shells and so forth. Ordering the cosmos so exactly gives its people a sense of knowing and belonging that spreads out into every aspect of their lives. Often these chains continue into recent history and look forward into the future, laying out a precise and orderly sequence of events that leads ever forward.

Numbers

Numbers often have important, sometimes almost mystical significance. One is the single, the indivisible. Two create a duality, two halves of a whole. Three form a triangle, or pyramid, a balanced shape. Four is a pair of pairs, and is often closely associated with nature in the number of elements, winds, etc. Five is the number of fingers to a hand, the most convenient way of counting. Six is two times three, gaining the powers of both. Seven is an oddity, often associated with luck. Eight doubles four. Nine is three threes. Ten is the highest one can count using fingers alone, and thus forms the basis for most counting systems. Zero is a fascinating concept – something to represent nothing. All can be used to bring additional meaning and flavor to a cosmology. A system of mystical belief built around numbers is called *numerology.*

Endings

Everything must come to an end, or so the saying goes. Yet in many cosmologies the ending is but another beginning. The concepts of renewed creativity or creative-destructive cycles are also often tied both to prophetic and divine elements in many myths. These are usually combined with other motifs: a final battle or judgment, the return or resurrection of a cultural hero, a natural cataclysm or unexplained divine retribution.

Endings are a common theme in heroic or fantasy literature, and can make spectacular splashes even in far-flung galactic empires. Final battles can be fought on scales varying from the personal to the universal. Cycles of societal birth, growth, death and rebirth can be played out in any milieu. Prophecy is often used by the gods to warn humans of impending doom, or to help them escape a tragic fate.

Final Conflict

Common to many cosmologies is the concept of a final great battle between opposed forces – good versus evil, light versus dark. In Teutonic mythology, this great conflict is called Ragnarok. More than a final predestined battle between the gods and the forces of evil, Ragnarok is the complete destruction of the universe, followed by its rebirth (see p. 15).

In other mythologies this conflict is continuous, and the outcome is not necessarily predestined. Often a final judgment or reordering of the universe is implied. Zoroastrian traditions speak of continuous warfare between good and evil, as personified by various spirits of both natures, until the final prophet conquers Angra Mainyu and all existing evil (see p. 52).

Creation Renewed – Recurring Cycles

Creation may be a cyclic event, a repetitive rhythm of creation and destruction. These cycles usually begin with a wondrous and beautiful world which

From Beginning to End (Continued)

For within Ginnungagap was Muspellheim, the Land of Fire that was the home of the world's destroyers. So fierce and hot was this land of flame that even the gods, the Aesir, stayed away. Upon its borders stood Surt, fiercest of the fire giants, and in his hands was a great sword of fire. From the beginning he had watched there, and he would be there at the end, at Ragnarok, the doom of the gods.

Also hidden within this void was Niflheim, a realm of ice, snow and freezing fog. At its center there surged and roared a mighty geyser called Vergelmir, the Roaring Cauldron, source of all the rivers that ever were. Elivagar was another fountain within the realm of Niflheim. From Elivagar flowed great rivers of ice which exploded and spread as great glaciers across the face of Ginnungagap. And from it also flowed a dark sludge, that formed great masses of black ice.

Continued on next page . . .

slowly decays as time passes. Slowly, dark, decadent and destructive forces gain power and influence, and spread throughout the world. Helplessly the world tumbles toward a final catastrophe, after which it is created anew, and life begins again.

Some worlds are continuously recycled, their creative divinities renewing them after each destruction. These cycles are incredibly long, and yet are sometimes precisely defined. The world of Brahma will endure 2,160,000,000 years – a mere night and day in the god's life. Then the world is consumed in flames, destroyed by the world-serpent Sesha and recreated by Brahma. This process will be repeated, until a hundred years of such days are gone, and then the whole universe, gods and all, will revert again to its primeval substance.

The destruction of the world in fire is also a favorite theme. This fire may be caused either by the falling sun or a fragment of the moon, by demons, by a mysterious spark from the sky, or by a trickster-god. In most versions, however, a few people remain alive to repopulate the earth (see *From Beginning to End*, pp. 11-15). Other traditions foretell spells of cold weather and onslaughts of ice and snow, which later melt and cause great floods.

Basic Forces of the World

Part of developing a cosmology is determining the role that the divinity plays in the world. In some cosmologies, gods are tied strongly to the forces that bind the world, and are subject to the whims and laws of natural forces. In others, these forces are actually depicted *as* gods. Or there may be no gods at all, the laws of physics being the only underlying principle. In this last case gods may still be worshiped, but they are cultural constructs, aiding humanity in understanding themselves and those forces of the world they do not understand.

Nature

The mysteries of nature are a continuing source of both fear and wonder. Most cultures have myths explaining weather, earthquakes, floods and other natural phenomena in terms of divine myth or legend. Earthquakes are commonly thought to occur when the gods or heroes who support the earth shift their position. The Burmese Shans held that the earth was a great sleeping fish which occasionally awoke and bit its tail, then writhed in pain, shaking the earth. Often specific aspects of nature are held to be the responsibilities of a particular deity. Norse Thor governed thunderstorms, the Irish Manannan was concerned with forecasting the weather, Greek Poseidon was originally called Enosigaois ("earth-shaker") and was armed with lightning flashes. Chalchihuitlicue, the goddess of flowing waters, was the spouse of Tlaloc, the rain god of the Aztecs; Susanowo was the Japanese god of the winds and thunder.

Nature is often viewed as either a deity or a mysterious force. Frequently it is seen as a feminine force, an extension of a divine earth mother. The cycles and seasons of natures are explained by a variety of myths and legends which usually involve some type of vegetation deity who is regularly slain and later reborn. In Greek legend, Persephone, daughter of the earth goddess Demeter, was sentenced to spend a third of the year beneath the earth, during which time all plants withered due to her mother's sorrow.

From Beginning to End (Continued)

After countless eons Niflheim's ice touched Muspellheim's flaming air. A great explosion rocked the void. The fire of Muspellheim scorched the dark sludge from Elivagar, and from this the body of a giant formed. For long ages this giant, who was called Ymir, or Aurgelmir the Mud-boiler, slept. A male and a female grew beneath his armpit and one of his feet mated with the other, creating a six-headed son. From these creatures were born the frost giants.

The scum that flew from Elivagar did not poison all the ice of Niflheim. Where the ice was still pure, yet melting from the fire of Muspellheim, a vast cow appeared in the thawing ice. Four rivers of milk flowed from the udder of this great cow, who was called Audhumla, the Great Nurse. Upon this milk was Ymir suckled.

Audhumla began to lick at the great masses of ice about her. In time she licked a complete man into shape. This was Buri, for he was beautiful and bright. Buri had a son called Bor. Bor's wife was Bestla, the giant Balethorn's daughter. And Bor and Bestla had three sons: Odin, Vili and Ve. Humans they made from the roots of an ash tree and an elm tree – the first man was Ask, and the first woman was Embla.

In time Odin and his brothers argued with old Ymir, but this was so long ago that no one really knows why they fought. But after a great battle they killed Ymir, hacking him to pieces. So much blood flowed that almost all of the giants drowned. And still the blood continued to flow, forming all the oceans, lakes, pools and streams.

The sons of Bor hacked and chopped at Ymir's body; from his flesh they formed rolling hills and wide plains. From his bones they made the mountains and from his hair they made the trees and bushes. From the soil of his flesh the dwarves crawled forth like maggots. The brothers threw Ymir's great skull into the air where it formed the high heavens. Four dwarves were made to hold it up. And when all those labors at last were done, they threw Ymir's brains into the air to make the clouds. Sparks and cinders from Muspellheim they threw into the sky also, and so the stars came into being.

Continued on next page . . .

Time

The ability to quantify time is important to any civilization. The movement of the sun, moon and stars, the continuing cycle of the seasons, the aging of humanity – all these involve the concept of passing time.

Aeon represented ages and epochs in the history of the world, and was often depicted as a winged lion-headed human entwined in serpents. The Greeks saw the lord of time as a primeval god, called Kronos (Cronus).

In Indian thought, Kala personified time as a cosmological force. Kala was his own father, and hence his own son. Kala was also associated with the god of death, a motif found in other mythologies. Thoth, an ancient Egyptian god of the moon, chronology and the calendar, is another example of a temporal god associated with death: as the protector of Osiris he was a guide and helper of the dead. Tai-sui-zing was a Chinese god of time; he was also "the star of the great year" – the planet Jupiter with its 12-year orbit.

The concept of time eternal is often expressed in vibrant symbols: the phoenix rising perpetually from the ashes of its own burning, the world-serpent continually biting its own tail. Both of these legends personify the concept of eternity, a process which has no beginning or end.

From Beginning to End (Continued)

Ages passed, with many arguments between the gods, and many battles against the giants and trolls and other evil creatures. Then one day Balder, Odin's son, began to have nightmares of doom and death; but none of the gods could explain why. Odin traveled to Niflheim to seek out the ghost of a seeress in Hel's great hall. Even she spoke of Balder's inescapable doom. Frigg, Balder's mother, refused to accept this. She searched out every living thing, making each swear never to harm Balder – all except the mistletoe, which she thought too small to be dangerous. The gods began to play a new game – they threw things at Balder and laughed when they did not harm him. Loki, the trickster, was angry and jealous, so he made a dart of mistletoe. He gave the dart to blind Hod. When Hod threw it, it pierced Balder's heart, killing him.

Frigg sent Hermod to Hel to beg for Balder's release from death. Hel agreed – if everyone and everything in the Nine Worlds wept for him. But one evil giantess – Loki in disguise? – would not weep, so Balder had to stay in Hel's halls.

The gods mourned for a long time, but eventually decided to have a feast. They did not invite Loki, but he showed up anyway, throwing insults. They hunted him down, and despite his trickery they caught him. They tied Loki across sharp rocks in a deep mountain cave and placed a great snake above him. His wife sat by him, holding a bowl to catch the venom that dripped from its fangs to torment Loki. When she moved the bowl to empty it, he writhed in anguish, shaking the earth.

Continued on next page . . .

Entropy

A common theme of many cosmologies is that the world (and all that exists) was created from a sea of undefined chaos, and will ultimately return to it. Entropy, or this return to chaos, is generally considered inevitable in these cases.

As a chaotic and destructive force, entropy is often associated with evil or malevolent deities. Many cultures develop rituals designed to appease these chaotic forces, staving off their final destruction. Fear of entropy can be a strong opponent to change.

But there is always hope. Most cultures believe that faithful devotion will ensure at least spiritual salvation.

Fate

The idea that the outcome of one's life (or at the least, life's major events) has been predetermined is common to many cultures. Often this concept is personified, and the agencies responsible for destiny are named *Fate*. Fate is generally seen as a supernatural, often capricious entity responsible for all that one finds unsatisfactory in life. Illness, misfortune, early death – all of these are explained and justified in terms of predestination.

Interpretations of fate vary greatly from culture to culture. Sometimes a distinction is made between a fate determined by an impersonal force and a fate impressed upon a person by a deity. Further distinctions involve the belief that one's fate may change: some cultures think one's fate is determined at birth, or that it is fixed annually, usually at the new year. Some hold that the pattern of the stars at birth determines one's destiny. Other forms of divination use physical signs, such as birthmarks, to reveal one's fate.

With the question of fate and destiny comes concern about free will and self-determination. Some cultures accept the loss of personal will, and develop a fatalistic world view. Others embrace the idea that their fate lies in the hands of the gods, believing that their life serves some greater purpose.

Karma

Karma is the belief that all of a person's acts have spiritual consequences, influencing the cycle of deaths and rebirths which an individual endures until he finally achieves liberation. Differences in social status, fortune, well-being and lifespan are all the result of past karma. Karma is both impersonal and inevitable, and often mental acts and thoughts are held to be as important in determining karma as physical ones. Some believe that karma falls under divine control and that devotion to the god may bring release from the cycle. Others believe that study, knowledge, works and discipline will allow one to achieve purification and eventual release.

Another interpretation holds that karma itself is a material substance, albeit a supernatural one. This matter becomes attached to the soul of the individual who is overly concerned with worldly matters. All actions causes some karmic matter to gather about the soul, but evil deeds produce a different type of karma which is harder to eradicate. Liberation and release are achieved through a combination of penance and abandonment of action. Inaction prevents the further buildup of karma, while penance removes that which has already accumulated.

Yet another concept of karmic interactions suggests that attempting or achieving something particularly good, evil or important to or with someone else can form a bond of karma which the souls must work out *together* in a

From Beginning to End (Continued)

The End . . .

Balder's death and Loki's evil acts herald the end of the world – Ragnarok, the doom of the gods.

With the coming of Ragnarok the quarrel between the gods and the giants worsens, and there is constant war on earth. Midgard freezes and all humans (except for two who take shelter in the branches of the world-tree Yggdrasil) die. The dread wolves Skoll and Hati swallow the sun and the moon, and the world falls into darkness, for even the stars go out.

Loki and the great wolf Fenris break their chains and join the giants, fighting against the gods. Hel brings the dead to fight on Loki's side; they attack Asgard. On the vast plain of Vigard, the gods face their enemies and destroy each other. Odin is killed by Fenris, who is killed by Odin's son, Vidar. Loki and Heimdall kill each other, and Thor slays the great world-serpent Jormungand, only to die from its venom. Thousands die in gruesome battle. The fire giant Surt throws flame in all directions, destroying Asgard and Midgard, and the earth sinks into the sea. All life perishes.

And Beyond . . .

Yet there is still hope. For while the Nine Worlds are destroyed, the world-tree Yggdrasil survives. A new green Earth rises from the sea. Lif and Lifthrasir (who hid in the branches) climb down from Yggdrasil and begin the human race anew. And before Skoll swallows the sun, she has a daughter who will light the new world.

There are even survivors among the gods. Odin's sons Vidar and Vali survive, as do Thor's sons, Modi and Magni. Balder, Nanna, Hod and Honir revive and begin a new race of gods that will live and rule in peace.

future life. A GM can use such bonds to bring or keep together a party with diverse interests, or to motivate a group to take on a particular quest. A bond between the characters and the primary villain can be particularly powerful!

Divination

Divination is the act of foreseeing the future. More generally, it is a means of determining the significance of future or present events and the role the individual may play in these events. Often divine forces may not be involved at all, if the culture believes that fate and destiny lie outside the influence of the gods.

Common to all cultures in one form or another, divination is notoriously subject to interpretation. A culture may use several means to obtain insight. Dreams, hunches, ordeal, tranced possession, augury, mechanical manipulations such as the casting of lots – these are but a few of the methods used.

Many forms of divination are systemized and mechanical, involving complex series of diagnostic symbols: the tarot, *I Ching* and astrology are examples of this type of divination. But it may also result from accidental signs and omens. For example, in some cultures, if twins are born, calamity will follow; if a person trips, or sneezes, or meets a cross-eyed woman first thing in the morning, then something momentous will occur later in the day. While this type of divination lacks an ordered arrangement of symbols, it still suggests a causal relationship between a minor event and a later, major occurrence. Many believe that all signs point to future events: if the signs are complicated, then a specialist or trained divinatory reader must be consulted. But it is from these smaller, personal instances of divination that superstitions of good and ill luck arise.

Prophecy

Prophecy is a specific type of divination, in which the will of the gods, or some force which supersedes them, is revealed. These prophetic pronouncements are often of grave importance, involving sweeping consequences that will result from the actions, or inactions, of a particular individual. Often, prophecies describe events which will affect the very gods themselves.

One of the most common themes involving prophecy is that of the "fatal child." Prophecies, before birth or at the birth itself, reveal that the child is destined to slay parent, grandparent, or even king. Although the child is abandoned or condemned, he manages to survive, usually by the intervention of a kind, humble person. Unaware of the prophecy, the child grows up in obscurity and proceeds to fulfill his destiny.

Other prophecies warn of calamity and punishment – but only if the warnings are ignored. Some great challenge or opponent must be met, and if it is defeated, great rewards will result.

Creation of Life

Along with the world and the forces that control it, the existence of life itself must be explained.

Substance

From what substance did life come? This is more than an interesting detail – it often gives important insight into the nature of all creation.

Deity's Image

The idea that man was made from a piece of, or at least in the image of, the prime creator deity is a common one. This associates life closely with the

The Fated PC

The GM might wish to involve the party in some fated or predestined event directly. Sometimes the best way to do this is to make a character an instrument of fate. While this option might reduce the free will of the individual, it brings up several interesting roleplaying opportunities.

Fated characters usually come from Unusual Backgrounds. Often they are abandoned at birth in an attempt to avoid some prophecy. Sometimes their parents know of their child's destiny and send the infant PC away to a safe place, or foster him in isolation with a mysterious teacher or hermit.

This teacher or stepparent might know nothing of the child's true past or parentage but often teaches him special skills that will be of great use later in life.

Fated individuals are often marked by circumstance, or bear an unusual birthmark. He might be the seventh son of a seventh son, or be born upon an auspicious day. All these things distinguish him in some way, and may warn others that this person is somehow *special,* predestined for some great purpose.

A fated character is destined to complete some action which will have long-lasting campaign effects. Often such a PC will have important, and possibly unknown, enemies who work against him. If the individual is fated to oust a tyrant from power, then that tyrant will watch him very carefully.

In some cases, the hero might even be fated to fail! Struggling against fate itself can be the most difficult, yet rewarding, type of adventure.

As an interesting twist on this theme, the GM might arrange an adventure that has the group working *against* a prophecy. Loyal PCs might not wish to see some star-touched upstart overthrow *their* lord.

The GM must be careful, however, to find out if the players are willing to put up with such a heavy hand on the part of the GM. Some players may become resentful if it appears that one player is "benefiting" too much from such GM attention. The GM must also consider what happens to a plot-line or adventure if a key PC is killed or otherwise incapacitated. Many epic quests end abruptly when a player quits, removing the PC from the game.

divine. Some myths grant only humanity this divine link, considering animals an integral part of the world's creation that need not be explained directly.

This belief can greatly empower people. As they are to the gods, the world is to them. They might even aspire to the power of the gods, since their forms are so close.

Lump of Clay

People and/or animals are made by breathing creative force ("life") into an existing element such as earth or clay. This associates life more closely with the earth and its elements, rather than with the divine.

African myths say that humanity was created from the five elements (stone, iron, earth, air, water). The Mayans held that men were first made of earth, but they were mindless, and thus were destroyed. Then they were remade of wood, but they lacked souls and intelligence, and were ungrateful to the gods, and so were drowned in a great flood. Finally the gods remade them of a maize gruel, and they grew and prospered.

This belief makes people a part of the world, rather than set above it. No matter what their eventual fate or powers, they can never reach beyond the elements which give them form.

Purpose

Central to humanity's self-image is the purpose for life's creation. The GM should consider the answer carefully.

To Amuse

Birds, plants, animals and people were created simply to make life more interesting for the deities. As such, people and animals are continually subject to divine whims, allowed to triumph or suffer, live long, or die young by the gods' choosing. The deities are worshiped in the hope that this will appease them, so they will decide to rain delights rather than disasters.

To Glorify

People are the ultimate achievement of the gods, created to express the divine will and power at its finest. Cultures with this belief tend to be arrogant, viewing themselves and their actions as reflections of the deity's will.

To Serve

All life forms, and people in particular, were created to perform certain rituals which ensure the continuance of the world and the deity in particular. Humanity alone is given the ability to choose how to serve, its position being the most important and complex. This belief tends to glorify the priesthood, as it is their task to interpret just what the proper rituals are, and to ensure that these are correctly performed.

Designing the Afterworld

Not all mythologies express a concrete belief in an afterworld. If the GM wishes to include one, it is important to match the afterworld and the culture rather than to create one at random.

If the religion stresses hard work and obedience in this life and a reward in the next, then the afterworld will often be a wonderful abode where food and luxuries are abundant and everyone lives happily ever after. There usually will be a place of punishment for the less fortunate. Sometimes the afterworld is simply a place of rest, where weary souls can sleep after their long lives.

Often the world of the dead is divided into different realms for different people. The manner of death might determine where the soul ends up. Souls of people who committed suicide might wander forever in limbo while warriors who died fighting may move on to some reward.

The realm of the dead might be a place where things go on just as they did in life. In Fijian belief *Nai Thombo Thombo* is a real place. A real road leads to it, and those who live in the villages that the road passes do all they can to make things easier for puzzled souls; all doors are built exactly opposite each other, and sharp implements are never left out where traveling souls might step on them.

Some souls might be reborn into the world after a suitable wait. Some afterworlds are transitional areas where souls wait before continuing on. The GM might decide that necromantic spells work only on those spirits that remain in this transitory realm – souls that have passed beyond are lost to the touch of the living.

Shamanistic societies believe in a number of otherworldly realms, only one of which is the realm of the dead. This land of the dead might be closed to all living persons other than special shamans guiding the dead. Or it could be a place to visit after a long hard journey.

Some afterworlds are nebulous, ever-shifting places. Others have great palaces and tombs, where kings still rule and servants still serve. Afterworlds often echo the organization of the culture that describes them.

Revenants

Common to most cultures is the belief that the dead can return to the realms of the living. These lost or restless souls have been somehow trapped in the mortal world. In some cultures this is because of violent death, or death before the "proper" time. In others, a bungled or missing funeral ritual will cause this. Or a soul might be trapped by an object or area that held great significance to the living person.

One common belief is that the soul has some final task which it must complete before it can continue on to the rest (or rebirth) which awaits it. Usually this is a task that the person felt strongly about. It might be avenging his own death, or that of another for whom he cared deeply. It might be the completion of a task that was interrupted by his death, especially if this task has religious or other deep significance. Or it might be a time of penance, which the deity has assigned the spirit before it can pass into the next world – a sort of "purgatory-on-earth."

Continued on next page . . .

Byproduct

Life just happened. Either the writers of the myth admit to ignorance, or they chalk it up as being an accidental byproduct of the rest of creation. People are no more or less blessed than any other element of the world.

Different Forms of Life

Plants, animals, and intelligent beings may have been created by different methods. In a fantasy world the origin of each of the different magical creatures (dragons, demons, etc.) should be considered, along with the different intelligent races.

Intelligence versus Animal

In almost every creation myth, people are considered superior to all other forms of life (probably reflecting the fact that man made the myth). Animals may be earlier creations, or they may be derived in a completely different way, untouched by the divine's special favor.

Alternatively, animals may be considered to be closest to divinity, in their instinctive understanding of the world, while people must attempt to reach this state on their own initiative. Even here, however, humanity's potential reward upon reaching this state of simple purity is much greater than that of an animal that was born to it.

Different Races of Intelligent Life

Some worlds will have multiple intelligent races. Perhaps each race will be the special child or product of a different deity, or they may form a progression of creations, each different, until a final form was found (usually humanity). Sometimes different races are thought to have been created for a particular purpose or task. Dwarves might be the remnants of an army of divine carpenters. Evil races might have been created as minions of darker gods, or for the express purpose of punishing or testing a "greater" race. In science fiction worlds, aliens might simply have been adapted to their world's habitat.

Some Eskimo tribes developed a myth to explain the different human races that entered their territories following the discovery of the New World. Their deity, so they say, shaped earth into humanoid forms and baked them in a great kiln until they were ready. The first batch she left in too long; these were burned, giving them blackened skin and hair. Worried, she didn't leave the second batch in long enough, and they turned out all pasty white. But on the third and final batch she left them in just the right amount of time, and they had the proper golden brown shade of skin.

Similar myths might separate the races of a traditional fantasy world.

Man versus Woman

The difference between the sexes can also be considered. Historical myths vary widely on the issue of whether man and woman were created together as equals, or one came first. The Bible speaks of Adam (created from the earth), with Eve created later from his rib bone. An earlier Jewish tradition says that Lilith was the real original woman, created at the same time as Adam. But she took umbrage when Adam required her to submit to his will, and she left Eden to explore the rest of the world. Eve was then created as a replacement. Greek myths say that woman was sent as a curse to men after they had angered the gods. Other mythologies suggest that woman was created first, with man coming later to serve her.

Whatever the GM decides is likely to have a strong effect on any difference in the roles that society ordains for the sexes.

Fall from Paradise

A common motif among first creation myths is that humans were created in a paradisiacal state, which they then lost through their own actions, bringing evil and suffering into the world.

Eve's run-in with the snake in the garden is a well-known example. The early Greeks also spoke of earlier ages of humanity, beginning with the Golden Age when everything was plentiful, devolving through the Silver, Brass, and finally Iron Ages. In each age, life became harsher and mankind became more wicked and greedy. Another Greek myth depicts Pandora (the first woman, in some versions) loosing the ills of the world from a vase given to her by the gods as a wedding present.

If there was once a paradise to fall from, where is it now? It may be the home of the gods, or it might prove to be a magically-protected place whose location is lost to memory.

Death/Transition

Once life has been explained, one must come to terms with death. In a mortal world, all living things die. The nature of death, whether it is to be feared or gladly embraced, may depend on a culture's views about survival of part or all of the person. If the culture believes that the individual continues to some new state, then how he gets there and what, if anything, he needs once there are important considerations.

Beliefs about death and the transition into some other world strongly affect funeral and burial customs. Some religions believe the body must be burned to free the spirit. In others the body must be returned to the earth, often earth specially prepared and sanctified to the deity, for the soul to begin its journey. Some cultures hold that wealth buried with the dead will gain them extra consideration in the afterlife. They created fine tombs which glittered with their earthly possessions. In other cultures the bodies of the dead are consumed by their living relations in a ceremony believed to transfer the power and wisdom of the deceased ancestor to the next generation (see p. 137).

There are two predominant views concerning the path of the soul.

Single Path

A new soul is born. It lives and dies. After death it travels to a distant realm where it is judged by its actions, wealth, or whatever other criteria the gods might set forth. This judgment determines the fate of the soul. Common motifs are a paradisiacal existence in the dwelling place of the god for the pure of heart, a wretched place of great suffering for the sinner, or an intermediary existence in which one must work off the evil deeds of life before ascending to the divine realm.

Believers in the single-path motif will often be more afraid of death, and more likely to seek personal immortality. They might also place more importance upon the judgment, since it will determine the fate of their souls throughout eternity. Some believers, of course, will long for death as an opportunity to enter Paradise.

Revenants (Continued)

Sometimes the revenant seems so lifelike that it is virtually impossible to tell the living from the dead. Only when the ghost or vision disappears before their eyes do the living understand just what they were dealing with. Irish folk tradition teaches that a corpse will rise from its coffin to take part in its own funeral.

Some apparitions are characterized by a wraith-like appearance. These spectral ghosts sometimes appear over the places their bodies lie, remaining until the body is properly interred. At other times ghosts appear with objects that have never been alive, like a favorite car. Visions of death coaches are common.

Ghosts and other revenants seem to be capable of most activities of the living. They frequently are very noisy, shouting, moaning, banging shutters or playing musical instruments. Often they wildly rearrange or even destroy the interiors of the buildings they haunt.

Religious rites can generally, although not always, put revenants to rest.

Ghosts and hauntings can provide classic adventuring. The party might be hired to rid an area of a ghost – but end up on the ghost's side, avenging a treacherous death. Or a party member might be haunted by dreams telling him of something he must do before a deceased relative can truly rest.

Judgment Day

Where a soul ends up in the afterlife often depends upon a divine judgment. Different religions define different criteria upon which a soul might be judged to determine its status in the afterlife.

Karma is the sum of an individual's actions. In most cases it is considered a negative quality. Deeds of avarice and greed that harm other individuals accumulate karma; deeds of selflessness and moral goodness dissipate karma. When a soul dies and is judged for its next life, the accumulation of karma determines whether the soul improves its lot in life, or finds it worsened.

Some religions judge purely on the faith and belief of their followers. Accepting the word of the deity as law and living accordingly will grant greater status in the afterlife, no matter what else the person may do. The greatest status is given to the truly fanatical and zealous. Cults of dark deities who require their followers to perform gruesome acts in the deity's name will often judge on this criteria.

Continued on next page . . .

Judgment Day (Continued)

Religions which hold personal achievement, wealth and prosperity highly may judge the soul by the wealth which it took to the grave. This will invariably result in larger and more ornate burial customs, such as those of the late-dynasty Egyptians.

Other religions, particularly those of ancestor veneration, judge the deceased by the sorrow, grief and piety of those left behind to lament. Thus, to slight the funeral customs or lessen the periods of mourning may have profound effects on the eventual disposition of the ancestors. Some religions teach that the prayers of the living can help the dead – or vice versa, depending on how the soul was judged!

Playing the Dead

If the gods have other plans for their faithful followers, death may be just another beginning.

Valhalla, for instance, might seem like the ultimate reward for the brave warrior – fighting all day, feasting all night, wounds healed at nightfall, the dead revived again in the morning. Yet there is a underlying purpose to all this repetitious activity – the gods are training an army to aid them at Ragnarok. Other gods might have similar plans for the souls that dwell in their afterworld realms.

When the realm of the dead is closely attached to other realms of the gods, adventuring could continue after death. A deity could reunite the deceased for one last grand adventure. Or they might wake up in the afterworld and then have to struggle to escape to the lands of the living!

Shamans rely upon the advice and help of spirits sent to them by the god. The GM, as that god, could send the spirit of a deceased adventurer to aid them. This would be an especially valid ploy if that person died with information the party needs. Animistic priests calling for divine inspiration might be haunted – or even possessed! – by friendly ghosts or ancestors. Magical clerics might manage to enchant a holy item with the spirit of a lost compatriot.

Another possibility is the unfulfilled quest. The ghosts of deceased companions might refuse to leave the party alone until the quest ends or until they are restored or laid to rest. And anyone betrayed by the rest of the party might have good reason to haunt those who failed them.

Recurring Cycles

Each soul repeats a cycle of existence. It is born, lives and dies. After death it travels back to the place it existed before its "birth," where it may be judged. This judgment may determine the circumstances of its next life. If the previous life was a good one, it moves "upward," the circumstances of its next life being better than the last. If the life was spent poorly, then the soul moves downward, perhaps even taking animal form. The soul is eternally reborn on this "wheel of life," though often a religion will promise eventual release from the cycle.

Believers in the recurring-cycle motif often have less fear of death. Their primary concern is usually to accomplish enough in this life to improve their next one. They often view advantages of birth as laurels earned in past times, while suffering is simply punishment for past misdeeds. They are, all in all, more fatalistic.

The notion of recurring cycles also brings up questions of access to information gained in past lives. Some religions view this as impossible – the soul goes through a cleansing which rids it of all past memories – but others strongly believe that these memories can be tapped and retrieved. A given soul may be marked or fated by its actions in prior lives (see sidebar, p. 16).

Immortals

Though in the "real" world all living things die, in many game worlds this is *not* true. Some fantasy creatures are thought to live forever unless killed. Often their ending is quite different from that of their mortal counterparts. Immortal races almost always have the "single-path" view, with the soul returning to a more primal state of existence upon its death. Or perhaps, having been granted immortal life on earth, when it ends they simply cease to be.

Afterlife

An integral part of the question of survival after death is the nature of the afterlife – where the souls of the dead go, how they travel, and what they do once they arrive.

Journey

Almost every culture that believes in survival pictures the transition as a journey from this world to the place of the dead. In some cases this journey is a simple transition, while in others it is a long, arduous task. Some cultures believe that articles buried with the deceased can aid them on this journey, perhaps making the difference between success and eternal unrest. Those who could *not* complete the journey often wander this world as ghosts (see sidebar, pp. 18-19).

Another common motif is the ferryman – a gatekeeper whom the soul must pass in order to complete the journey. The ferryman usually requires some token payment, a coin or some other item of value, before the soul can continue.

Judgment

The concept of judgment is also universal. One of a variety of fates befalls a soul according to its previous life. Generally those who deserve some sort of punishment suffer it, whether until they have atoned for their misdeeds, or for eternity. Those who have lived well may gain a life of splendor and happiness for eternity, or they may be reborn into a better existence. An exceptionally deserving soul might be lifted to a semi-divine state, either achieving oneness with the deity, or becoming a trusted servant.

Final Resting Places

In the single-path model, the soul must have somewhere to rest once life is done. The nature of these final resting places will often serve as the ultimate reward or punishment, even in the "real" world. For those souls who have lived a good life, or who have proved their worth by navigating the tortuous pathways to the afterworld, this is a paradisiacal place. For those who have failed in some way, their final rest might be a place of great suffering and torture, or it might be a return to the earth itself – forever excluded from the wonder of the true afterlife.

Even those religions that believe in a continual cycle of lives often have a final exit for those souls who achieve true enlightenment.

Final Service

Some mythologies incorporate the notion of a valued cleric or servant being taken to the land of the gods upon death, and being bound to some final service. In a world of many deities, it is possible that the different gods will draw their most faithful followers to them.

One example of this is the Norse Valhalla. Some warriors of great prowess were chosen by Odin to live in Valhalla until Ragnarok, when they would fight again, this time beside their lord. Others were chosen by Freya, who began her career as a goddess of battle; neither the Eddas nor the sagas discuss her purposes or criteria!

Reincarnation

If souls are reborn, then the method of reincarnation should be considered.

Generally the gods assign an individual to his next life, basing their decision on his actions in previous lives. But in some cases the soul itself is allowed to choose its next existence. Or the selection may be completely random.

Multiple Destinations

Depending on the cosmology of the world, it is possible for a soul to have a multitude of potential destinations. In a world of different races or faiths, each faith may have a different answer, and all may be perfectly valid. The will and belief of a soul may even be enough to impose its own choice. Some deities may reincarnate their followers, while others retire them after a single life, or call them to their sides. Deities may even compete over the final disposition of the dead, leaving little or no control in the hands of the individual.

Journey of Death

Many gaming opportunities arise if the GM decides that the afterworld is physically accessible to the living. Long journeys through dark and treacherous caverns might bring the party to the underworld. Egyptian belief, for example, holds that the underworld lies beyond a maze of passages and well-guarded doors, across a diversity of watercourses. Items entombed with the dead could aid the party on its quest. Those doomed souls that wander helplessly could either oppose or help the seekers.

Or the party might find the Isles of the Dead after a rough and dangerous sea voyage. They might accidentally come across the land of the dead and have to escape. Or they might seek it to recover a lost companion, speak to the dead, or regain (or return) a lost artifact.

When designing an afterworld adventure the GM can choose a motif from myths and legends that matches the flavor of the campaign. In one Greek legend, Aeacus, Minos and Rhadamanthus judged the dead in a meadow and consigned them either to Tartarus or to the Isles of the Blessed. In Tartarus they remained until they had atoned for the sins of their previous life. In the Isles of the Blessed they drew lots for their next incarnations and drank from Lethe, the river of oblivion, to forget all they had previously known. Those particularly favored retired to the Elysian fields to enjoy an eternity of bliss.

The Irish Celts believed in an Otherworld, sometimes imagined as being underground, and sometimes as islands beyond the sea. Their afterworld was believed to be a country where there was no sickness, old age, or death, where happiness existed forever and where a hundred years were one day.

The Inca believed that those who obeyed the Inca dictum "Do not steal, do not lie, do not be lazy" went to live in the sun's warmth. Those who did not conform spent their days in the cold earth. Those who remained in the earth were in reality still living, but had become invisible, implacable and invulnerable; hence a great preoccupation for the comforts of the dead arose. Eventually the great tombs became so large that they occupied more space than the habitations of the living.

DEITIES

2

Deities are beings of supernatural powers or attributes who are thought to control some part of nature or reality, or to personify some force or activity. In the male or general form, they are known as gods; in the female form, they are called goddesses.

The concept of gods or deities is universal. They are the center of most religions, the driving force behind belief and faith, the inspiration for the spiritual nature of a people.

When the GM creates a world, he should consider its deities early on, when defining the cosmology. The deities create the cosmos; their powers and attributes shape the world. Alternatively, the GM may decide that there are no supernatural forces, that deities are simply a construct of society, and that their worship might also be a construct – a means to gain power over others. But this in itself is a decision with consequences that must be considered.

An example of a deity created using this chapter appears in the sidebar *The Duality of Dhala*, p. 153.

Origins

Where deities come from is the stuff of creation myths and legends (see *Creation Myths*, beginning on p. 7). There are many different choices.

Finite

Deities were created by the same act which created the world. There will be no *new* gods. This scheme tends to foster powerful, unchanging deities of archetypal qualities. Since they are finite and determined, it is quite likely that they represent basic fundamental aspects of the world – the four elements, perhaps, or other abstract forces.

Sexual Reproduction

Deities are created by sexual reproduction among older gods. Usually this process begins with some sort of primal mother and father figure (Mother Earth and Father Sky, for instance) who produce offspring. These children then mate with other gods and goddesses (or even mortals) to produce new deities.

This scheme requires multiple divine forces, with strong anthropomorphic aspects so that they may reproduce in a "normal" fashion. (That may not restrict the manner in which the gods give birth however; offspring could be born through any part of the body, or even vomited out.) Often these deities are quite human, with temperaments, strengths and weaknesses to match. As they are "born," so, most likely, do they "die," and indeed it is possible for new deities to replace older ones. The cosmos of reproductive deities is a changing one of highs and lows, triumphs and defeats and mixed alliances. The Greek pantheon is perhaps the best-known example.

Accidental

Deities occur by accident, usually as a byproduct of some other action or force (often the creation of the world). There is an element of chance here, a randomness that will probably determine the nature of the deities. They were not necessary, or predestined, but accidental. Often these deities have limited powers, and are subject to higher powers of fate and chance.

GMing Deities

Whenever a GM decides to incorporate active deities and the religions that follow them into a game world, he must give some thought to the way the deity presents itself to its followers. The deities may walk the earth clothed in human forms, or not appear at all. If they appear, they may not always take the same form. They may make their wishes known in terms of visions and mystical occurrences. Perhaps they see their followers as flies they can swat at their leisure, or as objects of interest, or as real people with interests as diverse as their own.

So much depends upon the particular attributes of the deity that it is difficult to generalize. But truly *active* deities should be just that – active! They should not sit placidly in the heavens and wait for someone to summon them. They will have very definite interests, motivations and problems. They will set goals, and often feel free to prod the PCs in ways that suit their purposes. In short, they will act very much like any other NPC, except that they are much more powerful, and, in many cases, much more limited in what they can and cannot do. Often they must rely upon agents, even the adventuring group itself, to see that their will is carried out. They can be quite benevolent to those who please them, and utterly ruthless to those who do not.

Balance is, as always, an important issue. Gods make poor enemies – unless they have no direct way of retaliating. Limiting factors must be found, or the GM will quickly find the deities taking over the world, leaving little of value or interest for the players to contribute. Divine laws (see p. 37), limited access to the "real" world, and fear of or worry about retribution from other divinities can all combine to keep gods from getting too many fingers in the pie. The most interesting deities are often the most limited, for they must find ways to make the party do as they wish. All-knowing, all-seeing, all-powerful deities become boring quite quickly.

Divine Roleplaying

A twist on the standard party adventure is to allow each player to draw up one deity of a pantheon. Assign each one a particular area of influence as well as a general set of abilities, interests, etc. Deities can be drawn up as *Supers* characters, with 1,000 or more points, and fleshed out using the rules in this book. Additional advantages and abilities can be created at the GM's discretion. Or they can be drawn up as ordinary characters, but all damage they take or give is divided by 10. Or the GM may decide not to use dice at all!

The focus of this sort of roleplaying is on the interactions between the deities as they try to accomplish whatever goals they set themselves. The GM (or other players) can play the high-level clerics and followers, with maps drawn up to represent the areas of the world in which the gods hold sway. Battles can be fought, demigods created and destroyed, even gods killed as the pantheon goes at it. Or the GM can create outside influences that force the deities to rely upon each other and interact in new ways.

This can be used in the initial development of a world to create the basic mythological elements which later generations of player characters might worship or investigate. A GM might even have one group of players roleplaying the gods, while another group runs the followers, trying to understand and implement the desires of the first.

Many different variations on this theme can be tried, depending on the interests of the players and the GM.

Belief

Deities are created by the true faith and belief of their worshipers, or are personifications of an idea they hold to be true. These deities are completely dependent on their believers, their very natures sculpted by the fabric and substance of faith or thought. (See pp. 33 and 38.) But although they depend upon their followers, their powers and existence are still quite real.

A GM could make this the test for sentience – the ability to create and power a god!

Abstract Representation

Deities do not exist in any separate form, but occur rather as abstract representations of the forces of the world – time, the wind, the sun, the flow of a river. Their strength lies in the raw force of their particular element. The god, River, is an abstract power representing the wild fury of a raging river, the slow, irresistible force of the spring floods, and the life-giving nature of all water. Quite different from the God of Rivers, a supernatural entity who rules over the rivers of the world and their inhabitants.

These deities are created by the creation of the world, since they *are* the world.

Attributes

The purposes of the deity in the game world, the deity's powers, strengths and weaknesses, how the deity views its followers, what it asks of them, how actively it interferes in the "real" world – the GM must decide all of this and more for each of the major powers he creates.

Archetypes

Deities are frequently built on archetypes: primordial images, characters, or ideals of a society common enough to be considered universal. These may be elemental forces such as fire, water, earth or air, or facets of nature, embodying the characteristics of animals, plants, rivers, the sky, the sun, the moon, etc. Other archetypes are more abstract, concepts that represent the variety of human experience, such as mother, father, truth, justice, beauty, heroism, ferocity, or death. The true measure of an archetype is its ability to provoke the same feelings or reactions from a wide variety of different people. Listed below are some common archetypes, grouped roughly according to level of abstraction. These are presented as examples designed to stimulate further thought. Under no condition should this be considered a complete list of archetypes, nor a listing of necessary forces. Various archetypes might easily be combined in a single deity. Even the lines between categories are blurry at best.

Primal Forces: Creation, destruction, order, chaos, fate, prophecy or oracles, destiny, time, luck, death.

Abstract Natural Forces: Birth, death, undeath, light, dark, air, fire, water, earth, sky, sea, nature, animals, plants, spring, summer, fall, winter.

Specific Natural Forces: Dawn, twilight, day, night, sun, moon, stars (especially morning or evening star), north, south, east, west, wind, rain, weather, thunder, lightning, rivers, lakes, mountains, volcanoes, trees, forests, flowers, deserts, snakes, dragons, birds, insects, magic.

Abstract Societal Concepts: Art, beauty, smithing, carnage, crone, dance, disease, famine, fertility, guardian, handicrafts, harvest, healing, home and hearth, hunting, illusion, judgment, justice, law, learning, love, maiden, mercy, messenger, midwife, mother, music, oath or pledge, poetry, politics, peace, pestilence, prosperity, revenge, sickness, trade, victory, victim, war, warrior, wealth, wine, wisdom, witch.

Historical Personages: Deified historical persona, most often with associated myths and legends of their deeds. Ancestors, heroes, kings, saviors, saints, representatives of state and nation.

Extent of Power

In some cosmologies, deities are all-powerful entities who control the very fabric of the universe. In others, deities have very specific powers that they may only use in limited circumstances. The definition of exactly what each deity can do is important in determining what powers they can then pass on to their clerics and worshipers.

The Symbolism of Form

The physical forms associated with a deity are often symbolic in nature, helping to reinforce the deity's attributes in the minds of its followers. The GM should think carefully when selecting forms for deities. Strong associations can help players make the proper connections, and the symbolic aspect can enrich and enliven the game world. The symbolism commonly associated with a variety of forms, in a variety of religions and cultures, appears below.

Bull – A common symbol in Near, Middle and Far Eastern religions, most gods in Semitic religions are likened to, and represented as, a bull. The bull was prominent as an incarnation or attribute of Egyptian gods and kings. People have variously associated the sun, the moon, and the constellation Taurus with the bull. The Hittites associated the bull with thunder. It embodies divine rage.

Cat – The cat was sacred to the Egyptians because it was the primary form of the Egyptian mother-goddess, Bast. The goddess Freya rode to war in a chariot pulled by cats. Cats are commonly associated with dark magics and various forms of luck or chance.

Cow – Sacred still in India and once in Egypt and Greece as well, the cow, a symbol of life through the rich bounty of its milk, embodies divine beneficence. In Egypt, Isis-Hathor was the divine cow whose udder produced the Milky Way and all the stars. She personified the night sky, being named also Nut or Neith, with the stars appearing along her belly. In Greece, the white cow-goddess called Io, the moon, who wore the three sacred colors red, white and black, was the precursor to Hera, frequently called "the cow-eyed." Another of her Greek names was Europa, mother of the continent of Europe. Her name means "full moon"; she wed the father of gods while he wore the form of a white bull.

Coyote – The tribes of the North American Indian groups see the Coyote as trickster and sometimes creator. The Coyote is pictured alternately as a trickster who releases impounded game, imparts knowledge of arts and crafts, secures fire, daylight or the sun, and as a bullying, licentious, greedy, erotic, fumbling dupe.

Continued on next page . . .

The Symbolism of Form (Continued)

Dove – A symbol of peace and purity, the dove is sacred to early divinities of love and fertility such as Ishtar and Aphrodite. In some places doves are used as sacrifices for divination and love charms.

Eagle – The king of birds, commonly associated with royalty. In Greek mythology the eagle was closely associated with Zeus and his lightning. In the Indian Vedas, the sacred soma was brought to man by an eagle. Everywhere the eagle is noted for the speed with which it flies, the keenness of its sight, the marvelous height to which it soars, the inaccessibility of its nests, and the many years it lives.

Falcon – A funerary symbol, the falcon is sometimes associated with the souls of the dead flying away to the lands of peace.

Fox – Commonly associated with slyness and cunning, the fox is a common shapeshifter in many different mythologies.

Hawk – Ancient Egyptians recognized the hawk as a totemic form of the god Horus. In Greece the hawk was sacred to Apollo and hence, like the eagle, a sun bird. The hawk god Khu-en-ua was a conductor of souls, sometimes serving as the divine boatman ferrying the dead across the underground river.

Continued on next page . . .

Omnipresence

The deity is everywhere, capable of influencing all things. Omnipresence is common in deities representing primal forces (such as fate or time) that are universal. It is a common characteristic of a monotheistic divinity. Omnipresent deities have a great sphere of influence, but often their power is relatively weak in any one place or time. They tend to choose breadth over depth, and can often be overcome by more vital (although limited) deities for short periods of time. But they generally prevail in the end. Their power is an inevitable part of life; there is no place to escape it.

Omniscience

The deity knows all, sees all. This "all" may be just what is currently occurring upon the world, or it may extend into the past and the future, allowing the deity to know all possible outcomes of any given event. Omniscience is common in deities who represent truth and knowledge, as well as those who embody the primal forces of fate, prophecy and luck. Deities of light are often portrayed as omniscient, since part of light's symbolism is the shining brilliance that reveals all.

Omniscient deities will always know what their clerics and followers are up to. They are often approached for guidance or wisdom, though they often choose to veil their knowledge in riddles or ambiguous prophecies.

Omnipotence

The deity is all-powerful. Omnipotent deities are relatively rare in mythology, for a deity who can right any wrong must answer for all that he leaves undone. Often omnipotent deities are seen as harsh, cold and uncaring, with concerns that reach far beyond the humble lives of their worshipers. Indeed, a truly omnipotent deity may not need worshipers!

Generally, an omnipotent deity is seen as a fundamental force – creator, destroyer, and all that falls in between. Omnipotence does not necessarily mean solitary, though many omnipotent deities are the only supernatural forces in their respective cosmologies. A cosmos with multiple omnipotent deities can be quite interesting, especially if they choose, for whatever reason, to limit their interactions with their followers and concentrate upon one another. (Omnipotent gods who concentrate on vexing the followers of *other* omnipotent gods can also make life very interesting – especially for the followers!)

Limited Potency

Some deities are limited to a given area or locale, unable to extend beyond it. Others can touch any part of the world, but only in limited ways, usually related to the aspects they govern. For example, a god of wind can go anywhere, but his power may be limited to puffing and blowing, whipping up storms and mighty gales, carrying people or objects from one place to another, and so on. But he couldn't start a fire, build a house, or heal the sick. Other deities may be powerful at particular times, such as during the day, or in the winter, spending the rest of the time in a weakened state.

These limits might be natural, or self-imposed, or imposed from without. In some cosmologies even the deities must follow rules, particularly when interfering in the lives of their worshipers. This may be an absolute dictate that the deity may never violate, or a less-binding promise that tricky deities may seek to flout. Usually such restrictions aim to preserve some balance or primal force, with the understanding that deities who meddle too much can throw things greatly out of kilter. Deities may even be subject to limitations placed upon them by others of their kind, in the form of curses, geases, or binding oaths or laws (see *Divine Laws,* p. 37).

Physical Form

Once thought has been given to the extent of the deity's power, its physical form or manifestation should be considered. Does it have one constant form that it always takes? A variety of forms that it can choose between? Or is it completely mutable, taking whatever form it wishes at any moment? The more powerful the deity, the more likely that it has several possible forms. Static forms are generally found in the weakest of divinities (who don't have the power to change themselves), in those who represent some physical object from which they derive their form (such as the sun, a tree, or a mountain), or in the most powerful . . . where it might be said that the deity has no true form, but is found in all things. A deity's powers may change with its form, giving it good reason to switch from one to another.

Humanoid

The "made-in-the-image-of-god" concept is relatively widespread. Many deities have a form mirrored by that of their worshipers, and the gods may often reveal themselves in this form. An anthropomorphic form can make the deity much less intimidating to its believers, creating a common ground. Deities with strong personalities, or who represent particularly human archetypes or motifs, will almost always have a humanoid form. Certainly it would be hard for a human to see anything but an extremely beautiful woman as a goddess of love and beauty!

Animal

After humanoid, deities most commonly manifest physically in animal form. All of the Egyptian gods roamed the earth in animal forms. Animals are often seen as being closer to nature (and so the divine) than man is. Deities who take animal shapes also assume animal characteristics (see *Symbolism,* p. 66, and sidebar, pp. 25-29). Frequently the animal form is but one of many possible forms the deity might take (Zeus was notorious for taking animal forms during his amorous pursuits).

Archetypal

Another common thought is that the divine essence infuses the material which it represents. Thus a sun deity *is* the sun, rising each morn and setting each night. The spirit of the river lives within the rushing and roaring tumult. A volcano's eruption is a physical manifestation of the anger of the deity that lives within. Once again, the archetypal form might be just one shape the deity can choose to assume.

None

It is also possible that the deity has no shape whatsoever. This is especially true if the divine force is particularly abstract. Shamanistic divine spirits can affect the material world, but since they do not dwell on the physical plane, they have no physical bodies.

The Symbolism of Form (Continued)

Horse – Though only the Celtic Epona and the divine horses of Diomedes in Thracian myth retain the horse form among divinities, horses are closely associated with many gods, goddesses and demigods. Demeter sometimes appeared with a horse's head. Poseidon, Athena, Aphrodite and Cronus all had horse aspects at various times. Helios, among many others, rode in chariots pulled by horses. Horses are considered symbols of fertility, and in some cases are symbolic of the soul in journey.

Hound – Common companions of many gods and goddesses, hounds were often assigned to use their keen senses of smell to find and escort ghosts and, as guardians, to inspect the souls of the dead. In Babylon, the dog was the symbol of the gate goddess, Gula. The Celtic healer god Nodens took the dog for his zoomorphic form. Sirius, the dog star, was associated with Pan, whom Pindar called the "shape-shifting dog of the Great Goddess." In northern Europe, heavenly moon dogs carried away the dead. These were directly related to the hounds of Annwn and the great black hounds that scouted for the Wild Hunt of Odin and his ghostly company.

Jackal – In Egypt, the jackal was associated with Anubis and guided the dead to their otherworld destination. In Asiatic folk tale he provided for the lion, scaring up game for the lion to kill and eat, taking the remains as his just reward. From this he is sometimes termed "the minister of the king."

Lion – A symbol of royal power and strength, lions figure as attributes, companions and guardians of many deities. Lion statues are seen guarding the doors of ancient Assyrian temples. Lions symbolized the Babylonian god, Nergal, as well as the Egyptian gods Ra and Horus. Buddhists use the lion as a symbol of courage, nobility and constancy, and consider him to be the harbinger of good luck. Many ancient cultures used the lioness as the symbol of maternity and an attribute of the mother goddess. The Egyptian goddesses Bast and Sekhmet were lion-headed.

Owl – A symbol of wisdom and knowledge, the owl was associated with Lilith, Athena, Minerva, Blodeuwedd, Anath and the staring owl-eyed goddess Mari. To the Algonquin Indians, the owl was a bird of death and of the winter, creator of the north winds. To the Babylonians, hooting owls were ghosts of women who died in childbirth.

Continued on next page . . .

The Symbolism of Form (Continued)

Panther – The panther or leopard was a totemic symbol of Dionysus, whose priests wore panther skins.

Phoenix – A symbol of rebirth, the phoenix is originally associated with a god of Phoenicia. The sun, who flew on wings through the heavens, was constantly immolated and reborn from the fires of sunset and sunrise. Egypt's phoenix was associated with a heron-like bird sacred to Osiris, symbolizing both the human soul and the god's cycle of rebirth and resurrection. Sometimes the bird represented the morning star.

Ram – Rams are commonly associated with male virility and fertility throughout the world. The Egyptian god Amon was symbolized by the ram, which also holds a place in the zodiac under the name Aries.

Raven – In almost all cultures ravens are considered to be birds of ill-omen, harbingers of death and pestilence. The raven was considered a battlefield bird in old Irish mythology, and several goddesses appeared on the combat field in this form. The Morrigan in particular invoked war by simulating the raven's harsh cry. A Russian epic identifies the raven as the symbol of the enemy, and in Lithuania the raven is considered a bird of battle. However, in Yukaghir folklore, in the tundra and scrub zones of Arctic Siberia, as well as in the traditions of Northwest Pacific Coast tribes from Alaska down through British Columbia, the raven is a trickster.

Continued on next page . . .

Domiciles

If the deity has a physical form in this world, then that form may live in one place all the time, or may move to different locales. Supplicants may have to travel to address the deity, or it might come to them.

The GM must also decide if the domicile is the only place the deity has power, thereby limiting its sphere of influence. This may be true if the god lives within a volcano or a river, for instance. Or the residence may simply be the place where the deity has the most power, and thus chooses to settle.

Within the World

The divinity might be one and the same as the particular aspect of the world that it represents. The goddess of the river may reside completely within the banks that bound her domain. The sun god might live in the sky, the volcano deity in his fiery pit of lava.

The deity may live in all instances of its aspect, only in some of the largest and most spectacular, or in one particular place. This decision may affect the deity's sphere of influence.

Remote Locales

Another idea is that the deity resides in some remote location of the world. Mountains are perhaps the most popular, but at the four corners of the world, beneath the earth or the sea, and in the sky are all common locations. Anywhere that is particularly inaccessible will do, especially if it happens to be subject to powerful and inexplicable forces (earthquakes, volcanic eruptions, and so on).

Once again, having placed the deity, the GM must decide just how inaccessible its dwelling truly is. Epic quests which require direct dealings with the divine make great fodder for high-fantasy campaigns.

Wandering

Some deities don't live anywhere in particular, but rather roam hither and yon, according to duty or whim. Their particular aspect might require this wandering (disease, war and trade are all aspects that would suit itinerant deities), or it might just be the nature of the divine to be everywhere and nowhere at the same time. Many myths speak of deities who change shape into people or animals and wander the lands for purposes ranging from seduction to the completion of some goal or task.

If the deities wander, the GM should give some thought to how he will handle their direct interaction with characters. Most often those who see a god in physical form will have no idea that it is indeed a deity. (This is a good way for deities who are not omniscient to test the faith of their followers or clerics.)

Holy Places

Deities may reside in certain icons, shrines, temples, or other objects particularly holy to themselves. This is most common for deities whose scope is limited to a particular geographic area, and who depend upon their worshipers for their power. Believers are charged with tending the repository of the divine essence, and in return they are granted boons and special powers. The power of the god might be tied directly to the form or structure which houses it, or it might be much more resilient, simply choosing to take up residence in this place for convenience or some other reason of its own.

Other Planes

Another common thought is that some or all of the deities reside in some special area or plane beyond mortal ken. This might be the Greek Mount Olympus, the Egyptian underworld, the Hindu *Tap Loka* (Sphere of Penance), or the Immortal Plane.

If the deities live in another sphere or realm, what impact does that realm have on our own? Is it possible for a mortal to move from one to another, or can only a god make the trip? Myths are full of long, arduous journeys to the realms of the gods to ask some favor or gain some reward. Often there are a series of obstacles to keep out the unwary, a river or other "natural" boundary that must be crossed, and various other tests that only the truly worthy can overcome. Or perhaps the journey requires a special magic, like the ecstatic trance of the shaman, to pierce the realm of the divine – a journey made in spirit or soul as opposed to body.

Note also that different deities may control different realms. The concept of a deity whose task it is to supervise the souls of the dead is almost universal. And Mother Earth is almost always thought to reside within the earth itself.

Immortality and Death

In most cases, deities cannot die. Certainly they can ignore most, if not all, threats from mortals. Most deities are immortal – once created they will continue to exist until the end of time. Their full powers are far beyond those that any mortal can muster – so giving them numeric attributes or hit points is rather futile. They are not affected by normal weapons or magics. At best they might be bargained with, or weakened by disrupting the lives and worship of those who give them power. However, there are some exceptions to this general rule. The following sections cover instances in which deities might be weakened even to the point of true death.

Fading

Those deities who gain their powers directly from their worshipers can be weakened to the point of "fading" if all who pay them tribute are destroyed. A faded deity still exists, but does not actively manifest in the material world. Should its worship be resumed, the deity can be brought back, but this is a long, costly process that will take years, if not generations (see *Faded Gods,* p. 32).

Physical Deaths

Lesser deities (often little more than spirits) might be bound to some physical entity such as a shrine or holy object. Depending on the nature of the binding, destroying the object may destroy the deity. On the other hand, this might just set the deity free, possibly dissipating its powers until it can find another such object to reside in.

In other cases, a deity might choose to manifest a great deal of its power in a single form in order to complete some mission or task. This form, sometimes called an *avatar* (see sidebar, p. 38), will have but a fraction of the deity's true power, and is

The Symbolism of Form (Continued)

Ravens are also associated with prophecy, and "having the foresight of the raven" is a proverbial saying. The raven was the oracular bird of the Irish mythological Bran. Odin, All-Father of the Norse gods, had two ravens, whose Icelandic names meant Thought and Memory, who brought him news every day of all that men did.

Snake – Snakes are associated with female power and immortality. In India, the "Mother of All that Moves" and goddess of the earth was associated with a serpent. The Middle East used to regard the snake as the embodiment of enlightenment or wisdom, understanding the mysteries of life. The Siamese speak of Sarpa Rakta, the red snake who brings secret omens from the gods.

Stag – Closely associated with the Horned God of the mother-earth religions, The stag is generally considered a male forest spirit because of his tree-like horns.

Swan – Regarded as a symbol of maidenly purity, the swan is associated with the Vedic heavenly nymphs. The Vedic Brahma had the swan for his special vehicle or birdlike incarnation. Zeus appeared in the form of a swan to impregnate Leda. As well as being one of the birds of Aphrodite, the swan also symbolized the muses, and through them Apollo. The Norse valkyries wore cloaks of swan feathers, indicating that they might transform into that shape upon occasion. And the valkyrie queen Kara definitely had a swan incarnation, perhaps based on the Indo-Aryan goddess Kauri who appeared as the leader of the swan-nymphs.

subject to all laws of the physical world that the deity is not. This form may be given attributes and other character stats, and it may be affected by normal weaponry and spell magics. If this form "dies," the power within it returns to the deity.

Food and Drink of the Gods

The sustenance of the gods has long held a special fascination. In some cases the food and drink of the deities is reserved for them alone, granting special powers to those who might manage to sneak a nibble or a sip. In others, the drink of the gods is merely a favored drink of their followers, given to the gods in sacrifice and devotion.

The following are some examples from various mythologies:

Ambrosia and Nectar: The food and drink of the Greek gods of Olympus, they gave immortality to all who partook.

Amrita: The legendary drink of immortality in Hindu mythology, amrita was thought to be the lost water of life produced at the churning of the ocean. The name is applied to various Vedic sacrifices, but particularly to the soma juice (see below).

Mead: The favored drink of the Norse gods, supplied endlessly by Odin's goat, Heidrun, who fed on Yggdrasil. It is a fermented drink of honey and water, known to the ancient Greeks and Romans and common in medieval times throughout Europe. Mead was thought to be the early sacrificial drink of the Aryans.

The people of Rugen island (off the coast of Germany) used mead in the worship of their sun god. At each harvest a cup of mead was put in the hand of the idol. During the following rites the priest took the cup from the god and predicted the coming year from the liquid left in the cup.

Soma: The soma plant of India provides an astringent narcotic juice thought to have divine power. It was offered, mixed with milk, butter, barley and water, to the gods, but was drunk by all Aryans. Later only the three highest castes were allowed to drink it, and then only for religious purposes. The soma sacrifice became one of two main rituals to the deities. In game terms, soma is about as addictive as marijuana; the GM may decide that it grants a +1 modifier to shamanistic rituals or to miraculous magic (since the plant is worshiped both as a plant and as a representation of the god).

Reincarnation

In many mythologies, deities associated with the cycles of nature are assumed to die and be reborn in the normal order of things. Vegetation gods are usually described as dying each autumn to be reborn at winter's end. Sun deities might sink each evening into a sea of primal chaos, only to rise again at the dawn of the new day. Some Hindu gods were born, lived for thousands of years, and then died, to be born again during the next grand celestial cycle.

This is considered a normal part of the life of the deity, unaffected by mortal actions (though certainly the death and rebirth of the god affects the powers granted to its worshipers, as well as the whole nature of the deity's religion). Often the religion's power closely mirrors that of the deity – holding widespread influence during the height of the deity's strength, and diminishing greatly when the deity weakens (see *Changes Over Time*, p. 56).

Man may even participate in this cycle. Heroic adventurers could be prophesied to end the reign of a dark god . . . who then lies asleep for some preordained time before waking once more.

Transformation

Other mythologies speak of deities who seem to die, but are only reincarnated in a different form, often with different (and sometimes greater) powers. Once again this is a natural process that is likely to be reflected in the religion that worships the deity. The followers of the deity might influence this transformation in some way.

True Death

In some cases it *is* possible for a deity to die – but only at the hands of another deity, or a true and predestined hero. (The hero usually works at the behest of fate or destiny, and thus is in many ways a pawn in the hand of a greater force. This sort of plot should only be undertaken with great care and forethought.) Generally only anthropomorphic deities with limited powers can be destroyed in this way. Even a deity may hesitate to actually kill another deity, as this may have drastic effects on the fabric of the world.

A god that personifies an idea cannot be killed without wiping the idea out of the minds of sentient creatures. If sentient creatures still need the concept, this could prove impossible.

Attitudes

Every deity has a personality, be it kind, warm and loving or harsh, cold and cruel. Most deities will fall somewhere between the extremes. Often the attitudes of a church or religion of the deity will mirror the deity's own attitudes (although an inactive, unconcerned deity may find its religion developing attitudes that it does not necessarily embrace.)

Benevolent

The deity is kind and loving. It truly cares for the welfare of its followers and will do almost everything in its power to aid them.

Benevolent deities must be limited enough that they don't solve all their followers' problems for them. Perhaps the deity cannot directly interfere in the lives of its worshipers unless called upon (see *Divine Intervention,* p. 113), either due to divine strictures or physical limitations.

Some deities are only benevolent to certain people – their own followers, or those who follow their strictures and do as they desire – but cruel and intolerant to those who defy them.

Malevolent

The deity is evil and malicious. It cares for nothing but its own power base. It might even take pleasure in the misery and suffering of others. The problem with truly malevolent deities is deciding why anyone would willingly follow them. It might be that none *do* willingly follow, but are coerced by the power of the god (see *Maltheism,* p. 137). Or it might be that the deity offers great wealth and power to its direct servants.

A single deity may be benevolent to those who follow it, and malevolent to those who do not. (Mere dislike and intolerance does not constitute malevolence. A malevolent deity or religion takes delight in destruction far beyond the simple desire to weaken an enemy.)

Meddlesome

The deity is very active in the affairs of the world. It constantly checks up on its followers, offers advice, and uses its powers to affect the course of events – a cosmic busybody.

Meddlesome deities should never be particularly powerful. If they are, people will quickly realize that little that they do matters – since the deity is busily arranging things to suit itself. This personality attribute is more appropriate for a limited divinity who must convince its followers to do those tasks it sees as necessary.

Meddlesome deities will often communicate with their followers through omens, answers to prayers, even full divine manifestations. Particularly intrusive ones might offer their followers bonuses on their Divine Intervention rolls (see *Divine Intervention,* p. 113), though GMs should be *most* cautious about allowing this sort of boon.

Indifferent

The deity is not at all active in the affairs of the world. Either it has other matters which concern it, or it simply does not care, and will rarely (if ever) intervene on the behalf of its followers.

Omnipotent or omnipresent deities often possess this trait. Indifferent gods almost never answer their followers in any sort of concrete way, preferring that those who desire enlightenment find it for themselves. Followers of particularly indifferent deities may have to take penalties on their Divine Intervention rolls (see *Divine Intervention,* p. 113) to reflect their god's extreme dislike of meddling in earthly affairs.

Although a deity may be generally indifferent, certain events might attract its interest. A deity might also be indifferent to normal goings-on, while concerning itself greatly with the activities of its higher-ranked clerics. Or it may truly not care, letting its worshipers muddle along as best they can on their own. Some may take great delight in watching the unguided bumblings of man, considering them an eternal source of divine amusement.

Apotheosis

For those few who achieve true enlightenment, there is the possibility of apotheosis – the raising of a mortal to a divine state. This implies that the individual has achieved true unity with the divine, and can freely tap the same power.

This is not a common thing, nor is it something that a PC should expect to accomplish. True apotheosis turns someone from an individual into a godlike creature, concerned with the greater matters of the world. In some cases, apotheosis cannot occur until death. In others, the individual transcends to a deified state while still on earth. However, being more deity than man, he is no longer truly interested in the day-to-day affairs of mortals.

In legendary cases of apotheosis, the deified person leaves behind any former profession to become a prophet and teacher for his religion. If truly divine, he may even shift to the home of the gods, dropping all trappings of mortal existence.

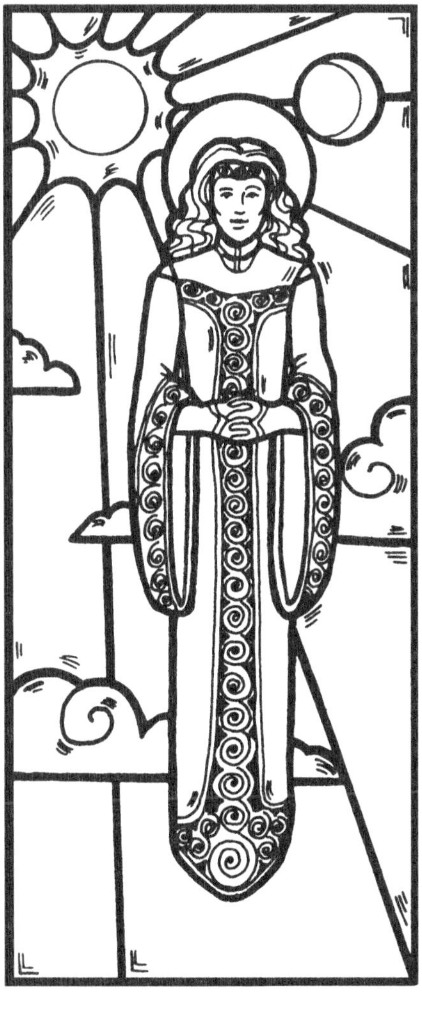

Faded Gods

Deities who depend upon followers for their power must take care of them. Should too many of followers be killed or converted to other religions, the deity may find that it is unable to sustain its own existence in the world, and fade.

Depending on the workings of the cosmos, a faded deity might be one who has simply lost influence upon the mortal plane (but still exists in whatever realm the gods call home), or it may be reduced to a set of potentials which either remain unfulfilled, or are taken over by another deity. Whichever the case, the loss of such a power might have visible effects upon the world. The earth may quake, rains fall for days on end, volcanoes explode, winds howl, and so on. If it was a particularly powerful deity, certain fundamental aspects of the world's workings may alter, causing shorter days, the birth of a new season, etc. Such disasters can be used from a historical view to explain the way things are now, or they may be true disasters and calamities that will affect the present world.

The GM may choose to center a prophecy around the destruction (or fading) of a god, threatening great horrors should the heroic quest be unfulfilled. Priests or fated heroes might easily be at the center of such campaigns.

Even should they fail, and the calamity come to pass, no god which has once existed and been followed is ever irretrievably lost. Its worship may pass into legend, its temples, religious texts and symbols turned into curious relics, and still the potential of its power remains. If there are those who desire to resurrect the deity, they may attempt to do so.

This can form the basis for a different sort of campaign – one in which the only apparent solution to the problems that beset humanity is to resurrect a dead (or faded) god. Such an adventure might require that questers to venture to the home of the gods to seek out the faded deity or its remains, and find a way of revitalizing them. Or it might simply be a matter of gathering enough interest and desire on the part of others to hold a large ritual wherein power is sacrificed to the deity to restore its power base. In some cases sacrifices of food, animals, or even willing members of the congregation may be necessary.

And if it turns out that the god is quite *different* from what the adventurers expected . . . a whole new quest may begin.

Observant

The deity closely watches all that occurs within its domain. If it is not omniscient, then it cannot see *all,* but what it can see it pays attention to. This does *not* mean that it necessarily acts on the information that it gains (that would require a meddlesome streak), but it will watch everything that it can.

Most actively-worshiped deities are considered to be observant. People like to think of their deity as being intelligent and aware of the world.

A deity may have many reasons for not divulging what it knows to those who follow it. It may be testing them, it might be indifferent to their concerns, or it might be cunning and mysterious, preferring to keep its knowledge wrapped in obscurity.

Oblivious

The deity pays no attention to the activities of the world. It cares little for day-to-day events, generally focusing its attention on the workings of whatever force or power it represents.

Oblivious deities are generally the more abstract ones who represent some simple primal force. They are not concerned with events in the world that do not directly impinge upon them.

Oblivious deities almost never answer scrying or informational questions, and often do not even have a divination aspect to their religion. They are quite content to let the world continue on its course without their aid. Oblivion and indifference are attitudes which go together well.

Forthright

The deity's nature and purpose is clear to all. Indeed, the deity may go out of its way to ensure that all know what its worship means, trying to spread the truths that it has to offer. Forthright deities often spawn proselytizing religions who wish to convert the ignorant to their brand of enlightenment.

Deities of aspects such as light, truth and knowledge are commonly forthright, as well as those postulated by the more philosophical religions. Abstract forces have little to hide, though they may be difficult to fully comprehend.

Mysterious

The deity drapes itself, its purpose and its followers in mystery. It keeps its true nature well hidden. Even clerics may not truly understand the deity they follow, until they reach the very highest levels. A mysterious deity may simply be incredibly secretive, forcing vows of silence and confidentiality upon those privy to its secrets. Or it might actively spread confusion about its nature and purpose, engaging in tricks and other hocus-pocus to confuse and befuddle.

Deities of illusion, thievery, chance, dreams, fate and prophecy are often mysterious. Mysterious deities are sometimes associated with the darker forces, as the darkness, too, seeks to hide and obscure. But one should not make the mistake of equating mystery with evil. In some societies *all* deities are mysterious in nature, revealing their secrets only to the initiated, and then only as the secrets are earned. Clerics of mysterious deities do not necessarily share this attitude, though they are always sworn to hide the secrets of the deity from the public view.

Codal

The deity follows strict codes of behavior. Its likes and dislikes are clearly defined and codified, and laid down as law for its believers to follow (see *Codal Systems,* p. 133). Depending on the deity's other attitudes, these laws may be anything from rules for the benefit of its followers, to specific details on capture, torture and ritual butchery of human sacrifices.

The churches of codal deities almost always have a rigid organizational structure, from the lowest lay member to the highest-ranking cleric. Each has his specific title, duty and responsibility to those both above and below him. Such deities are very intolerant of aberrant behavior. It is better for a follower to hold to the codes and fail than deviate from them and succeed. Indeed, the laws and codes of the cult may have the force of a sworn vow, and bound by personal honor. Such deities invariably have nasty ways of dealing with those who violate their laws.

The Mesopotamian goddess Tiamat, who is referred to as "the dragon of chaos," handed down law as part of creation. In Norse mythology, Odin upheld order against Loki and his children, the forces of chaos. The idea of order as good and chaos as evil comes from Zoroastrianism (see sidebar, p. 52).

Random

The deity has no strict codes of behavior or belief, comporting itself in disorder and confusion. This can be a friendly, carefree sort of disorder, or the vile unconcern of one who is as willing to destroy as to create. Such deities are random in their actions, often doing things for no particular reason or cause.

Note that the unenlightened may not be able to tell the difference between a god working toward a mysterious goal and a god being random.

Random deities usually spawn chaotic religions with little structure or organization. In some cases there is no real religion at all – followers pledge themselves to the deity and go merrily on their way doing whatever they like in its name. In other cases the religion is simply a facade for anarchy. Those who rise to power might be those who wield their influence most effectively, or they might just be those who happen to catch the deity's fancy. The only thing certain is that there will be no rhyme or reason to the entirety.

Chaos-worship may or may not be a purely fictional construct. Even for Michael Moorcock, who codified "Gods of Law" and "Gods of Chaos" for his works of fantasy, the concept wasn't totally clear. The chaotic elements in a religion are not simply echoes of an over-used convention which most gamers don't truly understand – those elements don't even match the gaming convention. For differences between religious and roleplaying ideas of chaos, see the sidebar on p. 138.

The Power of Faith

In some cosmic views, supernatural power exists in abstract forms which can be shaped and given true life and power by fervent belief. Thus, societies may truly create the gods according to their own imaginings – gods with real substance and power, but completely dependent upon worshipers for continued existence. If the belief falters or fails, then their existence slowly loses reality, sinking back to the initial abstract form, until some other strong faith gives it shape.

A GM using this structure can create many godly factions. Different cultures will likely form different beliefs, which in turn create different gods to be worshiped. Each people's gods are as real as the next – they're just different!

The nature of the deities will likely change as the people's faith matures, and their society and world changes. Or, once given life, it might be that the divinity is immune to further changes, and will require that the people hold by the reality they have created for themselves.

Cyclical Deities

Other worldviews will create cycles of time during which a god's power grows to a high point, and then slowly wanes to a low point, after which it will begin to grow again. Deities of Nature are particularly likely to have cycles of strength and weakness.

The cycles may be as short as a single day, in which the Sun god has little power at night, while the dark god has little power over day. Or they may be tied to the seasons, or even longer, multi-year periods. Some mythologies tie the powers of the gods to the heavens, defining spans of times in terms of tens or even hundreds of years when the stars align to grant power to a particular deity, only to replace it with another at the beginning of the next cycle.

Times of transformation from one power level to another can make for interesting gaming. Followers of a preeminent god might not be happy to find their place usurped by heavenly prerogative; they might seek to change the natural order. Or the cleric of a deity whose power base is particularly weak might find his influence growing steadily, along with his duties and responsibilities to those he serves.

Strengths and Weaknesses

All deities have strengths and weaknesses. Any character strength or flaw can also characterize a deity. It may be wise, greedy, peaceful, selfish, devious, generous, jealous, proud, honest, inquisitive, arrogant, rash, aggressive, protective, gullible, cunning and so on.

Relationships

When defining multiple deities, the GM must define their relationships with one another – how the various elements of the cosmos interact and what the politics of the heavens are. This includes establishing who their friends and enemies are and what guidance they give their followers in dealing with other religions about them. There are several common cosmological models, which can be combined for interesting results.

Allies

Deities form alliances from necessary circumstance, familial feeling, or mutual need.

Multi-Faceted Deities

One common divinity is a dual-or triple-faced deity where each "face" is a separate and distinct divine entity. For example, the goddess Hecate may be composed of the trinity Maiden, Mother and Crone. The Hindu god Ishvara consists of Brahma the creator, Vishnu the sustainer and Shiva the destroyer.

Quests and Geases

Now and then a deity will come upon a task that must be completed. This task might be a mere whim of the deity – the desire for some new expansion of its religion, or to recover some lost artifact or holy place – or it might be something essential to the continuation of the religion as a whole. If the deity cannot accomplish this task with its own powers, or that of its supernatural servants, it might turn to its dedicated followers for aid.

In most cases the deity will manifest itself before those it wishes to place under a geas, to provide some explanation of the quest and request their service. Those who refuse are likely to suffer the deity's anger and retribution. In some cases the deity does not directly manifest (depending on its powers and the nature of the world), but rather provides a prophecy, omen, or other sign of what it wishes. In any case, those who accept this service must do so completely, with the understanding that they will dedicate their lives to its completion.

Such quests are the bread and butter of epic fantasy novels, and can be the foundation of a fantasy campaign. Quests provide a long-term goal that will motivate the characters over a series of individual adventures, eventually resulting in a final confrontation and climax. And once their task has been completed, the adventurers may find themselves heroes of great fame, or enemies of great infamy (depending, of course, on the nature of the quest).

GMs must be wary, however, of organizing the entire actions of a party around one motivated individual, lest his death or removal leave the rest of the group bereft of purpose. Generally it is better to place the geas on several members of the party, whether they be faithful servants of the divine or not.

By their very nature these individual deities are allied, even though their purposes are often at odds (such as the creator and destroyer aspects of Ishvara). They may never war with or seek to destroy one another, as to do so would cause their own destruction. At times this presents a paradox, with contradictory forces as two sides of a greater coin.

This sort of "alliance" can never be altered, shifted, or broken. Though the deities may act separately (the relative balance of powers within the alliance perhaps shifting over time), and even squabble among themselves, they will live or die as one.

Dependencies

Even deities have hierarchies and interdependence. Some lead, others serve. Some must draw upon the powers of others to feed their own strength. The goddess of Shadow is dependent upon the sun, the moon, or some other source of light to turn darkness into her own element. The deity of rivers may very well be subservient to the deity of water. The harvest must have cooperation from the earth and the sky (in terms of weather) to reap her bounty. Storms cannot occur without wind.

Most deities are content with their place in the cosmos, whether it be master or "servant"; their divine interdependence is mirrored in their religions. Some, though, are less satisfied, and seek freedom and independence, or even a shift of the scales. They may plot and scheme, using their followers and clerics to seek ways of freeing themselves or gaining more power.

Family Ties

Anthropomorphic deities often have traditional familial relationships – that of father, mother, wife, husband, son, brother, sister. In some cases these relationships are all but ignored, but in others they create lasting bonds.

Strongest are the ties between mates or consorts. Sometimes mating bonds are made at the time of creation and never change. Other times they are formed during times of invasion and conflict – just as in earthly politics, where an alliance is formed and bonded with marriage. Children generally feel strongly for their parents, though they may covet and attempt to usurp their position and power. Siblings often squabble, and may be close or far apart. Parents may hate, ignore, or dote upon their divine offspring.

In some cases, there may even be multiple families of gods who scheme, plot and war against each other. The Norse mythologies have an example of this. There existed two families of Norse gods, the Aesir and the Vanir, whose members eventually intermarry for mutual benefit. Some anthropologists believe that this shows the influence of encroaching Aryan culture on indigenous northern Germanic cultures. If true, it would be clear evidence of myth following culture – or, in a game world, of the gods being influenced by the actions of their people, rather than the other way around!

Deities within a family setting are more likely to grow old and even die.

Political Alliances

Alliances may also be more fluid things, forming to suit the situation at hand, breaking when circumstances alter. Deities with human characteristics are often pictured playing politics with one another, vying for power and position, making and breaking alliances as needed. Generally these activities are mirrored upon the earth, where one church might unite with a traditional foe against a common enemy.

SF Deities

How does one incorporate the concept of a supernatural entity in the rational, scientific world of science fiction? Moon bases and galactic societies seem far away from the mysteries and superstitions of godlike powers. But even as people reach toward the stars, they risk discovering new things as mysterious and inexplicable as the creation of the universe was to our ancestors. Supernatural entities, or "gods" could easily be a part of this.

Perhaps the most common theme in SF religion is the meeting of humanity with an intelligence or alien race which is so far advanced that it is for all intents and purposes god-like. It may be benevolent, seeking to aid humanity's efforts to better itself, or it may not be so kind. Malevolent powers could demand worship, at the threat of utter extinction – a situation quite similar to our primitive ancestors contemplating their doom by forces beyond their control.

Another alternative is the creation of machine intelligences which so far exceed our own that they become "god-like." Future generations might not even realize that it was man who originally created their new masters. (Or see *Flatliners,* beginning on p. 144, for a variant.)

Or it might be that through scientific exploration, we discover a force or intelligence that underlies the fabric of our reality. Such a thing can be studied and analyzed, perhaps even fully understood, thereby attracting advocates who wish to use the truths learned therein to reach whatever ultimate fulfillment the universe provides.

Study of psionics and other mind-expanding techniques may contact god-like entities that exist on other planes of reality. (See *Disciples of Change,* beginning on p. 151, for an example of a "religion" that might lead to such a result.)

Enemies

As most deities have friends and allies, so, too, they have their enemies. Animosity might be caused by simple dislike, or particular events that have set the deities at odds, or fundamental antagonisms between the forces they represent.

Opposing Forces

Deities whose powers are mutually contradictory are opposed to the point that they cannot possibly coexist peacefully. Such deities are natural enemies; they cannot help but conflict.

Common examples are deities of light and darkness, good and evil, or life and death. Each by its nature destroys the other. Together they create a balanced whole, but always they must fight, each trying to subdue or destroy the other. Their religions and clerics will almost certainly be like-minded. This is the stuff of eternal conflict, often leading to long, epic battles for dominance.

Given the nature of their powers, it is impossible for both these deities to be dominant in the same place at the same time. Rather, it is a zero-sum game where one will always be weakened in direct proportion to the amount the other is strengthened. Clerics of one will likely acquire special modifiers in dealing with the believers of the other.

Feuds

Other deities have long-term feuds which govern their relationships. They simply do not get along. A deity of the hunt should not be expected to get along with a deity of the hunted! A goddess of mercy and healing will do her best to combat a god of famine, drought, or disease. And an agriculture deity will certainly not think very highly of a god of trade and commerce who promotes the interests of man over nature.

Generally these deities (and their followers) will battle wherever they might meet. But it may be a subtle sort of combat – dragging in other "neutral" deities on one side or another, and specializing in subterfuge rather than warfare. Outright bloodshed is not *necessarily* the only answer. Persecution, intolerance, social snubs or discrimination may also work in places where the two are forced to coexist. But they will never be friends.

Sibling Rivalries

Some deities that should otherwise be friendly may develop rivalries. They might fight over power, the right to certain followers, a coveted person or object. Perhaps it is a matter of personality differences, or of jealousy. These rivalries are generally more subtle than are direct feuds, especially since quite often the deities in question are supposed to be friendly (if not outright allies). Norse mythology gives us the foster brothers Loki and Odin who fought more than they aided one another. This rivalry can be mutual (two deities who compete against one another), or one-sided (one deity takes a dislike to another who still feels friendly or allied).

Coexistence

When the spheres of influence among the deities overlap, their relationships with one another must be considered. Sometimes a competition will result, with each trying to win over the followers of the other and gain complete control of the sphere. Or they will divide the powers, duties and responsibilities of the sphere in an equitable fashion, each content with its own piece. Multiple gods of death might argue, each stealing what souls it can find while figuring

Deities of Horror

Deities that inspire horror are generally those whose power is directed toward the dark side, either in terms of monstrous forms, alien intelligences, or the darkness within each of us.

Monsters or demons of horrible visage and immense power are the most popular – bug-eyed aliens from the void, animals of stupendous proportions and true intelligence, dark gods. Any great power with evil intent can easily find those who fear it enough to provide it with worship. Such deities may possess their followers, or simply direct their efforts. The only intelligence necessary is cunning, and even this may not be needed if the entity's powers are tremendous enough.

These monstrous deities could be new inhabitants of the world, either created by man's tampering with natural laws, or recently arrived from elsewhere. Or they may be incredibly ancient, fundamental aspects of darkness and evil born at the world's creation that have recently been unearthed, or whose worship has continued in secret for generations. Their powers can be as many and varied as the GM desires. (The Cthulhu mythos is a marvelous source of inspiration.)

But monster deities are not the only alternative. Forces of madness, insanity, chaos, and entropy can be just as horrific, and might not have forms at all. Worshipers are drawn to such forces by their own destructive desires, or by feelings of duty or tradition. Some even feel they sacrifice themselves for the general welfare, since without evil true goodness cannot exist.

Modern horror often draws upon the beast within, making supernatural entities out of man himself in such forms as vampires and werewolves. While often feared far too much to be worshiped, such creatures could be at the center of a constructed religion.

And, finally, there is the mystical, mysterious god with dark potential and unknown desires. Fear of the unknown is quite real; even if the entity is benevolent, a horrible visage or an inability to make itself understood might create a situation of fear and worship without the "god" truly desiring it.

ways to weaken the others. On the other hand, they might split the duties, assigning one to manage the underworld, another to escort dead souls, and yet another to "recruit" from the living.

Often how well deities coexist depends upon the nature of the power and the deities themselves. Deities of war are unlikely to peacefully cooperate, while those of peace and mercy are just as unlikely to come to blows. The splitting of powers and duties might be preordained at creation, or might change with the whims and desires of the deities in question.

Indifference

Deities might not care one way or another about each other. If their spheres of influence do not overlap or oppose, and their worldviews do not clash (or at least do not come into direct contact), then deities can go merrily on their separate ways without having to worry about one another. Some deities may not even form an opinion of a fellow god until some sort of interaction is required.

Shifts in the Balance

Things change. Deities rise and fall in power. Feuds may occur and eventually be resolved. Alliances may break and scatter. Rivalries may grow between former close allies. New deities may replace old ones. Sworn enemies may be forced to work together to defeat a common foe. Without change, the world stagnates. When developing a cosmos and the deities within, it is important to consider not only the way things are now, but the way things have developed since the early beginning, and the ways they might change in the future. Long wars and early devastations that shaped the world into its current form are recurring themes in many mythologies.

Fate/Destiny/Prophecy

A common theme is the prophecy which predicts major changes in the current balance of things in order to defeat some recognized evil, or to achieve some desired goal. It might be an alliance between forces with a history of bitter conflict, or a betrayal by a trusted ally; perhaps it is the coming of a new deity that will unite the others, or the death of a central figure that will throw the rest into conflict. In short, it is anything that upsets the whole, bringing a new and (possibly) better order.

Fated final battles are another recurring theme among mythologies. Ragnarok is well known (see p. 15). Generally the final battle constitutes the end of the world, which is then reborn.

Divine Laws

Sometimes the deities themselves recognize the need for rules. If deities can war with one another, then they can also sign treaties and enforce limits upon one another's behavior. A group of squabbling deities may become subject to a greater authority. Of course, all deities may not abide willingly by the law. Some require constant monitoring by their fellow divinities, and spend much of their time trying to slip the bonds of their confinement.

This is a situation rich with potential for limiting the powers of deities, especially as regards their ability to influence the world their followers live in. Cosmic politicking and wrangling can create interesting effects upon the "real" world – causing conflict between religions that were once at peace, or generating intrigue where there was none before – or vice versa!

In the House of the Gods

Some adventures may require the characters to visit the realm of the gods. Usually the PCs are seeking divine assistance beyond that usually available, perhaps even beyond the limits of the gods' power in the mortal realm. Or the adventurers may be seeking a deity for some other reason – hoping to find and resurrect a faded god, or even kill an existing one.

Whatever the case, the GM has several problems. First, how are the travelers getting there? Is this an actual, physical journey, or one of the spirit or mind? Often such lands are guarded by tests of physical prowess, mental capability, or spiritual strength. Guards may even include demigods or divine allies. If this is a required step in an epic quest, the GM must formulate trials that will truly test the mettle of the party members, without presenting insurmountable obstacles.

Then too, the GM must determine the general geography of the place. Is it fixed, or does it change to suit the whims of its inhabitants? Are the deities tied to particular locales, or do they move about? Are there other deities there besides the one that they seek? How difficult will it be to find their goal?

Unless the party is visiting a very minor god, or has some special artifact that renders them invulnerable, combat is unlikely – deities are much too strong to be dealt with that way. Still, the deity may require a test of strength, making the group defeat its servants, or some human/monster form of itself, before speaking with them.

Avatars

Avatars are living manifestations of the deity within the mortal world. In some cases they are wholly and completely of the divine, but more commonly they are some person, animal, or thing that the deity has chosen to invest with its presence and power. Some deities will always have one or more avatars, while others will only create them in times of need.

Human avatars are often chosen from people with special bloodlines, or with a divine mark or favor that renders them more accessible to the power of the god. Avatars will often have divine blood somewhere in their ancestry. The deity may choose to "possess" them for particular times and instances only, or the possession may be a permanent thing, leaving the person no independent will or existence of his own. Some gods might even breed children on mortals specifically for this purpose (see *PC Avatars*, below).

Animal avatars are always chosen from animals that have symbolic meaning or spiritual ties to the divine. Often the deity itself will be thought to have the animal form of its avatars, and the deity's followers will consider those animals to be particularly holy.

Continued on next page . . .

Worship

Most deities will have a following – a body of individuals who take inspiration from the god or divine force and apply it to their daily lives. The number of followers may be small or large. Their worship may be single-minded and devotional, or a matter of respect and offering. But some people, somewhere, must know of the god, or its existence may eventually be forgotten.

What Deities Get From Their Followers

Besides recognition, deities may or may not stand to gain anything from their followers. It may be a two-way link, in which each depends on the other . . . or the divine entity may be eternal and all-powerful, with no need at all for the worship its followers give. These are the two basic options.

Nothing

The deity gains nothing from its followers. It is eternal, independent of any need to be worshiped. It may ignore its followers completely, or it may choose to focus on their actions, meddling in their lives for its own reasons.

Religions worshiping these sorts of deities are driven almost completely by the spiritual needs of the people. The deity may, at any time, choose to turn its back on its followers, or it may decide to torment and punish them if they do not do as it wishes. The lack of a reciprocal need makes the deity all-powerful in regards to its followers.

Followers of eternal deities may find them uncaring and perhaps even cruel if the deity is indifferent or oblivious. They can offer nothing the deity craves. The unequal relationship might make the followers humble and subservient, wishing only to please a force to which they can offer nothing but their worship.

Alternatively, a benevolent deity may succor its followers and shower them with benefits just because it can.

Everything

The divine being requires the worship and belief of followers in order to survive. It may be that the deity is simply a potential force, existing without power until fueled by the fervent belief of others. Or it might be that belief actually *creates* the divine force. Or perhaps the deity has great power in an abstract sense, but can only focus its power through the faith and worship of others. Or it might have no ability at all to influence events in the material world except through the beliefs and actions of its followers. (See pp. 24 and 33.)

Deities empowered in this fashion are, by definition, limited. Their influence exists only while they have worshipers. This necessary dependence on their followers must affect the nature of the religion. Most likely the deity will take great pains to care for its followers, but a malevolent deity might use cruelty and torture to inspire the fear and respect it needs.

What Deities Give To Their Followers

In order for a deity to gain advocates, the faithful must in turn gain something tangible by worshiping it. Deities (and their associated religions) with nothing to offer their followers will soon find their worship extinct.

Answers

The most common thing a follower gains from his deity is peace of mind. The deity, through the religion that worships it, provides a framework in which to interpret the complexities of life. This framework explains the beginning (a creation myth), advises on dealing with problems that confront the believer, and, in some cases, prophesies an ending (see *The Cosmos*). It answers the common questions that plague humans . . . what kind of creatures we are, where we come from, why we are here, why the world is the way it is, why we suffer and die, and what happens to us after death. And the lifestyle, ceremonies and rituals of the people reflect the deity (see *Symbols*, beginning on p. 65). Where the deity does not directly answer these questions, or provide the necessary guidance, its clerics must extrapolate from divine inspiration, and find acceptable responses (see *Hard Questions*, p. 47).

Avatars (Continued)

Being a personification of the deity in the "real" world, avatars have powers far beyond those of normal humans, but are still less than the god they represent. Avatars, for instance, may be defeated in battle, though this simply destroys the mortal form, freeing the divine energy to return to the deity. Destroying a deity's avatar may, however, weaken the deity for awhile, until the deity can recover the freed energy and turn its attention back to mortal affairs.

PC Avatars

PC avatars should be rare – the powers they represent are strong and their occurrence is potentially unbalancing. GMs should think *carefully* before allowing a player character to become an avatar of a god. Among other things, when the deity possesses the person, he will no longer be in control of his own actions. Instead, the GM takes control of the character. Few players will appreciate such a move.

In some cases the PC will have control over the coming of the deity, able to summon its presence when desired, while in others the deity will "possess" him at times and in circumstances of its own choosing. When not "possessed," the adventurer will generally have no special powers or abilities. Only under the control of the deity (and the GM) will he gain divine powers. Thus, being an avatar has no cost or benefit in terms of character points.

Divine Messengers

In cosmologies where deities either cannot manifest directly in the mortal world or find it quite difficult to do so, they often depend upon divine messengers to see that their wishes and desires are heard. These messengers may be separate demigods that serve the deity for one reason or another, or small, individual manifestations of the god that have separate form and will. Clerics of such deities will be used to dealing with these messengers and often mistake a messenger for the deity itself.

When used with care, divine messengers make excellent GM tools. They are assigned a particular purpose by the deity, but may have to deal with adaptations and variations in the "plan." The deity might even decide that a messenger should oversee the orchestration of one of its plans. It is thereby consigned to the mortal realm for an extended period of time, during which it will likely take on more and more human attributes. (GMs must be careful not to let the messenger take over the adventure in such cases.)

Depending on the circumstances, the messenger might appear in a blaze of light and glory, send the recipient of the message a vision or epiphany, or simply disguise itself in a familiar form so that it may converse with others. GMs can use divine messengers to instigate major quests and adventures, or use them to steer parties back to a more profitable course.

Alternatively, messengers might be sent to disrupt the activities of groups working against a particular deity, in which case they will either have to fight the messenger (much easier than taking on the deity), or work around them.

Love and Pride

Some religions stress the care their deities lavish on the faithful. This can be a source of great pride to their followers, who feel raised above the rest of the world by their god's attention.

Protection

The deity may offer protection from other deities, or even from itself. Malevolent deities commonly promise to destroy their followers last.

Powers

If the gods are real, then they have true powers, which they can grant to their special servants (clerics). The outward display of true power, as well as the opportunity to channel powers beyond those available to normal man, will draw many people to a religion.

Particularly devout servants may even be elevated to semi-divine states so that they can better aid their god.

Divine Manifestations/Intervention

Depending on the nature of the cosmos, the deity may not appear to its followers at all. Deities might not be allowed to manifest upon the material plane, either in physical form or by direct intervention. They might not have the power necessary to "appear," and be able only to make suggestions and influence their followers through visions and dreams. They may be able to appear, but not act, their manifestation little more than a phantasm. On the other hand, they may be able to manifest quite freely in startling and "miraculous" ways, limited only by their own interest and will.

A deity who can and does manifest easily must be carefully handled. A meddlesome, omnipotent deity would have little need for others to do its bidding, and will be likely to organize the world to suit itself very quickly. A limited deity with few abilities once manifested, or a disinterested one who rarely feels the need to exercise power, is more manageable. Remember, also, that deities may manifest for reasons having nothing to do with their followers. Oblivious deities may arrive on predetermined schedules or at inconvenient moments. Deities may even appear in unexpected forms or in ways that are completely unknown to their followers – this is particularly true of those with random or mysterious natures.

Deities with little or no ability to manifest in the world must keep their followers by faith alone. They will generally have less control over the form and practices of their religion – if they care at all. Those that do care will have to find more subtle ways to reach their followers, and wait for them to act.

A central concern is whether the god initiates the intervention by his will alone, or only at the call of a cleric or other believer. How often the deity can influence events directly, and whether there are any limits on the type and form of the intervention, are other matters the GM must decide.

At the God's Will

The deity manifests at its own discretion. While perhaps most likely, this must be handled carefully to avoid detracting from the accomplishments of the god's followers. This works well with deities of limited influence, as with those who are oblivious or indifferent. Another factor that might be used to limit this is only allowing the deity to appear before true believers. Thus the deity can manifest on its own initiative to request certain actions, behaviors, or sacrifices. It might appear to punish, or to bless.

At the Follower's Will

The deity manifests only at the call or invocation of the follower (usually a cleric). The deity could actually possess the follower for a certain amount of time, or the follower might simply call into his presence forces much greater than he could hope to achieve on his own. Generally the follower is allowed to specify a particular goal or task he wishes of his deity. This request is, of course, interpreted by the deity as it sees fit.

Alternatively, a deity may select one or two "chosen" individuals to whom it will appear, answering only their calls.

The simple desire for the deity's intervention is usually not enough to guarantee it. Usually rituals or special invocations are needed (see p. 113). And even then the deity may choose not to answer. It might be busy with some other task, or it might not find the summoning to be of interest. Never should a call for intervention be a "sure" thing – deities are not at the beck and call of their followers, no matter *how* much they may depend on their worshipers.

Frequency

If manifesting requires a great deal of the deity's power, then it will not be willing (or perhaps even able) to do so on a regular basis, or several times in quick succession. The price of summoning the deity's aid should be high, reflecting the cost that the deity must pay in order to answer (see *Divine Intervention,* p. 113).

Limits

The deity should be able to intervene according to its nature and power. Limited deities are, of course, restrained in the effects they can generate. Other factors, including divine agreements and "laws," may limit omnipotent deities (see *Divine Laws,* p. 37).

Temple Guardians

Another common use for divine servants is as temple guardians. In this case, their sole job is to guard and protect the sacred shrines of the deity. (See also *Demigods,* beginning on p. 42.)

Temple guardians spend most of the time either invisible or in static forms where their power drain is minimal. They only manifest upon detection of hostile intent, at which time they appear or awaken and set about their business. Since they are assigned to a single task, the deity usually takes pains to ensure that they are prepared for its eventuality – guardians are some of the nastiest of divine servants to tangle with. Most of their abilities will be combat-oriented, and they will never surrender or flee.

In most cases, the guardians are also backed up by real temple guards. In abandoned temples or remote shrines, the area might be completely devoid of life except for the guardians.

In order to give a party a fighting chance, the GM might come up with obscure and little-known weaknesses that the party can research and use against the guardians. Or, if the guardians are completely separate entities, it might be possible to break the contract that binds them in service to the deity as guardians.

DEMIGODS

A demigod is an immortal spiritual being, semi-divine in nature. Sometimes it is thought to be the offspring of a deity and another creature (animals, humans, other lesser beings or forces). Or it might be a "proto-god," needing only sufficient power and worship to reach full divinity – which happened frequently. Or it may be an altogether inferior being who serves the true deities. All types of spirits – angels, devils, demons and so on – fall under the general category of demigods – greater than humans, less than gods.

Demigods are defined by their attributes and their relationship to the world and the divine (if they serve one). Many different types of demigods may exist within a single world. Each deity may have its own lesser servants, or this privilege may be reserved for only a few deities. Or the world might be full of freely-roaming spirits which may choose individually whether to bind themselves to a deity.

GMs should keep in mind that most cultures don't refer to these beings as "demigods." They are referred to as gods, lesser gods or children of the gods.

Attributes

The essential nature of the demigod, its powers, form(s) and personality, may vary nearly as much as those of gods.

Limits to Power

Each demigod will have specific powers. In no way should these powers approach those of a true deity, even if the demigod is independent. Generally they are limited to a single area or aspect, though this varies directly with the power of the deities they serve. Demigods of an omnipotent divinity are likely to be much more powerful than those of a more limited deity.

Elementals: Elementals are lesser powers commonly found in fantasy worlds. Each elemental embodies the particular attributes of one of the four (more or less) elements in the world. Salamanders or ifrits characterize the essence of fire, undines that of water, golems earth and sylphs wind or air. New elements along with their elementals may be defined – shades for shadow or darkness, elementals of swamp or desert, and so on.

If deities that control these elements exist, then elementals will most likely serve those deities. If not, the elementals might be bound by some greater force (such as Nature), or might be free to do as they like.

Spirits: In an animistic worldview (see p. 127), a multitude of spirits fill the world, each controlling one specific thing. There are spirits of healing, of sickness, of anger, of justice and so forth.

Servant Entities: Some demigods are merely lesser manifestations of a greater deity's power. These demigods have whatever fraction of power the deity chooses to grant them. Their purpose is entirely to serve the whim and will of the divine by performing certain acts it ordains, which vary widely in scope. These may even have been clerics or devoted servants who have been elevated to a higher sphere of power.

Lesser Gods: A demigod might be an inferior deity, controlling some smaller aspect of the world much as a normal deity would do, but without the same amount of power or influence. Independent-minded lesser gods could watch over some of the more abstract realms of the world, like music, mischief, or midwifery. Sometimes a lesser god is limited to a certain locale.

Ancestors: Some believe that the human soul, upon death, ascends to a higher state of being. One's ancestors might then wander the world, watching over their lands and descendants much as they did while alive. If they followed a particular deity, they might become its servants. Otherwise they might be worshiped on their own as lesser powers.

Physical Form

Demigods may have any physical form. It is less likely that a demigod can change its form, although many can and do.

Domiciles

Demigods may live in the physical world, in the dwelling place of the deity they serve, or in another plane of existence all their own.

Immortality and Death

Like deities, most demigods are immortal. The only way to "kill" one is to find the source of its power and destroy it. However, when they manifest themselves on the material plane (the world), they *are* subject to physical types of damage (of one kind or another – this will vary according the individual demigod). If their physical manifestation is destroyed, then their power is dissipated until they can regroup and reform, which may take hours or millennia depending on the demigod and the situation.

Personality

Demigods often take on personalities which closely mirror the source of their power. They may share many of the same personality traits as the deity they serve, or they may be completely different. See *Attitudes,* p. 30, for ideas.

Relationship to the Divine

Demigods will generally have some kind of relationship to the divine, whether it be service, fleeing from service, or the jealous coveting of power. Those who do not seek service with a deity are either free-roaming sorts who wish nothing more than to be left alone, or would-be gods working on their own. Distinguishing factors are the demigod's source of power, its desire for more power, and its willingness to involve itself in the workings of the world.

Messenger

The demigod serves as the eyes, ears and mouth of the deity in the physical world. When the deity wishes to disclose omens or other indications of its desires, it may send the demigod in its place. When it wishes to know something, it sends its messenger to investigate. When not "at work," the messenger will either wander the world observing, or remain near the deity.

Missions

The demigod is sent to perform particular tasks at the deity's request. It will not return until the task is complete or it has irrevocably failed. The task may be anything of particular interest to the deity, and may require the demigod to get help from other deities, demigods, or mortal followers. In some cases the deity is quite specific about what may and may not be done; in other instances the demigod has almost total free rein.

Demigods with tasks are almost always *servant entities* (p. 43), though the mission might be payment for some other favor, or penance for some wrong. The child of a god was sometimes given a series of tasks to prove himself to his parent, in order to gain status.

Retribution

Servants of retribution are the divine police squad. They are sent out to deal with those who have particularly angered the deity – whether it be a follower who has transgressed against his faith, or a nonbeliever who has desecrated a place or object holy to the deity. Their powers are tailored for annoyance and destruction. They may just harass their target for some length of time specified by the deity. They might cause weapons he touches to shatter, make his golden coins turn to lead, haunt him with voices and eerie visitations, or generally make every aspect of his life miserable. Depending on the nature of the deity, they might injure or even kill him.

Servants of retribution inflicted on player characters can be treated as a standard *curse* (see p. 95). GMs should never allow one to kill a PC without at least offering him a fair (though not necessarily equal) duel, unless he stupidly asked for it (such as following a lie with "May the gods strike me dead if I lie").

Escorts

Escorts often wait at the fringes of the deity's home to bring any who might venture there before its lord. Others may perform other escort duties as determined by the god, including bringing newly-dead souls to the lands of rest.

Sycophants

The demigod exists to fawn upon and flatter the deity. Particularly common in a cosmic court of the gods, sycophant demigods might serve as courtiers, handmaids, entertainment, or simply as higher entities worshiping the deity in their own fashion. Sycophants will rarely, if ever, leave their duties of praise, and thus almost never answer calls from followers.

Guardian

The demigod guards some place of great import to the deity. Guardians are perhaps the most common sort of divine servant, and next to those of retribution, the nastiest. Some common guardian positions in various mythologies:

Temporal Guardians: Those who protect the holy places of the deity, their temples and shrines, from desecration and defilement.

Guardians of the Dead: Those who guard the final resting places of the dead. Such guardians ensure that only those who belong enter, and that they remain as long as necessary (often eternity).

Guardians of the Realms of the Gods: Those who guard the home of the deity. They exist to keep out those who would seek to disturb the divinity. Some bar all passage, while others will offer puzzles or riddles that may be solved in order to gain entrance.

DEVELOPMENT

3

How religions begin and develop, how other cultural influences affect them and how they change the culture around them are all issues (among many others) that the GM should consider when designing a game-world religion. Looking at the role religions play in our world can give a GM some ideas on where to start.

Building a Religion

Once the GM has decided on the cosmology and gods of the game world, it is time to create the religions. Often it is easiest to work backward: figure out what the religion *is,* then decide how it got that way. The GM needs to consider not only the basic nature of the religion, but also how it fits into society. The most obvious expressions of a religion are its ceremonies and symbols (see *Symbols,* pp. 65-87). But how does it interact with society and other religions? Answering these questions will help add a sense of realism and depth to any campaign.

Beliefs

The first step in designing a religion is to decide what its central beliefs are – what view of the world it gives to its followers, how it answers the fundamental questions of life and how it treats those who question it.

All religions have tenets. These can be traditions, scholarly writings, oral histories, commandments and laws. These *doctrines* form a system of principles and laws which state the fundamental beliefs and policies of the religion.

A *dogma* is a doctrine accepted by the followers of a religion as a god-revealed truth. A dogma bolsters the present position of the religion and is supported by both tradition and scripture, as well as being compatible with other accepted doctrines.

Purpose of Life

Perhaps the first questions that anyone might ask concern why we are here, who created us, and whether it was for a specific purpose, on a whim, or by accident. In many cases, the answers tie directly into the mythology of the religion. The creation of life is just another step in the creation of the world, and life's purpose is probably told in myth and legend (see *Creation of Life,* pp. 16-21).

Some religions impose harsh servitude upon their believers, forcing discipline and great sacrifices from them. Others encourage only what people desire anyway – wealth, power, health, prosperity. Some, like Hinduism, define clear-cut paths that restrict each person to a particular position in society.

As important as what the religion teaches its people about the purpose of life is the effect of the answer on believers. Those who believe themselves to be the chosen of the gods are more likely to put their own interests and survival ahead of others. Those who are taught that they are superior to other life forms may abuse them, or may see themselves as shepherds or caretakers. Those who view all life as interrelated are more likely to be tolerant of others.

And not all answers need be steeped in mysticism or "faith." A future religion may use rational or scientific answers: The world was created according to various principles or "laws" of nature. It lives and breathes and continues according to these same laws, no event being independent of a cause or an

The Knights Templar

A classic example of the conflict between State and Church – and how both may change drastically over time – can be seen in the history of the Knights Templar.

The Knights Templar was a crusading order which took part in a religious war in the Holy Land. Originally called "The Order of Poor Knights of the Temple of Solomon," it was founded by a group of pious soldiers around the year 1120. They protected pilgrims and lived under religious rule, taking oaths of poverty, chastity and obedience. The organization grew rapidly at a time when trained knights were rare, its greatest strength being its feudal associations. They did not recruit from the upper nobility, but from the more obscure warrior families. In the beginning, distinctions of class were somewhat vague, but by the 13th century an aspirant to the order had to be the son of a knight and his lady.

As the need for trained troops grew, the ethical considerations of the order were laid aside. Different rankings – similar in tone to feudal ones – grew. Beneath the rank of Knight there came to be *sergeants,* also know as serving brothers; esquires; *freres casaliers,* rural brothers; and *freres de metier,* servant brothers. The knights came to live a life even more privileged than the secular nobles. By this time the Templars had become the companions and servants of royalty, their humble origins virtually forgotten.

By the end of the 13th century the Templars had drawn a great deal of criticism, most notably by William, Archbishop of Tyre. They had gained a reputation for pride and greed. In addition, they had made the serious political mistake of remaining loyal to the Church during conflicts between the Papacy and Emperor Frederick II.

Continued on next page . . .

effect. A divine force may have created these laws to serve itself, or there may be no divine at all. Man's sole purpose may be to survive.

Hard Questions

Another common question is why we suffer; there must be a reason the young die, sickness comes, and famines, droughts, floods, and all manner of disasters strike. And there must be something we can do about it.

Suffering might be caused by gods warring among themselves. Perhaps a malevolent power causes suffering and disaster, seeking to destroy those who follow a more beneficent deity. Evil could be a necessary opposite to good, neither able to exist without the other, and both essential to the balance of the whole. Perhaps suffering is the deity's punishment for those who would stray from it, a measure of divine displeasure. The deity could be willful, sending miracles and disasters as it sees fit. Or suffering might be a test, to strengthen the souls and minds of true believers.

Each answer offers a different view of the world. Evil forces may be fought. Pain as a necessary part of the whole requires acceptance. Punishments can be avoided by the pious. Willful deities are worshiped avidly, given sacrifices and homage to incur their favor rather than their wrath. Tests can be overcome to gain rewards.

Death

People often wonder what happens when we die – whether death is an ending or a beginning, to be welcomed or feared, whether the spirit moves somewhere beyond to face judgment or remains upon the earth to aid or haunt, or if this life is the sole experience, with nothing after death.

By far the most common religious belief is that some sort of afterlife exists. Most often the soul is judged by its actions in this life, and sent on to face the consequences – those who lived a good life will retire to a paradisiacal existence, or be reborn into a higher state, and those who lived badly will be assigned fates to fit their sins. Those who serve the gods are often given special consideration, and may even be recruited to some future service after their deaths. Some may be denied death by divine blessing or curse until their earthly work is done. Others may ascend to the divine presence without dying at all.

Worship and veneration of spirits is central to many religions. Even religions that do not actively seek communication with spirits and ghosts often have beliefs concerning them, or ceremonies and rites to appease or protect them. (See *Death/Transition,* pp. 19-20.)

Natural Phenomena

In addition to the all-important questions of life and death, religions usually attempt to resolve questions about the world as a whole. Generally these kinds of questions are answered in myths, which can explain everything from the existence of the stars, to the color of grass or sky, to the occurrence of the seasons, earthquakes and lightning. Often such myths are veiled in allegory and parable. Or a religion might incorporate known fact and scientific rationale into its view of the cosmos.

The GM may want to decide how much actual truth there is in a religion's mythologies, or to leave the question open. (See *Basic Forces of the World,* pp. 13-16.)

The Knights Templar (Continued)

About this time it suddenly became common practice in the French court to denounce enemies for the practice of sorcery or witchcraft. In the Papal court, the fear of such plots was even stronger. On October 13, 1307, agents of the King of France arrested every known member of the Templar order – somewhere between 50 and 100 knights – on charges of heresy. But despite the fears of sorcery, this was simply a convenient excuse. The French government had for some time been demanding a fusion of the Templars with the Hospitallers, the other main military order. They wished to form a single great order that would be led by a son of the King of France. By laying charges of heresy (and ignoring Papal decrees that they had no right to do so) the French crown took control of Templar lands and coffers. The Templar trials were only one of many political arguments between the French government and the Papacy. But by the end, the entire order had been denounced and dissolved, most of its Knights having been tortured and burned at the stake.

The Druids

The Celtic world was an amalgam of people whose languages and traditions were connected, yet did not share any common origin. The Celts were identified as distinctive nations as early as 600 B.C. Each tribe had its own chieftain, but there was no ruler over all, no great Celtic Empire. The continuity of Celtic culture resulted from the influence of the *druids*.

The unity of Celtic society and its control rested with the "men of art," a triumvirate of learned men. These triumvirates were led by the druids, yet the druids were more than priests. They controlled the warriors, and through them controlled the tribes. In Gaul these triumvirates were the *druids*, *vates* and *bards*; their Irish counterparts were called *druidh*, *filidh* and *bairdh*. This form of authority illustrates the importance of triple motifs and symbolism in Celtic culture. Both the bards and the vates had religious duties; the vates actually carried out the sacrifices, at which a druidic priest had to be present.

According to Caesar's writings, Britain was the center of druidism. Druids were responsible for divine worship, the performance of ritual and sacrifice (both public and private), the interpretation of ritual questions, the settlement of disputes and the punishment of those who refused to accept their judgment. Those who disobeyed druidic decisions were often banished from the tribe or even the country, and might even become sacrificial victims.

Druidic acolytes were taught by rote; druidic secrets were chanted and sung back and forth between student and master until they were known perfectly.

The most important druidic belief was that the soul passes after death from one world to another. This does much to explain the Celts' famed bravery in battle. It is possible to be reborn in animal, as well as human, form. Magical transformations and metamorphoses are a common theme in Celtic tales. The afterlife was a very real concept and was seen as an extension of earthly existence where all the pleasures and joys of mortal living were somehow intensified. Warriors fought, yet lived to fight other battles; the slaughtered pig was alive the next day, ready to be consumed again.

Continued on next page . . .

Scripture

Scriptures are sacred writings. In most cases they began as oral traditions, passed down from generation to generation, often surviving centuries before being written down. During this time, changes occur; even the origins of the knowledge may be lost. To fight this tendency, sacred knowledge is often stylized – the meter, melody, chants and breathing patterns strictly governed and taught. The words themselves might become so sacred that they are whispered, or not spoken at all to any non-believer.

When oral traditions are transcribed, they often become holy objects treated with great veneration and awe. Fragments of these words may be worn as amulets, while recitations of certain phrases may impart blessings or curses. Sacred scriptures can safeguard their secrets by using puzzles, riddles, paradoxes, parables, exaggerations, contradictions, negations or secret languages. The languages used are usually archaic, and require those who would study or read the scriptures to learn an ancient tongue. Often translations of scriptures are discouraged or forbidden, as many consider the words themselves to be the medium by which the divine reveals knowledge to the faithful.

A GM can design scripture to give information about the world as well as the religion . . . or to hide it, making the protagonists puzzle out the meaning over a period of time. Scripture can provide color, background, clues and other valuable cultural information.

Scriptures help define religious identity and codify divine will. They usually include the creation myths of the religion, and often describe its laws and restrictions. These can be quite specific, with long lists of rewards, penances, punishments and compensations. Sometimes they describe covenants between the divine and its worshipers. Leaders and prophets are sometimes granted lost or hidden knowledge though scripture. Scriptures can also include long narratives and histories, and trace the genealogies of important people and families.

Often people believe that scripture reveals eternal and sacred truths. In some religions, these truths are more important than the divine itself; the deity is only a vehicle for enlightenment.

Interpretation of scripture is very important to many religions. *Canons* are those scriptures which have been named "official" by a religious authority. Sections of scripture are sometimes rated in terms of levels of validity and importance. Certain sections and passages are often the keys by which believers interpret the scripture as a whole.

Even written scripture can change over time. Editorial privilege, glosses and translations can affect the interpretation of written works. New scripture is sometimes added with the justification that older works were incomplete or unenlightened.

Religious Rank and Hierarchy

Just like military forces, religions quite often have elaborate hierarchies. The structure depends on the nature of the deity or philosophy, social and economic constraints, the number of worshipers and clerics and the power of the church in the community. The larger the church, the more likely that some sort of hierarchy is necessary. A church with five clerics and a scattering of followers has less need to concern itself with exact levels, positions and stations, though this will not necessarily stop it from doing so.

Most often the hierarchy (theoretically) represents levels of growth and wisdom in the faith. Each rank may reflect new and deeper knowledge of the faith, new spells or skills, and rituals and mysteries hitherto unknown. Or it may simply indicate different levels of duty and responsibility.

Advancement, and what skills, abilities or levels of experience are needed to advance within the structure, must also be considered. Advancement generates goals for clerics, and gives them a sense of achievement that can only improve their faith and devotion.

Often the different ranks will have different titles, garb, daily duties and responsibilities, etc. (see *Symbols,* beginning on p. 65). Not only do such things provide a campaign with color and depth, but they can be interesting roleplaying aids for clerical (and other) characters.

The Druids (Continued)

Astrology and astronomy were important facets of druidic knowledge. The druids claimed to have created the universe. The world was indestructible, yet at some future undefined time both fire and water would prevail.

The Celts as a people were devoted to religion. Sacrifices were both public and private. The Celts believed in capital punishment, but they turned it into a religious rite. Innocents were offered as well, and after a defeat a great leader would offer himself. Self-sacrifice was also common, intended to relieve fellow tribesmen. Sacrifices were made to ensure victory, and to celebrate it. Captives were often promised to the gods before battle, and so could never be ransomed, sold or otherwise given away. Human victims were often offered as foundation sacrifices (and buried beneath the building's cornerstone), or given to appease the god of blight and crop failure.

While the druids did not normally engage in battle, they were deeply involved in combat as magicians, prophets and advisers. They interceded with the gods, and their prayers were often thought to determine the outcome of battles. Druids had great control over the elements: they could send showers of fiery sparks down upon opposing armies, induce magical sleep and transform trees and stones into armed men. They practiced hypnotism; their rites often included long chants, incantations and dancing.

The Inquisition

While holy wars might be waged against those in distant lands, dealing with one's own followers is more difficult. As religious organizations grow, and schisms and "heretical" viewpoints develop, some religions find it necessary to seek out and destroy such contrary opinions. Oppression can become widespread.

The Inquisition was theoretically formed to deal with "heretics" within the church. Often these heretics had done little more than point out the excesses of the Church and its priests. By the 12th century, corruption was rife; reformers such as Pierre de Bruys and Frere Raymond Jean were burned, their views and objections suppressed.

By 1252 the power of the Inquisition had greatly expanded, and had become an elaborate extortion scheme. Property of accused persons was instantly seized by the Church, often to be sold even before a confession had been extracted. The accused actually had to pay for both their imprisonment and their torture. Terror and torture were the tools of the inquisitors. If a person confessed in order to avoid the torture, he was tortured nonetheless, so that his testimony might be "confirmed though ordeal." Even if a person resisted the torture, he might be held indefinitely, charged with *obduracy* for refusing to confess. (Torture remained a legal recourse of the church until 1816.) Trials were a mockery – the entire procedure was keep secret, witnesses were hidden and concealed, anyone who spoke in defense of a heretic was arrested as an accomplice, and any form of evidence was accepted with little question of its validity.

The Inquisition was especially concerned with the matter of "witches." The Inquisitor's handbook, the *Malleus Maleficarum,* and Bouget's *Discours des Sorciers* describe in great detail how such persons should be tortured, questioned and killed. During the period of the Inquisition, which pagans often refer to as *the Burning Times,* countless victims were given to the flames. Chroniclers report that entire villages were wiped out. Even in England, the country least touched by the terror of the Inquisition, an estimated 30,000 "witches" were burned between 1542 and 1736.

Orders

Not all hierarchies are strictly linear. Many religions encompass a number of different "orders." In most cases these orders will have differing types of responsibility within the religion – military, scholarly, healing, etc. The GM can be creative with the orders – the larger and more powerful the church, the more likely it will splinter into different groups. This is also a place for potential conflict within a religion – different orders may have almost completely separate hierarchies, and different interpretations of the faith as a whole (always emphasizing whichever area *they* specialize in).

Different orders will likely have different titles, different regalia, perhaps even different symbols to represent their particular areas of the church.

Recruitment

Young clerics must be trained. Often a mentoring or apprenticing situation will be created, whereby a new cleric is assigned to an older and more experienced member of the church, to learn duties and responsibilities by example. A would-be cleric may be required to pass ritualistic tests before being invested with the next level of rank.

No matter what the religion, the method of training new clerics must be considered in detail, for it will be a common background for all clerics of that faith.

Disobedience

Where there are rules, regulations and hierarchies, there must also be ways to deal with those who break them. A church's punishments will vary with the nature of the deity or philosophy worshiped. The GM may define lesser penance such as extra work, extra prayer and short-term vows, as well as greater punishments like long-term vows, expulsion, excommunication, geases, etc. (see *Penance,* p. 60).

Church and State

A religion may be widespread, but if it lays down laws it cannot enforce, it may find its authority questioned or challenged. In some cultures, conflicts between religious and civil authorities are common. In others, they are nonexistent. The GM must decide how church and state interact – how church and civil authorities get along (if they are separate), whether civil laws are based upon religious ethics or mores, whether church and government support one another and how they settle disputes between them.

If the religion *is* the state and the government *is* the church, the rulers are usually considered to be either actually descended from a deity or the divine's worldly representatives. It is this divine connection which grants them the absolute right to rule. The will of the government and the ruling hierarchy is the will of the gods, and must not be questioned. Defiance of governmental edicts is considered to be a religious crime, and the darkest heresy. The rulers of such religious states may be completely out of touch with the needs of their people. Or they could be very concerned with such things, putting a great deal of effort into meeting civic needs. Much of the religion's attitude toward society will depend upon the tenets of the religion. Large bureaucracies are likely to develop, each level of which has great power over those below. These organizations often end up buffering the divine leaders from the very people they rule.

Other state religions may hold that while the ruler is chosen by the gods, and rules by virtue of divine grace, the ruler is not the godhead personified and is thus capable of error. The ruler will need high-ranking clergy to advise him and interpret the will of the gods in difficult cases. This type of influence grants enormous political power to a religion, which might even be able to remove a contrary ruler from power.

Most state religions are notoriously intolerant. They might publicly denounce and outlaw competing religions. State religions are also sensitive to factions within their own ranks, and may go to great lengths to avoid schisms, denouncing or even killing those who object to church policy. The GM might want a tolerant state religion, but this raises more questions. Why is it so tolerant – from doctrine or practicality? Does it have an enlightened leader or is there no true competition? Or does it preach tolerance and then find subtle or underhanded ways to discredit its competition?

Sometimes a government might *adopt* a religion as the "official" or state religion. Such religions are usually chosen in order to manipulate or influence the general populace. If a government can say that its edicts and decisions are the "will of the gods," few will disagree for fear of calling down divine – and civil – wrath upon themselves.

The Reformation

This split within the Christian church resulted in great political upheaval and war. It began with a theological argument. Many people felt that the Roman Church should not be the sole interpreter of scripture. The rising sense of nationalism throughout Europe only encouraged division. The teachings of Luther, strongest in his native Germany, spread into Scandinavia, France and England. Various nobles and princes stood behind their favorite scholars, often switching sides as the political situation developed. In German Switzerland, civil war ensued between the reformers and those who remained Catholic.

Then Calvinism grew to be the greatest religious force in the Reformation, rejecting many of the standards of Luther and Zwingli. In England, many of the Catholic medieval traditions were retained, including territorial divisions and clerical hierarchies. Henry VIII's arguments with Rome resulted in the establishment of the Church of England, but there were few significant changes in worship or doctrine beyond the dissolution of the monasteries and religious houses. All of their wealth went to the Crown. The Bible was translated into English.

During the reign of Edward VI, the Latin mass was outlawed, and statues and images were destroyed. Catholic Queen Mary restored much of the Pope's power in England. Many English Protestants fled; others were tried for heresy and burned at the stake. Later Queen Elizabeth I brought about the final break with Rome, but not all Protestants felt that enough changes had been made. Many Puritans fled to Holland and America.

During this time a counterrevolution (also known as the Catholic Reformation) sprang up in Italy and Spain. Many new religious orders were established, including some that were concerned solely with the Roman Inquisition. Civil war broke out in Holland, with the northern states (under William of Orange) being Calvinist, while the south remained Catholic. In France, the Huguenots (Calvinist French Protestants) battled the Catholic majority. In the following century, the national churches struggled for power in political and religious wars. In the end, the religion of the monarch became the religion of the state.

In some cases the country is actually run by the church alone. Vatican City is an example; within its boundaries, the Pope holds both civil and religious authority. But in other state religions, civil authorities have only minimal influence in the church. While Queen Elizabeth is the theoretical head of the Church of England, she holds little religious power.

In a culture where gods are denied or are not worshiped at all, it is possible that the government itself will be viewed with near-religious awe, worship or even fear. Such cultures would probably put the needs of the state before all other social obligations. The state itself would become god, mother, father, spouse and friend to the individual. Governmental edicts would be sacrosanct. Religious fanaticism would be replaced by patriotic fanaticism.

Civil and Religious Law

Law is cultural knowledge that is used by authoritative agents to settle disputes. If church and state are indistinguishable, clerics might act as policemen and judges, handing down sentences based on religious law. There might be an entire branch of the church dedicated to the judicial system.

If the law of the land and religious law differ, which laws have precedence? Even if religious and civil law are similar, there could be arguments – it is not so much what laws have been broken, but rather who has the right to judge the case. Conflicts of this nature have led religions and governments alike to insist upon a separation of church and state. However, since civil laws are often based upon religious law and dogma, criminals might still be judged according to the standards and mores of the religion.

Civil and religious authorities also argue over who has the right to judge clerics who have committed a civil crime. Civil authorities often insist that the law is the law, and applies to all citizens. Many religions claim that these should remain internal matters, and that judgment and punishment should be left in the hands of religious authorities – a situation similar to diplomatic immunity. If clerics are granted similar immunity to civil law, ordinary citizens might become annoyed at such privilege, or seek to obtain it for themselves by joining the clergy.

Another source of conflict concerns people who break civil law because of religious belief. Some religions might teach their adherents to obey civil authorities, while others might preach resistance. If a person wishes to engage in a harmful or illegal practice for religious reasons, does the state have the power or right to interfere? In some cases, the state may declare children its wards because it believes that the family's religious practices endanger the child's health. Where is the line drawn?

Religion and Property

Power is usually related to land and money. If the religion has a great deal of material property, it may also have a great deal of political and social power. In some societies the church has all the power and responsibility of a feudal lord, complete with vassals, men-at-arms and tenants. Entire villages or cities might be under church rule.

In some societies, churches can accumulate land by convincing people to offer land and temporal goods in order to ensure their salvation or blessing. Or they may make the church the guardian of their minor children. If the church is able to convince a rich ward to join the ranks of its clerics, then his inheritance may go to the church.

Zoroastrianism

Zoroaster (also called Zarathustra) was a teacher who lived in northeast Iran sometime during the 5th or 6th century B.C. His teachings (transmitted in the form of hymns called *The Gathas*) extol the wisdom of God and love for the divine, naming him *Ahura Mazda*, the Wise Lord. Ahura Mazda is opposed by the *Angra Mainyu*, the Evil Spirit, destructive force against creative force. Zoroaster also retained some beliefs from the older Aryan religion. According to Zoroaster, every person must choose between these twinned, yet opposite, divine forces. (The later Zurvanite sect named these twin spirits *Ohrmazd* and *Ahriman*.)

The holy book of the Zoroastrians is the *Avesta*. It was not written down until the 5th century, the result of years of codification by generations of scholars and disciples. Unfortunately, only partial texts remain. A number of other books were added in the 9th century in an attempt to defend Zoroastrianism against Christian and Islamic pressures.

According to classic Zoroastrianism, both conflicting sides have their own forces. Certain "aspects" of the divine, such as *Integrity*, *Immortality*, etc., became the *Amahraspands*; they sit before the throne of god and protect the elements of the world. The *Yazatas* are numberless other heavenly beings. Several important Yazatas bear remarkable similarity to the old Aryan gods. Opposing these forces of good are hordes of evil spirits and demons. The demons of *Apostasy*, *Anarchy*, *Hunger*, *Thirst*, *Disobedience* and *the Lie* struggle against the holy Amahraspands.

At death, the individual's life is judged. If predominately good, the soul passes onto heaven; if not, the soul travels to hell, where the punishment fits the sin. But hell is seen as a place of reform, for a good God could not allow eternal suffering. When all are finally pure, the devil and his minions will be destroyed, heaven and earth becoming one with God.

Continued on next page . . .

Other forms of income include the sale of penances, prayers and indulgences. A cleric might assign a sinful follower prayers as a penance, or the follower might have a special request of the god. The church might guarantee that a number of prayers or offerings would be made in his name in exchange for a donation of money. Churches might have associated markets where sacrificial animals, incense and other gifts could be bought. Many churches support a "tithe" – followers are "encouraged" to donate a certain percentage of their wealth on a regular basis. Some churches sell "indulgences" – official remittance of a penance, or a pardon for a crime, purchased for a set amount of money.

Other Religions

If there is more than one religion in a society, the government may deal with them all equally or it may afford one of them favored status. If other religions are at odds with the government favorite, the authorities may step in. And the religions themselves must cope with the presence of the others.

Religions can deal with each other in three ways – acceptance, indifference or intolerance. Some religions will accept others under the proviso that their own believers not change their practice. Others tolerate them while denying their validity. Still others are completely indifferent, seeing neither threat nor opportunity. Over time beliefs and customs may mingle, and in some extreme cases one religion might be totally amalgamated with another. Or a totally new religion might develop from the melding of the two. But unfortunately, as the many conflicts of history have shown, intolerance seems to be the most common choice.

There are many reasons why a church might resort to forceful means of proselytism. Religions that believe their own view is the only true way often spread their views at swordpoint, offering non-believers a "choice" – *convert or die*. New converts may be slain anyway, to "save" them from falling back into their old ways. Other religions hold that those outside their faith do not have any rights at all – a crime committed against an unbeliever is really no crime at all.

Holy wars often involve land and property, being little more than excuses for a religious state to increase its properties and holdings. Or holy wars are fought over a lost shrine or holy artifact. If the particular shrine is held sacred by more than one religion, then a war might continue for decades or even centuries, while control passes back and forth between the two sides. Other wars may be fought over doctrine, or scriptural interpretation.

If a religion crosses national borders, and the religious hierarchy has political or military influence in both countries, two otherwise opposing nations might cooperate in order to wage war upon a third. In many cases, the driving force behind a holy war is a combination of religious and political factors.

Intolerance does not always result in outright violence. Unbelievers might be looked on with pity, and subjected to helpful attempts to convert him. Or believers might refuse to associate or do business with those outside their own religion. Insults and false rumors might be spread, all subtle ways of trying to force an individual to either abandon his belief or leave to avoid the derogatory barrage.

Roots

Once a GM decides the nature and the present status of a game-world religion, his next step is to work out how it got there. Legends and origin myths are often nebulous, with many different versions existing even within the same

Zoroastrianism (Continued)

The religion of ancient Iran was therefore a mix between the old Aryan faith and Zoroaster's teachings, holding a great deal of influence in its culture, especially during the times of Darius and Xerxes. The Magi were the hereditary priests; their teachings carried Zoroastrianism throughout Iran. It is believed that Roman Mithraism later grew out of these teachings.

Zoroastrianism survived the development of Islam; many smaller cults unified to deal with the threat posed by that religion. Many faithful Zoroastrians moved to India during this time, though small communities remain in Yazd, Kerman and Tehran to the present day. Many modern theological scholars feel that early Zoroastrian belief greatly influenced Jewish (and later Christian) concepts of the devil, heaven and hell, the resurrection and the end of the world.

Messianic Religions

Some religions believe in the coming of a messiah – a great leader, prophet or holy teacher who will deliver the faithful from their oppression. Some believe this will be done violently; others hope for a messianic age of peace and prosperity.

Many religions have a messianic element; often the belief in a messiah is only one of many tenets. Judaism is particularly well known for this belief; almost every prophet in Hebrew scripture has predicted a reign of peace, prosperity and understanding of God. In modern times, Reform and many Conservative Jews feel this will come about gradually, as humanity is slowly enlightened.

Historically, there have been several messianic movements. When the Jews were banished from Spain in 1492, mystical traditions grew in popularity, as did messianic belief. Later, during the 17th century, Sabbatai Zevi was hailed by many as the messiah, with Nathan of Gaza as his prophet. Sabbatai Zevi eventually adopted the Mohammedan religion in 1666, and still retained many of his followers. What are today considered to be mystical heresies flourished during this period. There have been many militant messianic movements throughout history, many adopting a variety of extreme doctrines, wishing to cast off "the burden of Law and Commandments."

Many native North American religions also have messianic traditions, especially in southern areas. Oddly enough, this messiah was commonly described as a white man with a flowing beard. Some scholars believe that this may have influenced the Spaniards' reception in Mexico, Haiti, Yucatán and Peru. Similarly, Pueblo tribes welcomed the Spaniards, who disappointed them by not delivering them from their Apache enemies. The great revolt of 1680 eventually resulted. Later, native prophets such as Tenskwatawa, Kanakuk and Smohalla strengthened the spread of messianic fervor, although their individual teachings varied. Common points, however, included the resurrection of the dead and their people's return to their former glory. In the late 19th century, Squsachtun (John Slocum) introduced the Shaker religion to the native peoples. The Shakers were known for their twitching dances and trances and it is thought that this movement influenced the Paiute messiah and the Ghost Dance apostles.

Continued on next page . . .

culture. These beliefs are often the seeds of developing religions and are passed on from generation to generation in many ways. The GM should pick a starting point or legend, and determine how it was transmitted. Many ancient traditions greatly honor their teachers and scholars.

Holy Teacher

Many religions begin with the teachings of a single individual. This revered teacher may be a prophet chosen by the deity to bring a specific message. Or he might simply be a wise or learned individual intent upon solving the mysteries of the world. Such teachers might not die, instead being called to serve the divine. Others are deified after their deaths. Holy teachers are common in philosophical and contemplative religions.

The philosophy spreads as others come to the teacher to learn, or as the teacher wanders about speaking to any who will listen. Places where the teacher lived or taught might become holy sites and shrines. Often his lessons are written down, becoming "holy" as they are preserved for later generations. Others may write commentaries; different schools of interpretation may spring up. What began as the teachings of a single person might grow into a number of different yet related religions. If the original teaching disagree with or criticize other schools of thought, its followers might suffer persecution. Teachings of equality and freedom for all might anger governments that practice slavery, or vice versa.

Many different types of religions have holy teachers. Proselytizing religions often develop if the holy teacher was intent upon spreading his teachings, while a teacher who waits for students to come to him often founds a contemplative religion. But some religions develop different sects, both contemplative and proselytizing, each dedicated to a different way of practicing the religion.

Divine Descent

Some religions develop from acts of divine intervention and descent. A representative of the deity, or perhaps even the deity itself, comes into the world and walks among its chosen people. A deity may present itself with great fanfare, using powerful magic or miracles to announce its coming. Others might arrive quietly, becoming holy teachers, spreading wisdom among the faithful.

Sometimes this divine appearance is foretold in prophecy; other times few might notice, the word spreading slowly only after the deity is gone. Often he has a particular task to fulfill. Sometimes the divine sends an intangible spirit, to sanctify a leader or to inspire a chosen prophet. An ordinary person might become a holy teacher under such influence. Divine entities may depart once their work is done, or they may choose to stay and wander, or perhaps dwell within a holy shrine where their followers may consult them.

Ancient Ways

Often religious knowledge is handed down from teacher to student, father to son, mother to daughter and so on. These types of religions usually involve more personal or domestic rites and duties than communal ones. Often these rituals are hidden in mystery and are revealed only to particular people. Some rites may be exclusive to men, others to women. The knowledge may be passed on gradually, the individual learning more and more as he grows older and passes through a series of initiations.

The individuals chosen to hold and pass on this knowledge are revered and even feared by the rest of the society. Such teachings are generally not passed on freely; the applicant must first prove himself worthy. Shamanistic or magical traditions are commonly begun this way.

Such religions are an excellent choice for a GM who wishes to gradually reveal religious information to clerical characters. A cleric could spend a lifetime uncovering lost knowledge, seeking personal enlightenment and searching for the right student to carry on the tradition.

Constructs

Some religions begin as deliberate constructs. These are not necessarily "false" religions, but they are usually strictly structured. Such traditions are created to deal with a particular social pressure or problem. A culture that is constantly at war might develop cults of holy warriors who are specially chosen. The traditions and structures of these sects might survive as secret societies long after the original religion has been forgotten.

Constructed religions will generally be found in relatively sophisticated societies. Perhaps some sort of magical or technological knowledge would be used to convince people of the power behind the religion. Or there could be a massive propaganda campaign begun by a charismatic leader. If the GM decides that belief alone is enough to actually create gods, such a movement might succeed in doing that. If so, a constructed religion could eventually become mystically powerful in its own right – which might surprise its developers.

Messianic Religions (Continued)

The underlying principle of the Ghost Dance religion was the belief that the entire native race, living and dead, would one day be reunited on a regenerated earth. It exhorted a return to native ways and tradition and a deliverance from white oppression. Much of this doctrine was spread by the visionary Wovoka. Participation in the sacred dances could hasten this reunion of living and dead. This religious movement was seen as a serious threat by government and military alike; hundreds of participants were cut down by U.S. Army fire at Wounded Knee.

Death and Resurrection

Almost all religions have some sort of death story or myth. Souls usually have some place to retire to, either for the rest of eternity or some shorter time while they await reincarnation. In a campaign where magical techniques for resurrection exist, the GM must decide how each religion will view this, in accordance with their own personal beliefs about death.

For the most part, religions which teach that their believers may ascend into the presence of the god, or travel to some paradise to enjoy the rewards of a well-spent life, will consider resurrection to be the ultimate heresy – a great perversion of the desires of the deity. Clerics and faithful followers of this religion will object strongly to being resurrected! Why should they return to the pain and suffering of life when they can retire to the loving embrace of their god? What karma is accumulated by a soul which is yanked back into a worldly existence from which it had escaped? At the very least the person will be disgruntled. In extreme situations he may kill all who so defiled him and then commit ritual suicide, hoping to commend his soul back to the deity.

It may likewise be important that certain rites and rituals are handled correctly for a deceased character. Such a character should be sure to properly instruct those he travels with (if they happen not to share the same faith) of all particulars – just in case the worst should occur.

Fanaticism

Fanatics are those who believe completely and utterly in the teachings of their church. No sacrifice is too great to preserve the faith, and they stint nothing. The church is their world, the deity the only one whose opinion matters.

Fanatics can be difficult to deal with, even for those who follow the same religion, since they take everything to the extreme. Indeed, in some cases, the fanatic may take things *too* far, interpreting the divine will in ways that pervert its intent. Fanaticism is a temperament trait more than a true measure of understanding or communion with the divine. Nothing guarantees that the fanatic has a truer vision of the deity or the religious experience than anyone else.

There is little more frightening than a fanatic with a *mission,* especially someone with an obvious enemy to fight against – for he will stop at nothing. Many of the greatest calamities in epic fantasies have been precipitated by fanatics whose beliefs have strayed beyond the realm of reason.

On the other hand, fanaticism is a common trait among those dedicated enough to devote themselves to the service of a religion. Not *all* fanatics are unyielding extremists, just as not all fanatics are intolerant of those who do not follow their particular religion. The only true constant among them is the fervor and devotion they grant to their calling, and the depth of the sacrifice they are willing to make in its name. (See also the Fanaticism disadvantage, p. B33.)

Changes Over Time

Religions, like their cultures, are not static. They change over time. The GM should keep this in mind when determining both the history of the game world and its religions. What happened in the past will determine how religions (and their clerics) get along and what their future motives are. A religion's future can be influenced by world-shaking events, slow culture changes or the actions of a single determined cleric.

Growth and Maturation

Religions grow and spread in many ways. This depends upon the teachings and beliefs of the adherents, as well as the influence of other religions and cultural elements.

Proselytism

Proselytizing religions actively seek new recruits, and their members put great effort into spreading the word. These clerics might stand on street corners or go from door to door, promising temporal success and eternal salvation. Other religions are content to let their charitable works and accomplishments draw people to them. Food might be free at a soup kitchen, but often the appetizer is a sermon. Proselytizing religions which have great political strength or influence often deny other religions equal opportunity for free speech, or spread their beliefs at swordpoint.

Missionary religions grow as a result of systematic efforts to preach and perform social works. Missionaries spread their beliefs either through proclamation (outright preaching) or through dialogue (which invites intelligent discussion and comparison of differing beliefs).

Some religions are strictly non-proselytizing to the extent that they openly disdain new converts and require them to undergo long training and purification before being accepted. Such religions might require that the potential convert undergo some form of testing or great ordeal to prove their worthiness and enlightenment. Others are seemingly indifferent and merely wait for new members to find them.

Propagation

A religion may spread in slow, piecemeal steps. Buddhism came to China by means of translated scripture and preaching, but the process took 500 years. The spread of Buddhism into China brought a new type of social organization – the monastic community – that became vitally important in medieval Chinese society. To accomplish this, the church needed the patronage of the elite, which took several centuries to obtain. But by the 5th century, the Buddhist church had formed an intellectual clerical elite that posed a serious challenge to the native Taoism. Buddhist writings – scientific and philosophical, as well as religious – were translated from their Indian sources. Kumarajiva, with the patronage of the Emperor, created a corps of translators that far exceeded anything that had previously existed in China. During this time, Buddhism was itself influenced by Taoism, developing a number of purely Chinese sects.

The Common View

The true strength of most religions lies in their followers. While the clergy may have great supernatural or political power, the mass of followers makes up the body of any religious organization. The belief of the common folk is often a subtle thing, but it is that belief that spreads the religion from generation to generation. Once a religious belief becomes widespread it is extremely difficult to suppress. Even if the religion loses its political influence and the clergy is outlawed, as long as its beliefs are held by the common people, the religion will survive in some form. Clerics will be hidden by their followers, holy objects secreted in obscure places, children taught in private. Nothing is more difficult to remove from a devoted believer than faith.

There is a difference between a devoted worshiper and a follower, however. Devoted worshipers hold their religious beliefs and practices to be of tantamount importance. Their religion is their strength, something they build their life on, something they turn to in times of trouble and need. Little will deter them from the practice of their religion, even physical danger. Saints and martyrs are the ultimate examples of devoted worshipers.

Followers are often less enthusiastic. They may be reverent and take part in all the expected rituals and ceremonies. But when push comes to shove, they falter. Followers lack the binding faith of the devoted worshiper, and often put their life and other possessions above unquestioning faith. They may question and doubt, or simply shrug in indifference. Some religions value doubts and questions, for they believe that if a religion cannot be studied and analyzed it is worthless. But often the devoted worshiper and the casual follower will conflict, the first seeing the latter as weak or flawed, while the follower sees the more fervent worshipers as closed-minded fanatics.

Decline

Religions are similar to growing organisms . . . they develop and they die. Sometimes this decline is the result of external pressure and oppression. Sometimes it is a gradual decay from within. As time progresses, cultures change and sometimes religions do not change along with it. If the values and beliefs of the religion clash with the accepted values of the culture, then followers will begin to question. When they doubt, and begin to reassess their beliefs and involvement in a religious organization, the religion weakens. Followers lose interest in the rites and celebrations, and at best give only lip-service to them.

As a religion weakens with the loss of followers, its social influence also wanes. Followers might also leave if a more appealing religion comes along. Religious values that have become cultural standards might survive long after the religion itself has perished. Other religious elements might be absorbed by new religions. Or the religion might split from within, and survive in some new form.

Adaptation

What happens when a religion runs into something unexpected? Great social change, war, competitive religions, magic, technology – all of these can be serious threats to a religion; all of these must be dealt with – or explained – somehow. Sometimes religions die; other times derivative religions develop. Often schisms result. But something always changes. It is the *how* that the GM must determine. Some of these conflicts may be history, but still have modern repercussions. Others may be present threats. Bringing such concerns into a campaign is a useful GM tool and can result in some interesting situations for both clerical and other characters.

Proselytizing and Party Unity

Clerics of proselytizing religions have a duty to bring the word of their god to all the people of the world. In most cases, proselytizing religions believe that anyone who does not follow their god is damned to a life-after-death of misery. Their clerics have a duty to those they meet, and especially those they form close bonds with, to convert them to the one true faith.

On the other hand, the player must recognize (even if the character will not) that other characters will hold other beliefs equally fervently, and may not be willing even to listen to endless repetitions of the "message," let alone fully convert. It would seem that one or the other (or both) is doomed to frustration and endless argument that can get in the way of party interaction and playing enjoyment.

This is not necessarily the case. Most proselytizing priests are not stupid – they recognize that other people hold strong beliefs, and that endless repetition of the same message is unlikely to do anything but annoy them. A much more common technique is that of conversion by example. By simply following his faith as closely as he can, the cleric believes he will eventually demonstrate its superiority. A quiet comment made at an opportune moment can have more effect than continued barrages. A realistic cleric will realize that he can only expect to save a small number of souls – making each one all that more precious.

If this sort of rationale will not fit with the character concept, then, at the very least, the player can have the character go through the whole speech once, and then simply refer to it on future occasions. This will save the nerves of the other players, even if it doesn't improve the interrelations between characters.

Martyrs

Martyrs are people who are killed by their political or religious enemies as a result of their unswerving conviction and devotion to their beliefs. Often martyrs serve as powerful symbols of oppression or persecution which may stir up both common and religious sentiment.

In some religions, martyrs are worshiped as holy or privileged individuals. Usually celebrations are held upon the death-day of the martyr.

Sometimes miracles occur at the burial sites of martyrs, or are associated with their relics. The teachings of martyrs often sway people, for if it seems that there must be *some* worth in beliefs that someone is willing to die for . . .

It is worth remembering that someone must perceive the martyr's death in terms of sacred sacrifice. A person who tells of the death in these terms, and a religion that embraces the tale, may have a vested interest in protecting the mythic nature of the death. They may do so without regard to historical reality or the beliefs of either the martyr *or* his slayer . . .

Natural Change

As a culture changes, so do its mores and behaviors. Religions also change as time progresses. Honored traditions can become hide-bound. If the populace sees the church as old-fashioned or inappropriate, they may abandon it. In order to maintain their influence upon the society, religions may change to increase their popularity and maintain membership. Over time, many religions become more willing to deal kindly with outsiders, often permitting open discourse and more friendly relations. Sometimes this requires a new look at old doctrine; sometimes new translations of scripture are made. Old restrictions, such as those against the investiture of women as priests in some Christian churches, may be lifted. If there are those within the religion who object to these changes, a schism might result.

Conquerors

Many religions have faced conflict and violence over the years. Often a religion is oppressed or outlawed by a conquering nation, and its adherents persecuted. Some religions change under such pressure, melding two cultures, creating an entirely new religion from the mix. Hinduism has its ancient beginnings in two distinct sources – the Indus Valley civilization and the oral traditions of the Aryans. The Vedic scriptures gave Hinduism much of its formal structure and myth. These traditions and beliefs, brought by the Aryan peoples who invaded northwest India, were quickly assimilated into the decaying Harappan cultures.

Other times, it is the religion of the conquerors that changes. In order to make the conqueror's religion more feasible and attractive, elements of the defeated nation's beliefs might be subsumed. All over Europe and the British Isles, many Celtic deities and their associated holy places were assimilated into Christian belief and culture. The Irish goddess Brigit became a Christian saint, her holy shrine at Kildare, a convent of nuns. The popularity of religious mystery and morality plays in medieval Europe echoes those popular in Greek and Roman cultures. These plays began as religious rites and slowly slipped into secular hands, though they were performed to celebrate religious festivals.

Some conquerors ignore the native religions unless they perceive a direct threat. The Romans were notoriously tolerant of native religions, so long as their own beliefs were not threatened. They also took many of the Greek gods as their own; Zeus became Jupiter, Hera became Juno, Aphrodite became Venus, and so on. But even the Greeks adopted the deities of others. Hellenic myths suggest that Athena, worshiped by the Romans as Minerva, was originally the Libyan triple goddess, Anath. Aphrodite, previously knows as Asherah or Astarte, was an ancient Syrian goddess famed for her temples, like those in Paphos on Cyprus.

Magic

The GM must carefully consider the role of magic in the game world. Does magic exists? Does it differ from divine aid? Are there magical deities? Do clerics use divine aid, magic, neither, or both?

If magic is seen as a gift of the gods, then it is possible that everyone with talent for magic will be brought to or trained by the church. In a church state, magically gifted individuals might be *required* to register in some fashion. In any case, the church would be most concerned with any individual who uses magical abilities without the sanction of the church.

Magic performed without the sanction of the church is often considered a threat both to the organization of the church and to the privileges of the god. Few clerics will be fond of the mage who blithely dazzles the populace with magic when the cleric is speaking of the all-powerful god.

If the church views any display of arcane power that does not come from their deity as "evil," then the conflict might be serious indeed. If the church has great political or social influence, there may be pogroms and persecution aimed at mages (see *The Inquisition*, p. 50). Even if the church doesn't have a great deal of political power, the individual mage might still have to be wary of clerics determined to destroy him.

Many religions will not have a magical aspect at all. They might be completely rational and scientific in nature, containing no divine element. Some deities could lack access to the material world, or might not be strong enough to share their power with their followers. Religions could be based on a unified worldview, a philosophy and belief rather than demonstrable power. In some cases the religion might suppose an apathetic or indifferent deity; others might simply speculate an unknown reason for the deity's lack of involvement in the world. Or perhaps there *is* no deity, and the church (such as it is) exists to provide what comfort it can amid logical explanations and philosophical rationalizations for the world.

However, a world in which magical deities exist will likely find that those religions without direct divine intervention will dwindle and fade. When the magical power of one deity is readily apparent, why should people worship one who lacks this measurable power? Rational philosophies and explanations hold little weight when compared to miraculous feats of supernatural power.

Paragons

Those in a state of communion with their deity are often considered holy men and women, great paragons of the divine virtue. These individuals remain quite mortal and are often swayed strongly by the events about them, but their viewpoint is at one with their faith, completely and totally embracing the teachings and views of their god.

Teachers, prophets, or warriors of great merit, these holy people have special status in the eyes of their deity through the purity of their actions. Though exactly how they conduct themselves depends entirely upon the nature of their chosen deity, they are as one with the personality, temperament, wishes and goals of their faith. Age is not an important consideration, though most often these individuals are older, having achieved true peace with themselves and an understanding of their place in the greater cosmos. Some cultures define a natural progression whereby anyone of advanced age and inclination devotes himself to the holy teachings, becoming a sage or wise man. Others believe that understanding is independent of age and experience, coming to any who are ready to devote themselves completely to the divine.

Given their elevated status, whether echoed by church rank or not, paragons generally receive special bonuses or divine blessings. At the very least their actions are more likely to find divine favor (with all appropriate bonuses – see p. 93), and often they are blessed with various special abilities.

Similarly, a world in which magic is real will tend to find little following for religions which fail to offer equal displays of divine power. This explains why such religions often need to associate demonstrable magic with evil deeds and intentions, for how else can they hope to hold the belief and faith of their worshipers? (See *Magical Clerics,* p. 112.)

Divine News

What happens if a deity changes its mind?

Since religions are collections of beliefs in a divine force or being, changes in the divine will have far-reaching effects.

If the deity is indeed powerful, and takes an active interest in its adherents, then it is likely that the religion will change to suit the deity's purposes. This might result in massive cultural effects, especially if a relatively peaceful god decides to launch a crusade.

If the deity does not interact with its followers or grant them direct power, but only speaks to a few clerics, then schisms and arguments will likely result. Some clerics might not believe that the god has changed, and will continue on as they were. Others will insist upon following the "new" tenets of the religion and form new churches or sects.

Even false religions are susceptible. The mortals behind the religious organization may adopt a new agenda, changing the religion to suit a new goal. Divine revelation will, of course, be the excuse used. Or perhaps a deity really *will* come into existence, or decide to "take over" a false religion, making use of an existing power structure.

Science

Technological developments may have great influence upon a religion. They may change the way a religion deals with the world, or shake the very foundations of belief. Before the advent of the printing press, many scriptures and holy writings were available only to clerics and other authorities. With the increase in literacy and the availability of religious material, followers were exposed *directly* to the doctrines of their church. Personal devotion and study became accepted practices. No longer was the cleric the sole dispenser of wisdom – now followers could read religious tracts and draw their own conclusions. Schisms arose as people questioned scriptural interpretation.

Penance

Penance is a means of reconciling a sinner and his god. In order to do penance properly there must be true sorrow – and a true resolve never to repeat the sin. Penance is both a form of punishment and an exercise showing repentance.

There are commonly three stages to penance – confession, acceptance of punishment, and absolution. A sinner might be required to make public confession as a part of his penance. Absolution can be a liturgical formula performed by the priest when the penance is done, or a divine pardon, which cleanses the sinner's soul.

Most religions (at least those that acknowledge the existence of sin) have specific rules for punishing misdeeds. Penalties range through the physical, mental and monetary realms. Various sects will require a penitent to spend a certain amount of time in religious service (from a few days to years). Some offenses are more serious than others; this will vary from religion to religion, or even among sects in the same religion. The GM should carefully consider just what will constitute an offense in the eyes of the deity and/or the church. Usually clerics are considered to be examples to other followers, so when they falter, their punishment is often more severe.

Some technological advances are taken in stride. Many modern religions proselytize through the media, reaching millions of potential converts. Other religions use the conveniences of science to aid in rituals of worship – prayer wheels might be run by electric motors, eternal flames are replaced by gas or electric light, sermons are delivered through amplified systems, electric organs provide music for songs and chants.

Other religions see the development of science and technology as a threat and do everything in their power to suppress new discoveries. The Romans ignored much of the astronomical works of Aristarchus, Hipparchus and Eratosthenes, who suggested a new order for the universe. Copernicus' works, first published in 1543, were prohibited until 1835 because they disagreed with accepted scripture. Galileo, whose works were first published in 1632, was forced to recant his discoveries and was later refused proper burial.

More recent developments, such as birth control, medical improvements and genetic engineering, have caused great argument and consternation among religious organizations who consider such advances to be contrary to divine will.

Many science-fiction stories have portrayed ultra-technological religious dictatorships, such as Robert Heinlein's *Sixth Column* and Frank Herbert's *Dune*.

Religion in Space

What happens when religions commute?

Just as religious purists fled to the New World to start anew, free from religious persecution, future space travelers may do the same. Entire planets might be colonized by a specific religious sect. Others who could not find their answers on Earth might seek them in the depths of space. Tours of the universe might become grand-scale pilgrimages for those seeking to view all the diverse forms of the divine. Proselytizing religions might send out their clerics to find new converts, even among alien races. And as human culture meets (or perhaps collides) with alien races, some religions may adapt and change while others strike out with xenophobic fervor.

Changing an earth-bound religion to suit a science-fiction campaign will be an interesting exercise for the GM. If, for instance, religious practice requires facing some holy site when praying, what direction do the faithful face when off the planet? Pilgrimage may become a near-impossible hardship. The church may be confronted with creatures not mentioned by their own scripture, or perhaps with the discovery of life created by someone else. Explanations of the unknown often result in shaken – or lost – faith. Some religions might find a way to amalgamate such knowledge, while others will deny its very existence. The church may need to decide whether to accept or seek converts, or even

Monasticism

Clerics who choose a lifestyle removed from temporal concerns so that they can devote their lives exclusively to religious pursuits are called *monks*. Most religions have some sort of monastic tradition.

Some religions develop traditions of monasticism based upon the wisdom of a holy teacher. Christian monasticism, for example, is based upon the teachings of Jesus that supported celibacy, poverty and total dedication to God. Monks achieve this through isolation, simple labor, meditation, prayer, and the study and recitation of scripture.

Christian monasticism has its roots in the late 3rd century. Celibate ascetics began to move into the desert. Eventually loose-knit communities of hermits formed; the monks lived alone but gathered together for worship and study. In the 4th century, two communities were formed, one by Pachomius in Egypt and one in Asia Minor by Basil of Caesarea. Pachomius' monks were very isolated, but Basil's monasteries were famous for their charitable works; they ran hospitals, schools and hostels. Prayer was always a central part of a monk's life, and by the 9th century Benedictine monks were famous for their prayers on behalf of the rest of society. New monastic groups appeared in the 11th and 12th centuries. Some, like the Cistercians, began a revival of the early Benedictine Rule; others such as the Carthusians formed new orders. Later, the Franciscans and Dominicans practiced mendicancy (living by begging).

As monasticism grew more popular, ordered regimens became increasingly important. Discipline not only focuses the mind, but also ensures a harmonious community. After Pachomius and Basil, the idea of a *rule* became a Christian monastic tradition. These rules govern all aspects of monastic life. Monasteries were viewed as large families, and were expected to be independent and self-supporting. Life was plain and simple, but not overly tiresome. The brothers (or sisters) were to elect their Abbot (or Abbess), who thereafter had complete authority. Monasteries were permanent communities; monks who professed to a certain rule were not expected (or usually allowed!) to move to other monasteries.

Continued on next page . . .

allow clerics, from alien races. Is a soul the same regardless of the body it inhabits – even if it is reincarnated as an alien? Will the spacefarers develop a reasonable dialogue with alien religions, or withdraw, denouncing all but their own belief? Religion may not even be part of a science-fiction setting; belief in science and logic might replace belief in a divine being. Or the wonders of the universe may prove to some that there must be a supreme being.

Schisms

Virtually every religion suffers from a form of schism at some time during its history. What happens when religions don't adapt – or only parts of them do – may affect how they resolve arguments and change later on. Some schisms are relatively peaceful, consisting of intellectual argument and perhaps a withdrawal of serious adherents. Many religions have sects that developed out of a desire to return to a "truer" form of worship. Other schisms reach into the secular world as well, resulting in political upheaval and wars that last generations.

Schisms are a realistic way for a GM to spice up a religion's history. A GM who may not wish to include numerous religions can still develop interesting political plots by allowing schisms to develop in the sole religion. In a world with many religions, the creation of sects will prevent predictability. Some sects might be friendly to outside religions, while others fiercely oppose them.

Divine Revelation

If the god hands down a revelation through a priest, some might suspect the cleric of ulterior motives. If there are already arguments within the church, no one would believe it if the opposing side claimed divine support! If the god descends to earth but does so quietly, without fanfare, will those who did not see the deity believe?

What happens when the *gods* argue? If the church supports a group of deities, who supports which side? Clerics might differ in opinion, thus splitting the church. Feuding deities might even manipulate and lie to each other's clerics, trying to gain new followers and cause problems for their competition.

If the divine is not particularly active, what happens when a cleric declares a revelation? What proof can be offered? Will everyone believe? Probably some will, and some will demand proof of the god's will. If an unpopular cleric is chosen for a position of power, others may object and oppose the god's will – if they even accept that it *is* the god's will.

Interpretation and Politics

Few things cause more argument than religion. Differing opinions about the practices of the religious elite often result in rebellious groups. Some clergy might object to trends and practices within their church for political or ethical reasons, or might favor the welfare of the common folk over the excesses of the nobility. Intellectuals within the clergy might question the reasoning of their teachers, challenging their authority. Others might favor a return to simpler times.

Monasticism (Continued)

Christian monastic rule could be divided into three areas: liturgy (which included the Eucharist and canonical hours); *lectio divina,* or sacred readings to support spiritual growth; and manual labor to help support the community. The rule was extremely detailed (Benedict's Rule consisted of 73 chapters) and described such things as a daily timetable (with seasonal variations), liturgy, diet, moral demands and guidelines for communal living.

Buddhist Monasticism

Buddhist monasticism is based upon the life of Buddha himself. Traditionally, the Buddha was a member of a royal family who renounced that position and left to seek a more lasting truth. The Buddha chose a middle path focusing on restraint, meditation and study.

After his enlightenment, the Buddha traveled to Magadha (part of northern India), where he attracted many disciples. Wandering truth-seekers took a three-month retreat during monsoon season and often gathered together during this time. Recital of the *Patimokkha,* a form of confessional, developed during this time. Eventually traditions of community life developed and once-temporary communities became more permanent. These monasteries, *Vihara,* became the keystone of Buddhist tradition. The *Patimokkha* developed into an extensive set of rules; 250 in the *Mahayana* tradition, and 227 in the *Theravada* (or *Hinayana*) tradition.

The *Vinaya* is a series of training rules; its most important rule is that the Buddha is the sole monastic authority. These monastic rules are broken into seven sections, according to the offense and its penalties. The first category involves serious offenses (sexual intercourse, stealing, killing) that result in expulsion from the order. Lesser offenses can result in temporary suspension or public confession.

Schisms often begin as reform movements started by disagreements in scriptural interpretation. In the 8th century a Jewish sect called the Karaites denied the validity of rabbinic oral traditions, preferring instead to develop their practices based solely upon written scripture. The Rabbinites (those who opposed the Karaites) believed that this sect threatened the unity of Jewish thought, so they opposed them in polemical writing. Attempts to disprove the Karaite position resulted in a number of new studies of the Torah throughout the Middle Ages. This is a good example of how a religious schism can cause people to re-examine their own beliefs, if only to prove someone else wrong.

Many reform-based schisms, however, cause great disruption, which overflows into the secular world. When those involved in a religious argument hold temporal power, the entire society can become involved. This is especially prevalent in societies where religion is an integral part of the culture. If there is little or no separation between church and state, then religious schisms become political schisms as well. A classic example of this is the Protestant Reformation (see sidebar, p. 51).

Some schisms begin gradually, as the result of expansion and external influences. If a religion spreads over a great geographical distance, it can be difficult to maintain contact. These new "outposts" of a church are often subjected to local pressures that the mother-church cannot understand. The new church makes decisions on its own, since consultation with superiors is difficult at best. Over time, attitudes and even doctrine can change.

Sometimes a single schism will lead to the establishment of many other sects. The first blow to Islamic unity began 25 years after Mohammed's death and was the result of a political, not religious, argument. This schism resulted in the establishment of the Sunni and Shiite sects. Over 70 splinter sects then sprang from the Shiites, most of which justified themselves on religious grounds.

Reunification

Not all movements are toward separation. Sometimes movements within a religion may wish to heal old theological wounds, seeking reunification of existing splinter groups. These factions feel that dissension with the church weakens it. Some might wish to present a unified front to the competition;

Sikhism

Sikhism is a faith which combines teachings of the Muslim *Sufis* with those of *Bhakti* Hinduism. All ten of the *Gurus* that Sikhism venerates were Hindu. Muslim influences came later – the caste system and idol worship were rejected and monotheism was emphasized.

The Bhakti cult dates back to the *Nayanar* and *Alvar* saints of south India during the 8th century, and the monism teachings of *Samkara*. The impact of Islam came with the advent of Sufi mystics; both Bhakti and Sufi traditions stressed the importance of ascetic discipline and the chanting of litanies under the guidance of a teacher.

In the early 16th century, Guru Nanak began to preach after a divine revelation. He built the first *dharmsala,* a "temple of righteousness." His following consisted of both Muslims and Hindus, many of whom called themselves *Nanakprasthas,* "followers of Nanak's path." Before he died, he appointed a disciple, Angad, to continue his work. A series of Gurus followed. The fifth Guru, Arjun, supported trade with Afghanistan and Turkey, becoming important commercially. His involvement in Muslim politics caused his arrest and eventual martyrdom. This caused a schism between Muslims and Sikhs, ending Sikh pacifism. Later Gurus raised armies and became active in the Himalayan foothills between involvements with the Mogul courts.

In the late 17th century Gobind Rai built fortresses and founded the *Khalsa,* a military fraternity with specific rules of conduct. All members of the Khalsa took a new common family name, *Singh,* meaning lion. Sikhs who did not join the Khalsa were called *Sahajdhari,* "those who take time to adopt." Those who later renounced the Khalsa were *patits,* or renegades. Gobind Rai lost all his sons fighting the Moguls; he himself was assassinated. According to tradition, he proclaimed the end of the line of Gurus just before his death. The Khalsa had been a strong political and military power and many Hindu peasants converted. During British rule the Khalsa were given special privileges in both the army and civil services.

In more recent times, the Khalsa tradition appears to be losing ground. Many members have cut their long hair and beards and have lapsed into Hinduism. Many Sikhs living outside of India are clean-shaven; Westernized Sikhs in India are following that trend as well.

others might wish to pool resources to deal with outside threats. Some might feel that they cannot help others while their own church is in such disarray. Many might feel that division within the church is a deterrent to converts. And others still may simply feel that the deity wants it that way.

Present-day ecumenical union in the Christian church, for instance, appears to have developed out of a feeling that the church's influence was waning. Many of the Protestant denominations have established councils of churches on both the national and world level. GMs wishing to run present-day or futuristic campaigns might wish to consider this sort of world-wide religious organization.

On the other hand, when the leaders of two churches agree to merge, there will usually be some followers of each who reject the merger. This leads to the existence of three churches – the new unified church, and the remnants of the two original churches!

Ancient Egypt

All of ancient Egyptian culture had religious origins. Astronomy arose from the need to time rituals; the oldest maps involved the geography of spiritual realms; most doctors and physicians were also priests. Religious commandments defined practices of hygiene. State administration was tied irrevocably to the concept of divine kingship; to serve the Pharaoh was to serve god. Judicial officials were titled "priest of Maat."

Egyptians monarchs were central to both political and religious life. A new era began with each new monarch; earthly and cosmic realms were linked through the royal personage. In its earliest stages, the Egyptian state unified neighboring tribes into *nomes*, each of which had religious autonomy. Originally there were 38 nomes; that number was later raised to 42, representing Osiris' 42 judges of the dead. During the Archaic period there were two separate groups of gods. Those of the first group were each linked to a particular place – these included the old nomes' gods and were usually worshiped in animal form. The other group of gods represented various cosmic or natural forces. Scholars believe that the theriomorphic (animal-shaped) gods originated with North African Hamitic cultures, while the anthropomorphic gods were connected with Western Semitic belief.

Early in the Old Kingdom, the monarch was seen as an incarnation of Horus. After the Fifth Dynasty, Horus was replaced by Ra, the sun god. During the Twelfth Dynasty, Amon became the state god. A period of monotheism resulted when Akhenaten declared Aten (another sun god, perhaps another version of Amon) to be the sole state deity. During the late period, animal cults became very popular, while during Ptolemaic and Roman times, Isis reigned supreme.

Throughout Egypt's long history, the religious state controlled much (if not all) of the country's commerce and trade. Agricultural product belonged to the gods; it was dedicated to them and stored in huge temple granaries, and later re-distributed to the various nomes according to guidelines developed from census information. Many revolts occurred when this distribution fell short of demand. Nome administrators were also priests; only they could release goods held in the temple granaries.

SYMBOLS

Symbols are physical representations of faith and worship. Ceremonies are symbolic acts. Both focus belief, and provide a familiar element which binds those of similar faiths together.

Symbolism

Symbols are of utmost importance in most religions. The essence of a symbol is the meaning it conveys. Symbols may be acts, sounds and objects, and will always have strong cultural significance. By granting the invisible or intangible a visible or tangible representation, immaterial ideals and concepts are more easily understood and recognized. Venerating a symbol shows respect for the beliefs it represents. Similarly, contempt or enmity for a belief or those who hold it can be shown by attacking or defaming its symbols.

Some symbols and labels are randomly adopted. These symbols are often variations on ancient motifs (see sidebars, pp. 66-69). If the same symbol is found in many wide-ranging cultures, it is called a universal symbol. Universal symbols may represent entirely different ideals or concepts, depending upon their cultural associations. For example, the color white represents purity in Western society, but deep mourning in Oriental cultures.

Symbolic Connections

The ideals represented by symbols range from everyday matters to ideas of cosmic importance. In simpler cultures, symbols often represent concepts of sex, fertility, creation, natural and supernatural powers. Associated objects and rituals are designed to induce good luck or ward off evil. In more sophisticated cultures, the symbolism may become more abstract, and often deals with personal characteristics such as greed, jealousy, hatred, love and envy.

Over time, symbols may gain new associations that are contrary to their original meanings. In most modern Buddhist cultures, the swastika remains a positive symbol of life and the sun, while most modern Western cultures vilify it as a symbol of Nazi Germany. Sometimes the presence of a universal symbol can indicate an old cultural influence, but tracing this can be difficult. The horned crown of the Assyrian kings, a symbol of power and divinity, began as a crescent crown worn by Suin, an ancient Babylonian moon-god. But since the crescent resembles horns, over time it came to be depicted as a horned crown, its celestial origins lost.

Graphic Symbols

Many universal symbols are geometric shapes. The wheel-of-life, the yin and yang, the various forms of the cross and interlacement of stars are all examples of common motifs (see sidebars, pp. 66-69). Some associations, like the sun and the circle, are virtually universal. The triangle is commonly associated with any triune deity or concept of a threefold (such as body, mind and spirit) cosmology. Squares, spirals, crosses, meanders (wavy lines), chevrons and scrolls are other common symbols.

Symbolic Acts

Gesture, posture and position often hold symbolic meaning, especially in a religious context. The posture of religious statuary may represent the mood or temperament of the deity. Gestures of benediction or blessing are often conveyed by the uplifting of hands or certain positions of the fingers. Worshipers

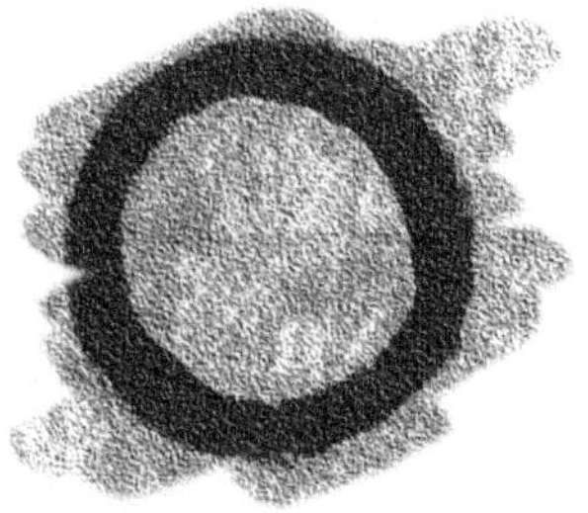

Round Motifs

The *circle* is usually a feminine symbol, associated with protected or consecrated areas. The cosmos is often seen as an unbroken circle. Circle symbolism is often used to convey a sense of equality of rank, such as with the Arthurian Round Table.

The *double wheel* is a symbol of eternity which represents the life cycles of the earth within an outer cycle of the cosmos. It often symbolizes a universal deity or elemental spirits.

The *spiral* is a symbol connected with the cycle of birth and rebirth. Sacred dances often follow spiral or circular patterns.

The *yang and yin* form a classic Chinese symbol representing opposing yet complementary and completing powers – male and female, light and dark, winter and summer, good and evil, and so on. Each half of the symbol contains a small spot of the opposite color, symbolizing the small portion of its opposite that each half of a dualistic pair contains.

often kneel in supplication; the god in a position of authority is often seated as a Judge. A finger placed to the lips to indicate silence, the "V" for Victory sign, a thumb down for death – all of these are symbolic gestures. Washing is a universal symbol of purification; breaking bread often indicates charity, or community.

Appearance and Dress

Color, fabric, style of dress and hair, scarification, tattooing – all of these may have specific meaning to a particular religion. Indeed, many religions have codes of dress and appearance. This places the individual within a group of worshipers, making him easily identifiable. Male Sikhs adhere to the wearing of the "five Ks." These are the *kesh* (uncut hair), the *kangha* (a comb securing the hair), the *kara* (a steel bracelet), the *kirpan* (a dagger) and the *kachh* (breeches which end above the knee).

In some religions, certain parts of the body must be concealed (or uncovered) at all times. Veils or headcoverings are often required (or removed, in some cases) within temples and churches. Malaysan Buddhists remove their footwear before entering their temples to pray.

Clergy must often adhere to stricter codes than secular worshipers, especially during religious services. Zoroastrian priests wear white robes, turbans and masks over their mouths during certain ceremonies. (See also *Clerical Garb*, p. 85.)

Particular colors are often sacred, or are worn at a particular ceremony or time of year. In the Catholic church white is used during Christmas and Easter, black on Good Friday, and blue or violet during Advent and the first four weeks of Lent.

Food

Plants, flowers, trees and fruits often hold particular significance to a religion. Rice is thrown at a wedding for luck, prosperity and progeny. The lily represents purity or death; corn symbolizes fertility. In China, long strands of vermicelli (representing wishes for long life) are eaten at birthdays. Bitter herbs and particular wines might be consumed at specific religious festivals, such as the Jewish Passover, in symbolic remembrance. Other foods, especially those of animal origin, may be considered unclean and therefore forbidden. Sometimes a particular plant or animal is actually considered to be a manifestation of the deity. The *haoma* plant is seen by Zoroastrians as the god Haoma on earth; in ritual the plant is pounded and the juice drunk, a bloodless offering representing the sacrifice at the end of the world which will grant immortality to all humans.

Animals

Often deities are associated with particular animals or natural motifs. Mithras, worshiped across the Roman Empire and beyond during the 1st to 4th centuries, was nearly always depicted slaying a bull. The cat was connected with the goddesses Bast and Freya, the cow with Hathor and Io, the ram with Amon and Aries, the sow with Astarte, Cerridwen and Demeter. All important animals either have some association

Cross Motifs

The *wolf cross* is an ancient Nordic symbol representing the first month of the year. A variation of the swastika (which was originally a symbol of life, light and the sun), the wolf cross also symbolized the turning of the year and annual sun cycles.

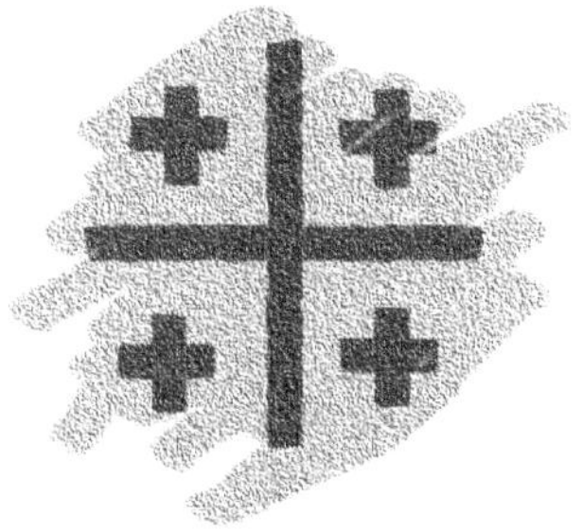

The *Jerusalem cross* was once a pre-Christian symbol called an "earth-center" cross. The subordinate crosses represented either the seasons, directions or four elements, depending upon the tradition. When Jerusalem grew to be the center of the medieval Christian world, this ancient cross symbol remained.

The cross became a well-known symbol as Christianity spread; this version is called the *Celtic cross*. Particularly common in Scotland and Ireland, it often serves as a grave marker. The Hindu *kiakra* is almost identical in shape.

The *Coptic cross* began as a sun-oriented symbol; the circle represented the sun, supported by four heavenly pillars. It was later adopted by Coptic Christians, who added the four "nails" to represent the crucified Christ.

Cultures of aliens with more than four limbs may have "cross" motifs with varying numbers and lengths of "arms," depending on their anatomy.

with the supernatural, are adopted as guardian spirits of some sort, or are identified with some cultural trait. In China the bat signifies good fortune, while in Europe it is associated with demons and vampires. The snake is a popular symbol, often seen as a wise feminine force. In other religions, the snake is diabolized, and seen as a corrupting beast. The European fox and Native American coyote are trickster figures. Various mythological creatures may also have religious significance, such as the well-known link between unicorns and purity.

Buildings

Temples and places of worship are often constructed to remind followers of aspects of the divine. The basic design, orientation, location and decoration may all have symbolic meaning within the religion. Christian churches often take the form of a cross, tall steeples pointing to heaven. A temple might have four towers, representing the four directions or elements; columns and pillars may specifically depict the deity or they may merely exist in numbers sacred to the religion. Buddhist *stupas* are often built in the form of a mandala, with three open, circular terraces within five closed square galleries. Doors and altars may be aligned in particular directions. A sanctuary to a solar deity might be constructed so that the light of the dawn pours in through the front door. Shinto shrines usually face south, or sometimes east; north and west are considered to be unlucky.

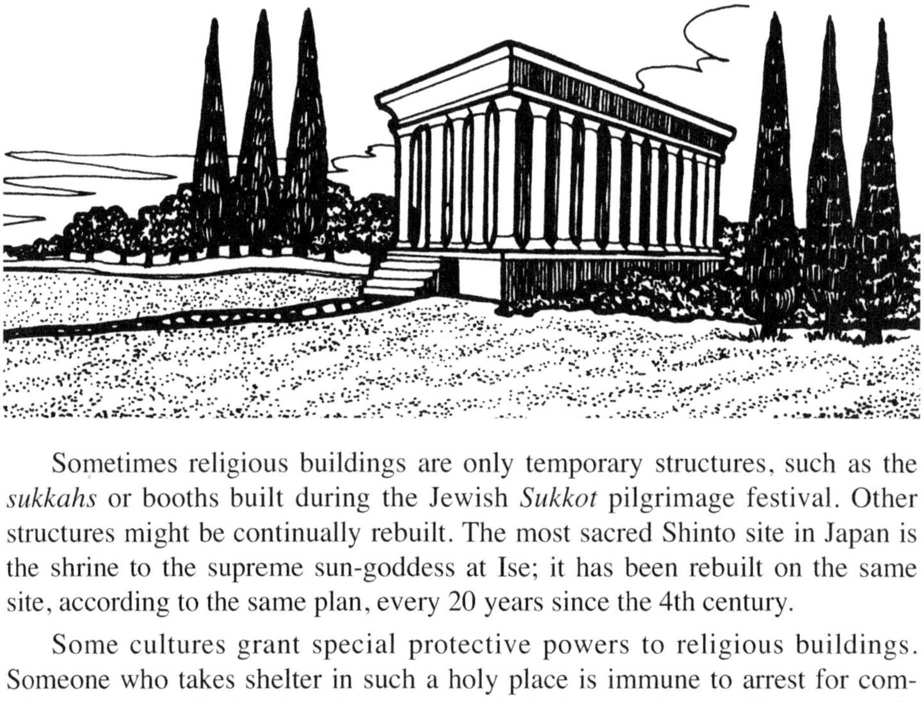

Sometimes religious buildings are only temporary structures, such as the *sukkahs* or booths built during the Jewish *Sukkot* pilgrimage festival. Other structures might be continually rebuilt. The most sacred Shinto site in Japan is the shrine to the supreme sun-goddess at Ise; it has been rebuilt on the same site, according to the same plan, every 20 years since the 4th century.

Some cultures grant special protective powers to religious buildings. Someone who takes shelter in such a holy place is immune to arrest for committing a crime, for holding divergent political views, and so on. This custom is called *sanctuary,* or sometimes *refuge*.

Tools

Objects may have symbolic as well as practical value. In addition, many items might represent the same ideal. A book, scroll or floppy disk may be used to represent learning. Scales and balances might represent justice. A chalice or flask might depict healing. In other cultures, one symbol may hold many meanings. Flame might represent knowledge, or torment, or destruction, or the warmth of the home.

Triple Motifs

The *triangle* is the most common triple motif. Triangle designs often represent the feminine principle.

Fate is often seen as not one, but three, linked entities and is often represented by a *triple triangle* motif. Single and triple triads (motifs containing 3s and 9s) are significant in many earth religions.

The *trefoil,* or three-leaf shamrock, is one of the oldest emblems of triune divinity, dating back to Indus Valley civilizations. This is a virtually universal symbol, but is particularly common in Celtic and Near Eastern religions.

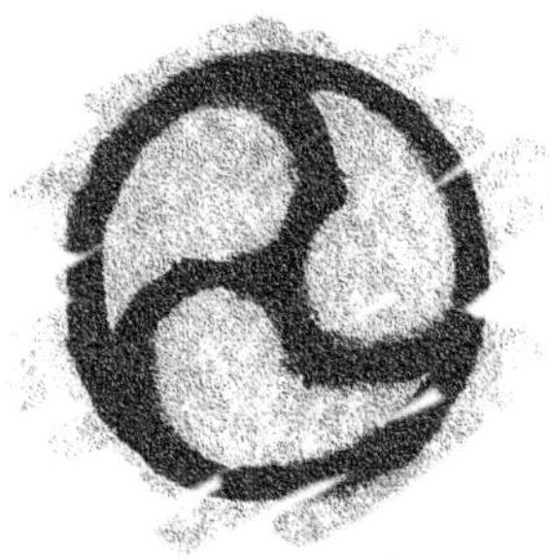

The *world triad* is an emblem of cosmic creativity, symbolizing both the threefold nature of fate and the eternal cycles of life.

Ceremonies

The terms "rituals" and "ceremonies" may generally be interchanged. They are formal symbolic acts which are defined by protocol, tradition and convention. Sometime these actions are mere routine and habit, and hold no deep significance to the participants. Indeed, over time, the actual meaning of a habitual action might be lost. But frequently they involve elaborate preparations and are performed with a great deal of pomp and formality.

What Is a Ritual?

Ritual is perhaps the most complex form of symbolic activity in any religion. These activities express religious belief in a physical way, and invite reflection and thought by their participants. Rituals can rarely be understood out of the context of religion and culture, and often puzzle – or even offend – outsiders. Rituals affirm the social position of the participant, and help define social boundaries, confirming one's place in the community. This sense of identity and community is vitally important to a religion.

The Done, the Said, and the Seen

Ritual is highly symbolic, and expresses concepts on many different levels. Language, gesture and physical objects involve all the senses. The taste of ritual foods, the smell of incense, the touch of anointing oil, the sounds of bells and chants – all these draw the participant's attention and strengthen the symbolism. The best way to understand a ritual is to consider it in terms of what is done, what is said and what is seen.

Ceremonies and rituals consist of a sequence of performed actions. Often a ritual re-enacts past events in the history of the religion, celebrating triumphs and remembering times of sorrow and misfortune. At times, rituals can be an emotional outlet and a means to deal with problems, by invoking religious laws and judgements, or offering sacrifices and penances. Rituals are small dramas, in which the congregations are the actors, the clergy are the directors, and the deity is the audience.

The vocal components of rituals are also important. They may be confirmations of faith, confessions, songs of praise and prayer, or the recitation of religious history and myth. What is said and heard enhances the meaning of the ritual.

Paraphernalia also reinforces the symbolism of ritual. Visual symbols are very common in rituals, and involve colors, numbers, shapes, vessels, vestments, animals and foodstuffs in complex combinations. A symbol can represent more than one thing, depending upon the ritual it is used in. Rituals grow, adapt and change according to the needs and traditions of the adherents.

Community Rituals

Ritual plays an important role in maintaining a sense of loyalty and community among members of a certain society. Rituals are generally performed publicly, according to oral traditions or scriptures. Special holy sites or consecrated buildings are the usual locations. Leaders of such rituals act as the liaison between the worshipers and the divine. These leaders are usually specially trained and consecrated.

Community rituals can also be performed by the laity. Jain temples do not hold images of gods, only depictions of their *Tirthankaras*. Images of these enlightened mortal teachers are bathed, sung to and purified during various rites

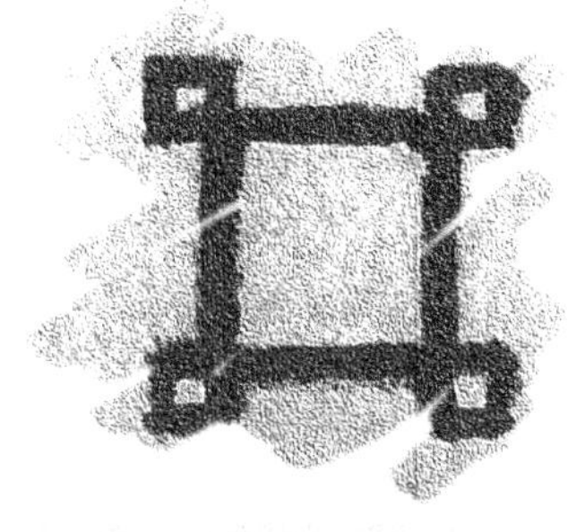

Four-Way Motifs

The *earth square* represents the nearly universal concept that the earth has four corners and four directions. It is thought to be inherently protective, for it also represents the four spirits, or earth-guardians, that stand at the corners of the world hold up the sky.

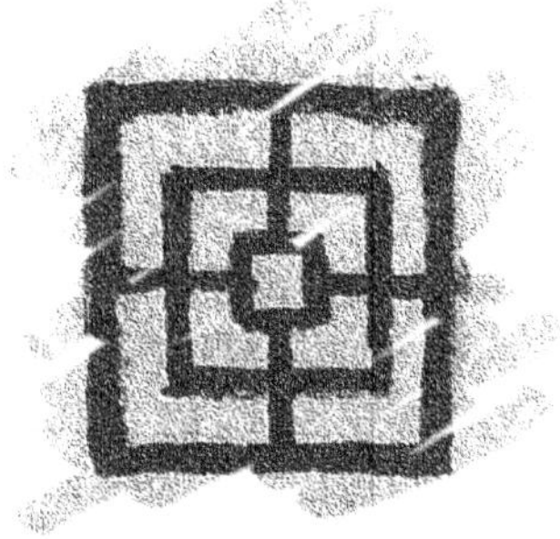

The *Morris square* (also called the Mill, or Triple Enclosure) is common to Celtic and earth religions. It represents the four elements, winds, directions, rivers and so on, all of which proceed from the holy center.

The *Nandyavarta* is a Hindu labyrinth design used in both mysticism and meditation. It symbolizes contemplation and revelation of inner mysteries.

The *world symbol* represents the four elements joined together by a central unifying force.

celebrating auspicious occasions. Communal meals, ranging from the temple gatherings of the Zoroastrians to modern Christian "potlucks," all help maintain community ties and strengthen religious fellowship.

Religious parades are another form of community ritual. Examples include the Corpus Cristi parades in Peru, the Islamic Ashura festivals in Kashmir, the Hindu marches devoted to Ganesh, and the well-known "dragons" paraded in Chinese New Year celebrations.

Defining Symbols for a New Religion

Symbols are important because of the associations they bring with them. When choosing symbols the GM must consider exactly what he is trying to convey. The GM should determine the key beliefs of the culture and pick a symbol for each. Using symbols that have common meaning can be a shortcut to help players understand the world. For example, to many people a sword will symbolize strength, knightly orders and chivalry.

If the GM wishes to create a new "feel," it is a good idea to choose symbols that do not already have strong connotations, or use older symbols whose meanings have been forgotten or changed. Reclaiming the older meaning of a symbol can be difficult, however. The swastika's present meaning (to Western cultures, at least) is far different from its ancient connotations of creativity and light.

If the GM wishes to create a totally alien "feel," then designing completely new symbols is an option. Such symbols should echo the structure of the alien society in some way.

Whatever symbols he chooses will play a strong role in any ceremonies associated with the religion. Symbols are inscribed upon altars and holy items, worn on priestly vestments and flown on standards at the heads of armies. Ritual gestures echoing the shape of the symbol will develop. Ritual responses might be repeated a holy number of times. (See *Numbers*, p. 12.)

Symbols do not have to be religiously significant – even atheistic societies will have symbols. A corporate logo might inspire loyal workers just as a religious one might inspire a true believer.

Clerical Rituals

Some rituals may only be performed by a sanctified or anointed member of the religion. These rites, sometimes called sacraments, are either so formal or so "holy" that only an invested cleric may perform them. Often clerical rituals are restricted by ranks. For example, a high priest invests a priest, while a priest invests a minister. Religions often require that their leaders undergo training, or that they be approved by the deity. Rites of passage are commonly considered clerical rituals, as are rites of initiation or ordination. Sometimes this investiture is only temporary and the individual serves for only a specific length of time, much as do the Elders found in some Christian churches. Young Buddhist boys in Burma usually become monks for a short period of time when they are about four years old. This particular ceremony is considered to be more important than a marriage or funeral and is intended to encourage the child toward the monastic life which is a Buddhist ideal.

Domestic Rituals

The home becomes a sacred place, and the parent (or elder) acts as the leader. A specially prepared place within the home is the usual locale for such rites. Domestic rituals are usually designed to involve the children in religious traditions. Religions involving ancestor veneration often hold their most important rituals in the home.

Personal Rituals

These rituals answer individual spiritual or emotional needs and link religion to everyday life. Solitude and privacy are often required for personal rituals. Techniques such as meditation, prayer, dreams and self-induced trances are often used. Such rituals do not require another individual to act as a liaison between the worshiper and the divine. The doctrine of Zen depends entirely upon years of disciplined meditation. For the Zen Buddhist, gardening, archery, tea-drinking and the enjoyment of nature are all personal rituals that contain the mystery of life and as such have the greatest religious significance.

Personal rituals are often repeated on a daily basis; the devout Jew begins and ends his day with the same prayer, "*Shema Yisroel Adonoi Elohenu, Adonoi Echod* (Hear, O Israel, the Lord our God, the Lord is One)."

Rituals of Healing and Exorcism

These rituals are designed to ensure the wholeness of the body and spirit. Often they act to restore health and purity, or to exorcise negative influences from the body, spirit or a particular location. The healer or exorcist uses symbolic systems, formulae and other skills to invoke the aid of the sacred; these are an important part of such rituals. He also uses techniques involving the "laying on of hands," praying, burning incense, and anointing with holy oils. Such rituals are thought to benefit both the individual and the world at large.

Festivals

Festivals are a popular and colorful form of ritual and are celebrated in all cultures in one form or another. Many festivals celebrate duality – the welcoming of the new, the ushering out of the old, mourning and rejoicing, fasting and feasting, and so on. There are two basic types of festivals: ecofests and theofests.

An ecofest is a festival which celebrates a seasonal or astronomical event. These are often rituals of remembrance, renewal and initiation. Spring and harvest festivals are classic examples of ecofests, as are celebrations marking the waxing and waning of the moon. Sometimes both seasonal and astronomical events are used. Ancient Chinese festivals were based on the old lunar calendar and the agricultural year, while the solar calendar was used for bureaucratic matters. Some religions, such as Judaism and Islam, still use lunar calendars.

Birthdays

Among peoples who have developed a sense of time, birthdays are important and often marked with special rites. Birthdays are times of transition and change, so many people believe that both good and evil spirits will try to influence the person at this time.

Ceremonies and games carried out at birthday celebrations are often seen as a symbolic wiping of the past. Trials of strength and skill often are performed as demonstrations of growth and progress.

The exchange of presents and communal feasting is a common custom. This strengthens communal bonds and ingratiates an individual both with the spirits and with his relatives.

The hour, date and place of birth are often very important, as they may be clues to the fortune and fate of the child. (See *Divination* and *Prophecy*, p. 16.)

Twins

In many parts of the world, the birth of twins is seen as an ominous or special event. Sometimes one of the twins is thought to be fathered by a deity, and one by a human parent. At other times, twins are thought to be evidence of adultery, with one man the father of each.

Often twin births bring great status to the father, as proving his virility. But among many tribal people, twins are destroyed, and the mother rigorously purified.

Twins are sometimes considered to be lucky, or to possess second sight. Often the fate of twins was thought to be interconnected – what happened to one was fated to occur to the other. In some cultures, twins were considered to be part of the same person, and were given the same name and referred to as though they were really a single person.

Ancient Aztec custom required the death of the elder twin at birth, in order to prevent the death of a parent. The surviving twin was considered to have great potential for evil, and was carefully watched.

Many cultures have twin motifs in their mythologies. Twin heroes are very common, especially among Aboriginal, South American and Native American tribes.

A theofest is a festival of theological significance, designed to celebrate some important event in the life of the deity or some other date important in the history of the religion. Many Catholics celebrate various "saint's days" and some still keep to the practice of abstaining from meat each Friday. The Jewish festival of *Purim*, celebrating their salvation from the persecution of Haman, is set on the 14th of Adar, the 12th lunar month.

Many festivals are a mixture of these two types, celebrating both a physical and spiritual event, often combining elements and traditions from older festivals. Sometimes the dates of these festivals vary from year to year, as they do not necessarily follow the modern calendar. The Christian celebration of Easter is such an example. Commemorating the resurrection of Christ, it is a lunar festival, occurring on the first Sunday after the first full moon after March 21st. As such, it falls sometime between March 22nd and April 25th. This formula was chosen in the 3rd century and is used today by most Christian denominations. However, the Eastern Orthodox church celebrates it according to the Julian calendar.

Easter is also a spring celebration; the name itself is thought to be derived from the ancient Teutonic goddess of dawn or spring, Eostre or Ostra. The association of eggs with Easter may well support this, as the egg was a holy symbol of that goddess.

Rites of Passage

Rites of passage are used to ensure spiritual safety at various times during an individual's life. Such rites also honor the participant. Common to all rites of passage are the concepts of separation, transition and entrance. These rituals include acts and symbols which illustrate the separation of the individual from a previous stage of life, the transition of passage, and the entrance into a new state of social and spiritual being. While some societies have literally dozens of such celebrations, there are five basic types of passage rites: prenatal, childhood, initiation into adulthood, marriage and death.

Prenatal Rites

These rituals confirm and celebrate the pregnancy, or even determine the sex of the child. Such rites are usually very personal, and are accompanied by prayers of both thanksgiving and supplication for protection. Often a woman will travel to a shrine or other holy site to ensure fertility and a trouble-free pregnancy. Some cultures require that a woman undergo some form of ritual purification after birth. Other cultures require rites to liberate and protect the woman from the special dangers inherent in childbirth.

Childhood Rites

Childhood rites include prayers for protection and blessing, rituals of naming and affirmation of lineage. Names have mystic and magical significance in many cultures. Infants may be given *milk* names that are used until the child reaches puberty. Families that have lost one child may give a new child an unattractive name so that evil spirits will not consider the child worth bothering. Children may be named after famous ancestors in the hope that they will grow up to be equally successful. Often naming rites are combined with other celebratory rituals, such as the child's first haircut.

While the child's parents or godparents may perform some rites, a cleric is usually involved. Many religions have rites which signify the deity's claim upon the child. Such rites usually involve some form of anointing or blessing.

Knots

The *knot* is an important part of many ceremonies, and rituals using knots can signify both joining and separation.

The knot is one of the eight sacred symbols in Buddhism, for it represents life, having no beginning and no end. Throughout India, knots are tied in the clothes of the bride and bridegroom in marriage ceremonies – in some places their clothing is actually knotted together. Roman marriages consisted of a series of knot-tyings and untyings. In Russia a net is thrown over the couple during the marriage ceremony, for no evil spirit can get at the couple without first untying all the knots in the net. In medieval Europe, it was commonly believed that if anyone tied a knot during a wedding ceremony, the couple would never have children.

Zoroastrian initiations consisted of the tying of a sacred girdle in symbolic knots. The sacred thread of a high-caste Brahman is tied in a special Brahma-knot at his initiation. In some Roman ceremonies it was vitally important that the priest have no knots or tangles in his clothing or hair.

Funeral rites often involve knot-tying, or rather untying. It is a common belief in many parts of Europe that knots would prevent a soul from leaving the body.

It is a common practice worldwide to undo all possible knots to facilitate childbirth. Knots have long been used in the causing and curing of disease. Multiples of sevens are especially potent, while nine-knot spells are considered to be most evil. Old Teutonic law severely fined anyone found guilty of tying nine knots. It is also a common custom to tie knots in the fringe of a shawl or scarf when friends and lovers must part.

Fishermen are particularly concerned with knots, and have many traditions about them. Fishers often "tie up the wind" in a knot, and then untie it to raise enough wind to fill the sails. Fishermen often buy a wind-charm from an old man or woman versed in wind-lore. Aeolus gave Odysseus the winds tied up in a bag before he set sail.

Rites of Initiation

Rites of passage involving initiation into adulthood are the best known. In most cultures these rituals involve tests, solitary vigils, purifications and anointments. Usually these occur at puberty, but in some societies an individual is not considered "adult" until marriage or the birth of a child. There are numerous other types of initiation rites which an adult may undergo during a lifetime: ordination in clerical orders, graduations, coronations and investitures of noble rank, knightings, hazings by secret societies and so on.

Many initiation rites involve symbols of death and rebirth. An individual may be required to "die," renouncing all previous connections and ties, to be reborn as a "new" person. Naming rituals are often included in such rites.

Rites of Marriage

The concept of marriage is a complicated one which varies greatly. Some cultures do not hold a marriage to be legal unless the union is sanctified and witnessed by a cleric. Other cultures do not even have words to describe the concept. In societies where marriage has religious significance, it is usually considered to be an honorable state instituted and blessed by the deity to ensure continuance of the race. The spiritual well-being of the couple is ensured when they celebrate their union with some sort of marriage rite.

Symbolic marriages between the cleric and the deity are common in cultures that consider marriage a holy institution. Such "marriages" may involve vows of celibacy and chastity on the part of the cleric. In some cultures, sexual congress between a cleric and a worshiper might be required, most notably for agricultural fertility rites. In other cases, proxy marriages might be required to protect the reputation of a pregnant woman. In India, temple prostitutes were married to a dagger. In classical Greece, it was common for a man to prefer to adopt a child born of a temple woman even over his own issue, for such children were considered both holy and blessed.

Funeral Rites

These rituals serve many purposes. They mark the passing of an individual from this life, appease his spirit so that it will not wander, and ensure protection from spirits. The idea that it is necessary to defend and protect the surviving friends and family prevails in many cultures. Funeral customs, beliefs and practices are greatly influenced by this.

The custom of wearing black, and other specific colors, developed from the belief that this would make the mourners less obvious and thus protect them from whatever spirits threatened the living. Similarly, throwing some object into the grave is often considered to "lay the ghost." If such a gift was omitted, people feared that the angry spirit would return to haunt the living. Many cultures believe that the dead envy the living, and so the living must do nothing that might inflame their wrath.

It is also important that nothing interfere with the orderly disposition of the body. Any interruption or delay might allow a lingering spirit the opportunity for mischief against the living. Thus funeral processions must not be interrupted or blocked in any manner. Even in modern society, a funeral procession has the right of way over other traffic.

It is the place of the cleric to ensure that all the proper rituals are performed correctly so that the living are not left in peril. He usually speaks the eulogy, although sometimes a good friend of the deceased is granted the honor. In many cultures this is the last opportunity to appease the lingering spirit of the dead.

Feng-Shui

Meaning "wind and water," feng-shui is the traditional Chinese technique used to select auspicious sites for graves, buildings and cities. The feng-shui practitioner sees the earth as a living being through which energy flows. Different locales have different concentrations of vital sky and earth energies. The patterns of hills, streams and plants show the presence of this energy.

Feng-shui theory is similar to traditional Chinese cosmology. The land exhibits *Yin* or *Yang* forms of energy. This energy can be classified as one of the *Five Agents*: wood, fire, earth, metal and water. In an ideal spot these agents are balanced, with perhaps slightly more Yang energy. The value of the earthly elements, however, also depends upon the influence of the stars and planets, so astrology is an important part of feng-shui.

If a grave is located at such a balance point, then the cosmic energy present will cause the bones of the dead to radiate this energy on behalf of their descendants. If a home or building is built on the spot, then all who dwell within will benefit.

A good gravesite is typically located halfway down a mountain slope, facing south and overlooking a body of water. Vegetation should be abundant and beautiful – it is important that the site be comforting to those who come to visit. A deficient site can be strengthened by building artificial mounds, pools and walls.

Feng-shui is not a religious technique per se, but it is necessary to ask the local deities for permission before proceeding with any construction.

Feng-shui was first developed in the Han dynasty (206 B.C. to 220 A.D.).

Scarification

Rites of passage and other ritual ceremonies often include some form of mutilation or scarification, such as circumcision, tattooing or piercing. This proves that the candidate is able to withstand stress and pain, and thus is old and strong enough to fulfill adult tasks. Sometimes the pain and blood involved in such rites is considered a sacrificial offering. In modern culture, many of these ceremonies have been reduced to functions such as the hazings and "hell weeks" suffered by college freshmen.

In other cultures, ceremonial wounds are prevented from healing, either by continual irritation, or by rubbing the wound with ashes or dyes. Other cultures bound the feet of young girls, or wrapped infants' heads in such a way as to ensure they would develop sloping foreheads. Such mutilations often appealed to both secular and religious sensibilities.

Many people regard such mutilations and scars as marks of distinction. In some cultures such scars provide visible proof that the individual is part of the community. This is not so different from the European students who boasted of their saber-duelling scars.

Prayer

Prayer is often a primary element of worship. Any address to a higher power is usually considered to be a prayer. Prayer serves many purposes: praise, adoration, confession, petition, intercession and thanksgiving. It can be a highly personal ritual between the supplicant and the divine, or a communal rite led by a cleric. In some cases the priest intervenes directly, praying on a worshiper's behalf.

Prayer can be spontaneous or ritualized. Ritual prayer can be as elaborate as a series of cadenced phrases and antiphonal response. (An antiphon is a responsive song or prayer.) Other prayers might be silent. Often prayers are not addressed directly to the deity, but rather to some figure who is asked to intercede, such as a saint or local spirit.

Prayers frequently consist of set forms recited at particular times of day, according to the traditions and demands of the religion. Prayer often also involves symbolic gestures such as genuflection, bowing and prostration. Islamic ritual prayer, performed five times a day (at dawn, noon, late afternoon, sunset and after sunset), begins with *wadu*, a purificatory washing. During the course of this silent prayer, the worshiper bows from the waist (*ruku*) several times and prostrates himself such that his forehead touches the ground (*sujud*).

The supplicant may beg, make demands or even reproach the deity. But many religions believe the more pitiful the speaker, the more effective the prayer. Such prayers often begin with a long list of self-effacing comments. Prayer is often accompanied by offerings and sacrifices.

Sometimes a prayer is neither spoken, nor silent, but is written down. Some Buddhist temples have huge guardian statues that are covered with bits of paper. Worshipers write their prayers down, and after chewing the paper, throw it at the statues. If the paper sticks, that is thought to be a sign that the prayer will be answered.

Sacrifice

A sacrifice is an offering of some value which establishes a relationship between the supplicant and divine beings, spirits, ancestors or other sacred powers. Such offerings may be gifts of thanksgiving, bribes or penances.

Sacrifice often involves the destruction of the offering – even the killing of animals or people, depending upon the seriousness of the ritual. Offerings might also be in the form of incense, food, flowers, drink, money or models of larger objects such as houses and ships.

Personal sacrifices are often seen to hold the greatest value. Monks might sacrifice their sexuality or speech by taking life-long vows. Other worshipers sacrifice part of themselves, undergoing mutilations or painful scarring. These are common during rituals of penance or mourning. Sacrifices in the form of self-torture and mutilation are sometimes required for initiation rites.

Blood and live offerings are common. Blood is often considered to be the "seat of life" and so is considered to be particularly valuable, as are other body parts. Australian tribesmen regularly make individual blood offerings, North American Indians offered their fingers, the Hindu goddess Kali was worshiped with self-decapitations. Even deities have been known to practice sacrifice – Tyr lost his hand in order to bind the wolf Fenris, and Odin exchanged his eye for knowledge.

Sacrificial offerings may also be symbolic, and substitutes and surrogates are commonly used. Animals might be sacrificed rather than humans; bread or vegetable carvings of animals are burned in place of the real thing.

In some cases a token sacrifice is acceptable. Ancient Greek libation was a few drops of wine. Practicality has led many Chinese to use paper models for most sacrifices, or food which is later eaten in a great feast. Sometimes there is no physical component to the sacrifice at all. Among poor Hindus, it is literally the thought that counts: a visualization of the offering during prayer is enough.

Performers and Recipients

Sacrificial rituals may be performed either by a worshiper in a private ritual, or by an intermediary on another's behalf. Such mediators are usually clerics or other sanctified individuals (such as an Elder or King). Sacred rulers (as in ancient Egypt, China, Japan and India) are especially holy intermediaries. Sacrificial rituals performed at a sacred time and place may require consecrated performers.

Fire, smoke, air or water conveyed offerings to the divine. Sometimes the deity requires sacrifices on a regular basis. Ancestors worshiped in mortuary religions require constant sacrifices. Cooked food is commonly given in such cases, often in the form of a special meal in which a portion is set aside and burned in a domestic ritual.

Human Sacrifice

Surrendering one's life is often considered the ultimate sacrifice. In many cultures such an offering was the ultimate gift a worshiper might make. This might not actually involve physical death, but rather a withdrawal from the world, with the worshiper devoting the rest of his life to the deity. In other cultures, the victim was actually slain.

The reasons behind human sacrifice are myriad. The victim might be considered a messenger to the gods, a hostage or securer of fertility, or a hedge against natural disasters such as flood, famine or drought. Captives or prisoners

Blood

Blood is seen as being of vital spiritual and magical importance. It is thought to be the seat of life itself, or the dwelling place of the soul. As a result, a great number of practices and customs involve blood.

Blood is often drunk to enrich oneself with the soul or essence of the donor. In battle, warriors will sometimes drink the blood of their fallen foes. Often the blood of fierce animals, such as lions and tigers, is used for the same purpose.

Many people also use blood for curative purposes. Leprosy was traditionally treated by bathing the afflicted person in blood. Bathing in blood is also thought to raise the dead or reanimate people who have been turned to stone. Sigurd became invulnerable after he bathed in a dragon's blood.

Some traditions hold that blood can act as an instrument of vengeance. It is thought by some that a body will bleed in the presence of its murderer. Often murderers bemoan that they cannot wash the blood of their victims from their hands or clothing.

Many offerings to the gods involve blood, not flesh, sacrifices. This may be real blood, or symbolic, such as that of the Christian communion ritual.

Blood is a powerful, binding agent. Thus blood covenants are considered to be among the most serious of oaths.

Ashes

The residue left after burning has important religious significance in many cultures.

Often ashes are thought to have purifying qualities, due to their close association with the mysterious nature of fire.

Brahmans rub their bodies with ash in preparation for certain religious ceremonies.

The lamas of Tibet mix the ashes of a holy man with clay and form images with them. They then place these in shrines and other places of devotion.

Ashes might also be scattered in the air, in the hope of bringing rain in time of drought. In Peru, they are used to disperse mist. In parts of Mexico ashes are thrown upon the water to bring fair weather. Often ashes are used as talismans against thunder and lightning.

The ashes of a sacrificed creature are often scattered over fields to ensure the fecundity of flocks and plenty of milk.

Ashes are often used in curative rites, or given to cattle to fatten them or to protect them from plague.

Mourning rites make frequent use of ashes. Many people strew themselves with ashes during funerals. Other cultures mix ashes with wine or milk and consume them in remembrance of the dead.

Ashes might also be used in divination or as protection against ghosts and other spirits.

might be slain in rituals of thanksgiving for victory in war. Other sacrifices are scapegoats, offered to appease a deity's wrath. Sometimes servants and spouses are slain as part of funeral rites. The bodies of sacrificial victims might be buried beneath the foundations of important buildings, or their bones and blood mixed into the bricks and mortar.

Human sacrifice is often closely tied to fertility, birth, resurrection and reincarnation. In such sacrifices the victim is usually intoxicated or drugged before the ritual. During the rituals the victim is actually deified, becoming the holiest of sacrifices. The Aztec priests of Xipe Totec wore the flayed skins of their victims as a symbol of reincarnation. Religions in which the cyclical nature of creation and life have great import often count human sacrifice among their most holy rites.

In voudoun (voodoo) and some earth-religion traditions, a worshiper opens his body to the gods so that they might walk the earth among their followers for awhile. The worshiper's soul may spend this time "sleeping," wandering or waiting between the worlds where the deities exist between visits to Earth.

Ritual cannibalism is often tied to human sacrifice, the participants believing that by consuming the victim they gain special divine benefits and blessings.

Dance

Dance seems universal to all cultures. Patterned, rhythmic movements of the body are used to express a number of emotions, most notably joy. Dance is often an important part of religious ritual, especially in tribal religions. In more complex cultures, dance is often either a performance art or a folk activity. Sacred dances are vital to many religious traditions such as Hinduism, Shinto and Confucianism.

Ecstatic Dances

Ecstatic or trance dances allow communication with divine forces and are used in rites of healing and exorcism. Often these dances are part of a shamanistic rite, accompanied by drumming, whirling and chanting. These activities are thought to induce a mystic trance which enables the shaman to aid the subject. Narcotics or intoxicants are often used. The shaman's spirit might leave his body during such a dance, to be temporarily replaced by an animal or ancestral spirit. The dancer is inspired to perform superhuman acrobatic feats, writhing, climbing, leaping and falling. Often the dancer becomes immune to pain; he might indulge in self-mutilation by fire or blade.

Some Hindu and Islamic sects practice ecstatic dancing as a form of moving meditation. Their repetitive movements induce trances which aid enlightenment.

Funeral Dances

Dancing is often an important part of funeral rites in which merrymaking is thought to please or appease a spirit. Specific dances might also be used to dispatch a lingering ghost. In cultures with shamanistic traditions, funeral dances become ecstatic rituals which aid the shaman in escorting the dead spirit to its proper realm. In some cultures these have been reduced to folk dances, although it is still considered to be extremely bad luck to dance certain Scottish reels and Irish jigs except at wakes.

Mocking Dances

These dances, also called *clown* dances, may re-enact battles or make travesties of history. The dancers portray supernatural beings or spirits of the dead. Speech is often distorted during such rituals (either reversed or falsetto) and combined with obscene gestures and actions. Demon or animal masks, usually made of wood or leather with long noses, beards, hair and horns, are used. The dancers wear shaggy or torn clothing and carry whips, bells, rattles and mock weapons. Medieval carnival clowns and fools arose from these traditions. Some North American Indian tribes use clown dancers to point out people's foolishness or pretension.

Astronomical Dances

Many agricultural and nomadic societies worship astronomical objects such as the sun, moon and stars. Astronomical dances are common at solstice and equinox festivals, and also might invoke benevolent forces to aid crops and hunting. Mummer's plays, the Maypole dances, the Eclipse dance of the Denne Indians and famous Sun Dances of the Plains Indians are all astronomical dances. Often these types of dances have multiple purposes – the Sun Dance also has curative and heroic aspects.

Battle Dances

Specific dances are performed in preparation for war or in celebration of victory. These dances strengthen communal bonds and boast of prowess and virility. Battle dances, most specifically sword dances, are often closely tied with agricultural rites. Such dances symbolize the cyclical death and resurrection themes associated with vegetation deities – crops are harvested (the god sacrificed) in the fall, but grow again (the god reborn) in the spring. Sword dances are often performed by men's secret societies, echoing sacrificial fertility rites.

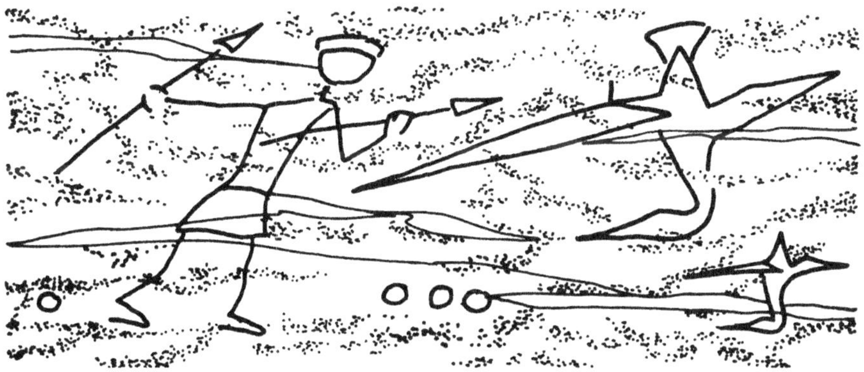

Holy Sites

Location can enhance rituals. Certain sites take on special meaning and importance. These may be holy cities, wells, rivers or simply consecrated buildings. Symbolic shapes, such as circles, crosses, triangles and spirals, can often be seen in the site – the circle of trees about a well, the triangular island within the joining of two rivers, the winding concentric path that leads up to a mountain peak. Buildings erected on such sites often echo the shapes revered by the religion.

Unusual natural formations are often seen as holy. Ayers Rock, in Australia, is one example. Monumental structures from lost cultures will usually be *assumed* to be holy, even if their true purpose is long forgotten!

Mistletoe

Mistletoe has been regarded as a mysterious and sacred plant from the earliest times. It is reputed to bestow life and fertility, and to serve as a protection against poison. The oak mistletoe was considered to be particularly effective, and has many medicinal and magical attributes.

The famous *Golden Bough* that Aeneas took to guard him on his way into the underworld was the mistletoe.

Mistletoe is especially sacred to the Celtic druids. Both Pliny and Caesar describe the rite of harvesting the plant: on the sixth night of the moon, white-robed druids cut it down with a golden sickle. It was not allowed to fall to the ground; instead it was caught in a white cloth. Mistletoe is still picked at midsummer in many Celtic and Scandinavian countries. (See *From Beginning to End*, p. 14, for its Norse associations.)

As a medicine, mistletoe is still called *allheal*, and is believed to cure sterility and epilepsy.

Mistletoe is often hung over house and stable doors as a protective charm.

Cake Customs

Many acts of sacrifice, worship and divination are associated with annual cycles. Cakes are used in many aspects of the life cycle, and are especially associated with baptisms, weddings and rituals for the dead. Cakes are often molded into the shapes of humans or animals, and offered as a substitute for the actual being.

In ancient Greece, dough cakes were thrown into chasms and crevices as offerings to Demeter and Persephone. In Egypt, dough cakes representing pigs and other animals were offered to Osiris and to the moon. Cakes were often left in tombs, as food for the dead. Millet cakes were sacrificed to Ceres and Mater Matuta by Roman matrons. Hindus feed the dead upon cakes covered with boiled rice, sugar and melted butter.

Cakes of various shapes were particularly popular in Greece. Cakes in the shape of girls or arrows were given to Helios at Delphi and Delos; Artemis was offered honey-cakes. In Athens, a twelve-knobbed cake was offered to Cronus every spring. At each full or new moon, circular cakes topped with candles were placed at crossroads in offering to Hecate.

Cakes are also often given away as charms, or used to drive away evil. In Scotland, children go from house to house upon New Year's Eve, singing carols and receiving oat cakes.

The Lenten season was ushered in by great feasting. Shrove Tuesday (or *Mardi Gras*) is celebrated throughout the Christian world by eating pancakes. On Good Friday, hot cross buns are a favorite treat said to bring good luck.

Hiding Ancient Symbols and Names

As religions diminish in power, their influence wanes as well. But sometimes ancient symbols and divine names live on in the practices and languages of later societies. GMs might wish to disguise such things in the societies they create as hints or clues to lost civilizations or faded gods. Often the names of lost or forgotten gods are seen in the names of days, months, or even humble everyday items. For instance, "Wednesday" derives from the phrase *Wodnes daeg,* meaning "the day of Odin (or Wotan)"; the term *cereal* is derived from the harvest goddess Ceres. Sometimes well-known religious terms become common idioms. Below are a few other historical examples of this subtle adaption.

Continued on next page . . .

Holy sites have mythic or historic significance. Someone of importance to the religion, perhaps even the deity, is believed to have visited that site, or performed a significant deed there. Many holy sites are also educational centers.

Pilgrimage

A pilgrimage is a religious journey to a sacred center or holy site. Such a journey is often considered to be a new beginning or turning point in the individual's spiritual life. Sometimes this pilgrimage is required duty. Every adult Muslim who possesses the means is expected at least once in his life to undertake the *hajj,* the pilgrimage to the *Kaaba* in Mecca. The actual ceremony he performs once there is complex and takes several days to complete. It includes both extensive prayer and sacrifice.

Pilgrimage may also be part of a healing or exorcism ritual. Pilgrims travel to holy sites that have reputations for miracles in the hope that they, too, will receive divine aid. From ancient to modern times people of various religions have traveled to sites like Bath, England, in the hopes of finding a cure for their affliction.

Other pilgrimages are made to petition the deity for a specific blessing. In southern India, many women travel long distances to ask *Naga* (a snake deity of fertility) to grant them a child. Frequently a second pilgrimage is promised should the blessing be granted.

Pilgrimages might also be journeys of hardship undertaken to redress some past misdeed. A pilgrim may travel to a holy site intending to make a special offering. During medieval times, many people sought Jerusalem for this reason. It was considered a "good work" by which they could acquire merit in the eyes of God. Christians, Jews and Muslims still travel to that city today for much the same reason.

Pilgrimages may also be undertaken for recreational or social reasons. Often great fairs and cultural centers develop around holy sites. Pilgrims may travel alone or in groups. Traveling together strengthens regional as well as religious identity. It might be particularly significant to visit a holy site or shrine at a specific time of year. It is not only important *where* something happened, but *when* as well. In Shinto belief, it is best to visit the Great Shrine of the Izumo Province (sometimes called the "land of the *kami*") during October when the *kami* from all over the country flock there for a grand meeting.

Some religions have festivals associated with ancient pilgrimages. Jews celebrate three such pilgrimage festivals: *Pesach*, *Shavot* and *Sukkot*. During these times Jews were commanded to go to Jerusalem to worship in the temple.

Holy Times

Particular days and times of the year may be considered special or holy. These times allow the adherent to make a connection between real, measured time and cosmic time. The solar year, with its solstices and equinoxes, and the lunar year, especially at the new and full moons, are nearly universal in their importance, especially in rural and agricultural societies.

Sometimes a specific day of the week is set aside as a holy day. Each day may also have junctures of ritual importance: dawn, noon, dusk, midnight. Orders of worship often contain series of rituals and prayers which are repeated at timed intervals. Astronomical and astrological measurements, such as the movement of moons, stars and constellations, often have ritualistic importance.

Solar Year

Solar festivals celebrate changes in the sun's course, especially its return at midwinter (about December 22nd). Themes concerning the birth or rebirth of solar deities are commonly celebrated at the winter solstice. New sacred fires are often lit.

The summer solstice (about June 22nd) is also called Midsummer's Eve or Night, and is celebrated almost universally with fertility and agricultural rites. Dancing, fire leaping, singing and other celebratory rituals play an important part in solstice rituals. Sun-deities that are born at the winter solstice frequently die or are sacrificed at this time, to be reborn again at the winter solstice. Restrictive laws and customs are often lifted for this single night.

Solstices occur in opposite seasons in the northern and southern hemispheres.

Equinoxes occur twice a year when the sun crosses the equator and day and night are of equal length everywhere. Usually this occurs around March 21st and September 23rd.

Lunar Year

The repeating phases of the moon have long been used to count the passing of time. Many calendars, such as the Mohammedan and Hebrew, are based upon the lunar month.

Hiding Ancient Symbols and Names (Continued)

Hurricane – Hurakan was a Mayan god of thunder and lightning. The Tainos of the West Indies and Bahamas spoke of an evil spirit who brought tropical storms; they named him *hurrican*. And the Galbi and Carib Indians used the word *hyorocan* when speaking of the devil. The Spanish borrowed from these terms when they coined the word *huracán* to describe the fierce storms they encountered in the New World.

Juggernaut – This word is an Anglicization of the Hindustani *Jagannath*, which means "lord of the world." The Jagannath is a large wooden statue of Vishnu that is treated with great respect and is clothed and bathed by worshipful servants. Each summer the statue is paraded through the streets; in the 14th century Europeans reportedly saw worshipers throw themselves beneath its wheels. Believing that this practice was part of the Hindu religion, the god was seen as barbaric and destructive and its name became equated with a force of blind destruction.

"In seventh heaven" – originally a reference to the Islamic multiple heavens; paradise is located in the seventh heaven or the realms above it.

Mumbo jumbo – derived from the name of an African god, *Mama Dyambo*; during religious ceremonies, someone would wear a frightening mask and rave about, making horrible nonsense noises to scare away evil spirits.

"Dressed to the nines" – a reference to the nine Muses, who were the epitome of creativity and beauty.

Typhoon – Typhon was an ancient Greek monster well known for his fierce battles against Zeus. The word was adopted into Arabic as *tufan*, meaning a violent storm. In southeast Asia it became *tai-fung*, which was adapted by the Portuguese as *tufao* and then by the English who made it *typhoon*.

Festivals and prayers celebrating the new moon and the reappearance of its light in the sky are virtually universal. Similarly, the full moon is viewed as a climactic period. The dates of many religious festivals are calculated as falling upon a specific day after the first full moon after the vernal equinox. The full moon nearest to the autumn equinox is often called the hunter or harvest moon.

Eclipses of the moon occur only when the earth is between the full moon and the sun. The shadow that results often has a reddish tint, which either dims the moon's light or totally eclipses it. These *bloody moons* are often considered dire omens. Other customs and superstitions relating to the moon are often agricultural in nature. It is considered best to plant above-ground crop under the light of the full moon, while root crops should be planted in the dark of the moon.

Sacred Items

Almost any object can be dedicated and sanctified to service or worship. Sacred items are objects which symbolize some aspect of the religion. These items are often specially created and consecrated to allow their use in religious services and rites. A sacred item does not necessarily have to be a Sacred Vessel (see p. 105) or Holy Object (see p. 106), although many will be. Sacred items are usually not worshiped in and of themselves, but rather are venerated as symbols.

Altars

An altar is a raised structure or platform which serves as a place of ritual or worship. Offerings and sacrifices are often placed upon an altar, in full view of the deity and worshipers. Altars are frequently either rectangular slabs or tall tripods. Some altars are also tombs, where offerings are made to deified ancestors. Altars used in personal rituals can be quite small or even portable. Sometimes relics and other sacred items are placed within or upon the altar.

Animals

Animals play an important role in many religions. The animal may be used as a offering. This offering is not always a sacrifice – sometimes the animal is dedicated to the god and lives out the rest of its life on holy ground. Many Hindu temples in India have preserves of elephants, deer or snakes and some Shinto shrines have ponds of sacred goldfish.

Some deities are associated with a specific animal; depictions of this animal will be frequent in religious art. The image of a lamb, representing Christ as the Lamb of God, is commonly seen in Christian churches.

Arks

An ark is a box or chest in which sacred items are concealed and carried. The ark might resemble a coffin, a flat-roofed building, or a boat. Often arks are transported by multiple bearers who carry it by means of poles passed though rings. In Hebrew tradition, the ark is considered so holy that is it hidden behind curtains or screens, and it is considered sacrilege for any but the highest clerics to look upon it.

Banners

Banners, decorated with religious symbols and themes, often hang in religious buildings. Sometimes, while the banners may be dedicated to the glory of

Symbols and Common Meanings

Every culture will have symbols to represent or define abstract concepts. Below are some traditional meanings; this list is by no means complete, nor should it be taken as absolute.

Acorn – Life, fertility, immortality.

Anchor – Hope, steadfastness, stability, good luck.

Ankh – Egyptian symbol of life and knowledge.

Axe – Solar symbol of sky gods, power, thunder, sacrifice.

Bell – Consecration, protection against destructive powers.

Candle – Light in the darkness, uncertainty, prayer.

Cauldron – Nourishment, abundance, fertility, renewal, transformation, rebirth, feminine power.

Cave – The womb of Mother Earth; the heart, the union of self and ego, rebirth, initiation.

Chalice – Inexhaustible sustenance, healing, salvation, faith, feminine power.

Clouds – Sky, air, rain, fertility, lifeforce.

Continued on next page . . .

the divine, they are looked upon as mere decoration. In other cases they are venerated as being inherently sacred. They are often carried in religious processions.

Beads

Strings of beads are often used as a memory aid when reciting long series of prayers, chants or devotions. Many religions have liturgies of repeated prayers. The Catholic rosary is a well-known example of this. Small carvings and other symbols held sacred to the deity are sometimes strung with the beads. They are often important worship aids for the laity as well, sometimes becoming an accepted part of secular dress. Throughout much of China's bureaucratic period, court officials wore heavy necklaces of 108 beads, a number sacred in Buddhist belief.

Bells

Hollow vessels that are sounded by striking them with a stick or hammer are called bells. Some bells are sounded by being struck by an internally-hung clapper. Bells are usually made of metal; they can vary greatly in size.

Smaller bells are sometimes worn upon garments to protect the wearer from evil spirits and other harm. Bells may also be rung to call for rain or a good harvest. Ceremonial and temple bells are often inscribed with holy symbols and rung as part of the worship service. Bells were publicly baptized, named and dedicated throughout both medieval Europe and Japan.

Bells are also used to warn and to summon, and to call out the hours of the day. Often long rituals, involving both prayer and sacrifice, are used in the creation of bells.

Chalices

Bowls, cups and chalices are commonly used in rituals. Sacred bowls catch the blood of sacrifices, or are used in divination rites. Cups are associated with symbols of resurrection and rebirth, and were raised to salute the divine and assure the worshipers that the god had received the proper homage and portion. Oaths are often made binding by the act of drinking from a common cup. Sometimes the cup is shattered to show that the oath can never be changed, for the vessel that witnessed it is no more. Cups are also associated with rites of purification and healing.

Drums

The drum is the most widespread and ritually significant musical instrument. Drums are often used in religious ceremonies, particularly in communal rituals involving divination, exorcism, healing, fertility, prayer, singing, dancing and marching. Drums are common in shamanistic and tribal traditions.

Symbols and Common Meanings (Continued)

Crescent – Symbol of the Mother-goddess; feminine or lunar principles.

Crescent and Star – Divinity, sovereignty.

Crook/Crozier – Authority, faith, mercy, jurisdiction, guidance.

Crown – Sovereignty, victory, honor, dignity.

Crystal – Purity, perfection, knowledge.

Cup – Immortality, plenty; when overturned, emptiness and futility.

Date – Fertility, abundance.

Dawn – Resurrection, hope, illumination.

Desert – Abandonment, isolation, desolation, contemplation, revelation.

Dew – Spiritual refreshment, blessing.

Dice – Fate, chance.

Distaff/Spindle – Spinning, time, creation, fate.

Door – Hope, passage, initiation, revelation, opportunity.

East – Dawn, spring, hope, youth or childhood.

Egg – The life principle; potential greatness, hidden knowledge, cosmic time, resurrection, hope, creation.

Ewer – Purity, innocence.

Eye – Omniscience, divinity, light, knowledge, vigilance, protection, enlightenment.

Feather – Truth, speed, space, flight, the soul.

Continued on next page . . .

Symbols and Common Meanings (Continued)

Fire – Purification, renewal, power, strength, transformation, protection, passion, illumination, destruction, truth, knowledge, emotions, fervor, revelation.

Girdle – Sovereignty, wisdom, strength, virginity, purity, binding, dedication, protection, fidelity.

Gold – Incorruptibility, wisdom, illumination, the sun, nobility, honor, wealth, prosperity, light, immortality, masculine power.

Hammer – Symbol of thunder gods; masculine principle, vengeance, justice, sovereign power, divine creation.

Heart – Physical and spiritual center; love, compassion, understanding; pierced, it represents penance; flaming, it symbolizes religious zeal.

Hearth – Feminine principle, warmth, bounty, food.

Helmet – Protection, preservation, hidden thought.

Horns – Divinity, supernatural power, royalty, victory, protection, virility, abundance.

Hourglass – Time, death, fate, temperance.

Ice – Brittleness, impermanence, frigidity, rigidity, hardness of heart, absence of love.

Iron – Strength, firmness, durability, inflexibility.

Jade – Purity, benevolence, justice, music, loyalty, good fortune, prosperity.

Continued on next page . . .

The construction of ceremonial drums is particularly complex and ritualized. Drums are highly decorated with carvings and painted holy symbols. Often charms and other holy objects are attached to the frame of the drum to increase its effectiveness.

Drums were also used in some places as a means of secret communication and as instruments of execution and expulsion. Criminals are often drummed to their hangings, and disgraced individuals might be drummed from their homes into exile.

In some cultures, drums are considered to be so holy that taking refuge in a drumyard (the outdoor compound where drums are kept) is similar to taking refuge in a church or temple (see *Buildings,* p. 68).

Fetishes, Charms and Amulets

These objects are believed to hold magical properties to protect and aid the wearer. Fetishes are not truly sacred objects, as they do not usually represent the divine. Rather, they are magical in nature. They are commonly found in religions that combine magical and spiritual traditions. Amulets and charms are predominantly magical items also, although these small ornaments might be inscribed with prayers or holy symbols rather than magical protections. Often amulets are made of a particular substance thought to have inherent protective abilities.

Font

A font is a receptacle for holy water, usually of a size which is not easily moved. Often a font is dedicated in the same way an altar might be, and is used as a focal point for religious ceremonies, most notably baptisms and investitures.

Gongs

Gongs are convex metal plates, sometimes with a central boss. Unlike clapperless bells, gongs are struck in the center, not upon the rim. Gongs are used in many religious ceremonies to drive out evil spirits or to control the winds. Drinking from a gong after taking an oath is a binding and sacred rite in many cultures.

Holy Water

Water which has been ritually purified or blessed is often referred to as *holy water.* Water is commonly seen as a purifying substance in and of itself – water that is blessed is thought to be even more effective when used in purification or healing rituals.

Icons

Icons are religious images painted or drawn upon flat panels of canvas, parchment, wood or some other substance. These images are drawn in a particular style determined by the traditions of the religion. Icons usually depict the deity or events in the history of the religion in a way that aids both public worship and private devotion. Some religious sects, such as the Eastern Orthodox Church, venerate icons and even worship them directly.

Idols

An idol is an object that is made to either imitate the shape of the deity, or to house the deity's spirit. Effigies of dead ancestors are often thought to hold the ancestor's spirit, so by addressing the effigy the supplicant addresses the ancestor directly. Statues and idols are often highly decorated and draped with precious offerings and other rich items. In Ireland, many roadside and other isolated shrines have statues of saints that are bedecked with such offerings.

Lamps and Candles

Lamps are typically symbols of enlightenment, and are often kept burning perpetually within a shrine or temple. Many religions venerate an "eternal flame" as a representation of the deity's presence. Candles are also commonly associated with ritual. A Jewish mother blesses Sabbath candles at the beginning of that holy day. The lighting of a candle is often linked with the preservation of the soul, seen as a small bit of light within the darkness of death. Candles are often lit in great numbers, and vary greatly in both color and size. Sometimes candles are placed in multi-limbed candelabra; during the Jewish festival of Hannukkah the eight candles of the *menorah* are lit on successive nights. The lighting of candles is sometimes offered as a sacrifice, in gratitude or supplication.

Symbols and Common Meanings (Continued)

Kiss – Peace, good will, faith, sealing a pact, reconciliation, fellowship.

Knife – Vengeance, death, severance, freedom, sacrifice.

Lamp – Divine light, revelation, immortality, wisdom, guidance, intellect.

Lance – Strength, victory over evil, divine wisdom, masculine power.

Loom – Weaving of destiny, fate, time.

Mace – Absolute power and authority.

Mill/Millstone – Fate, heavy burdens, martyrdom.

Mirror – Truth, wisdom, the soul, self-knowledge, purity.

North – Obscurity, darkness, night, coldness.

Pen – Learning, intellect.

Rain – Divine blessing, revelation, purification, fertility.

Rainbow – Heavenly glory, transfiguration, bridge between worlds, reconciliation with the divine.

Ring – Power, sovereignty, protection, delegated power, strength, commitment, fulfillment, union, royalty, eternity.

Rock – Permanence, stability, strength, refuge.

Rod/Scepter – Divine or royal power, justice, authority, dignity.

Salt – Life, incorruptibility, permanence, wisdom, the soul, knowledge, purification.

Sand – Instability.

Scroll – Learning, knowledge, law, destiny, the passage of time.

Scythe/Sickle – Death, time, mortality, harvest, rebirth.

Shield – Preservation, protection, strength, chastity, feminine power.

Shoe – Liberty, freedom, control.

Silver – The moon, divinity, virginity, purity, brightness, eloquence, feminine power.

Skull – The passing of life, futility, death, time.

South – Fire, warmth, youth.

Spear – Fertility, prowess, the masculine principle.

Staff – Authority, dignity, judgement, magical power, travel, pilgrimage.

Star – Eternity, divinity, constancy, immortality.

Sun – Cosmic power, all-seeing divinity, justice, glory, splendor, royalty, illumination, radiance, destruction.

Sword – Power, protection, royalty, leadership, justice, law, courage, strength, victory, destruction, martyrdom, vigilance, the masculine principle.

Tower – Ascent, vigilance, the inaccessible.

Continued on next page . . .

Symbols and Common Meanings (Continued)

Twilight – Threshold, uncertainty, ambivalence.

Veil – Darkness giving way to light, inscrutability, hidden knowledge, secrecy, ignorance, mourning, protection, submission to authority, modesty, chastity, renunciation, separation.

Water – Fertility, refreshment, purification, life, rebirth.

Well – Healing, wish fulfillment, salvation, purification, feminine principle.

West – Autumn, middle age, the dying sun.

Wheel – Solar power, cycles of life, rebirth, renewal, time, fate, karma.

Whip/Lash – Authority, government, domination, punishment, fertility, lightning, strength that drives away evil.

Wine – Revelation, truth, vitality, sacrifice, fertility.

Wings – Divinity, spiritual enlightenment, air, flight, freedom, victory, speed, communication.

Yoke – Balance, control, union, humiliation, slavery, toil, patience, obedience, law, sacrifice, agriculture, fertility.

Mandala

A mandala is an art form based upon symmetrically arranged geometric forms, usually circles, within larger concentric forms. Typically a mandala represents a central figure surrounded by a pantheon of subordinate deities. A mandala might be called a "spiritual blueprint of the universe" and is used in both public rituals (as an icon) and private meditation.

Masks

Masks can be made of all kinds of materials. They may be painted, carved, or both; they vary in size and complexity. Masks can be highly symbolic in design, or disturbingly realistic. They may be either worn or carried, and are often used in conjunction with holy dances. Masks are used in rituals for many reasons – to arouse specific emotions, such are bravery or fear; to frighten and exorcism harmful spirits; to teach; to entertain. Those who wear masks are considered to be representatives of the divine. Masks are used in sacred drama and rites which recall the activities of the gods in past times.

In the traditional societies of West Africa, masks are especially associated with agrarian and funerary rituals, as well as in ceremonies that recall the mythical origins of the tribe. Among the Dogon, each adult male becomes a member of the *awa* – the village's society of masks. When not in use, the masks are hung together in a holy cave. In addition to their ritual use, they are often venerated themselves, receiving regular sacrifical libations.

Mirrors

Cultures which believe that one's reflection is a vital part of the soul often see mirrors and other reflective surfaces as either "soul catchers" or doorways into other worlds. Mirrors can be used in divination rituals, and are particularly holy in lunar goddess traditions. The moon is often described as a mirror which reflects all that happens in the world. Copper mirrors are thought by some to be especially effective in healing rituals.

Phylacteries

Phylacteries are small amulets, pouches or boxes which contain fragments of holy writings or small relics. In Hebrew tradition, phylacteries called *tephillin* are worn upon the body, tied or bound to the arms, forehead, or over the heart. Other traditions, such Orthodox Christian, use small reliquaries in a similar fashion.

Prayer Books

Prayer books are collections of prayers, readings, songs, scriptures and other holy writings. These books are used for private devotions, on a schedule defined by the traditions of the religion. Hebrew tradition calls for two prayer books: the *siddur,* used for Sabbath and during the week, and the *machzor,* used for festivals. Books used in clerical or community rituals are often more elaborate and richly decorated. The *Book of Kells* was made for such rituals. Often these books must be made following strict guidelines; the Jewish Torah must be

handwritten without error on a flawless parchment and is considered to be inherently sacred. Other books, such as modern-day hymnals, the medieval "Books of Hours," and orders of service, are considered simply aids to worship.

Prayer Wheels

The most common form of prayer wheel is that of a prayer-inscribed cylinder upon a shaft, with a weighted cord to act as a flywheel. The worshiper rotates the cylinder as prayers are offered. Hand-operated versions vary in size from a few inches to several feet. Some great prayer wheels may be 20 feet in height. Such large wheels, which are found at shrines and temples, may be powered by wind, water or physical effort. Long stands of multiple prayer wheels are turned by a continuing series of worshipers – as one tires another takes his place.

Fragments of sacred texts are written upon each prayer wheel; sometimes entire collections of sacred writings are inscribed upon the largest wheels. As the wheels turn, each rotation is a separate prayer offered on behalf of the worshiper.

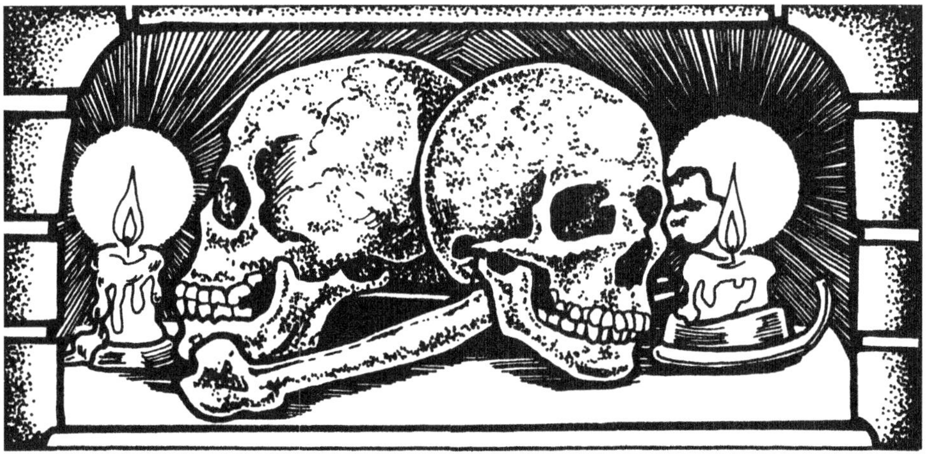

Rattles

A musical instrument that makes percussive sounds when objects enclosed in it are shaken is called a rattle. Rattles may be created from a great variety of substances, and may be attached to a dancer's body or clothing, to a staff, or may simply be held in the hand and shaken. They are common in tribal and shamanistic traditions and are often constructed of materials holy to that tradition, such as bone from a particular animal. The sound of the rattle is believed to be the voice of the spirits, and is used to curb or entreat supernatural forces. Often a specific type of rattle is used for a specific ritual. South American Indian shamans use *maracas* (rattles made of gourds) for healing and fertility rituals, while narrow stick rattles are used for visionary and divination rites.

Relics

A relic is an object which is venerated because of its past association with an esteemed or holy individual. Relics are usually physical remains, such as bones or teeth, but might also be remnants of clothing, skin or hair.

Relics play an important role in many worship services, and are housed in specially made and sanctified containers called reliquaries. These reliquaries vary greatly in both size, shape and the amount of decoration. The reliquary which houses the arm bone of an ancient martyr might be constructed of gold in the shape of an arm raised in blessing, and carried before religious processions.

Relics are often associated with miraculous healing.

Clerical Garb

Most religions have traditions (or even laws) which define the clothing their clerics wear. Classic examples are the Eucharistic vestments of the Catholic Church.

The *chasuble* is a sleeveless, often full-circle cape-like garment worn draped over the shoulders.

The *stole* is a long, relatively narrow band of fabric of varying lengths worn about the neck; Eucharistic stoles hang down nearly to the ground.

The *dalmatic* and *tunicle* are simple sleeved tunics; the dalmatic has wider sleeves than the tunicle.

The *humeral veil* is worn about the priest's shoulders during certain parts of a Mass or Benediction.

The *cope* is a floor-length, full-circle garment worn over the shoulders and falling straight at the front without overlapping. It may or may not include some form of hood.

Mitres are shaped, usually heavily embroidered hats that are worn by bishops and archbishops.

Continued on next page . . .

Clerical Garb (Continued)

The *High Mass* set of vestments includes the chasuble, dalmatic, tunicle, double stoles and humeral veils. Copes are optional. A *Low Mass* set consists of the stole and chasuble. A *Benediction* set includes a cope, stole and humeral veil. There are numerous sets of these garments and drapings, one in each liturgical color.

When vesting (dressing for a ritual), a priest first puts on the *amice,* a neck cloth that fills up the space left by the neckline of the chasuble. The *alb* follows; this is a long linen tunic, usually with decorations at the wrists and lower hem. The *girdle* gathers in the alb at the waist; it is usually a white linen rope with tassels. The stole is worn in various ways; priests cross the ends and use the girdle to hold it in place, bishops wear it with the ends hanging straight down, deacons wear it over the left shoulder and tie it under the right arm. Last comes the chasuble; a bishop will also wear a dalmatic over a tunicle beneath the chasuble, along with gloves, cope and mitre. Deacons wear the dalmatic; subdeacons the tunicle. Both wear the amice.

Thrones

Thrones are ritual seats, typically very elaborately carved and decorated, which are reserved for selected people. While they exist primarily in secular buildings, thrones are also found in the holiest of temples, reserved either for the deity itself, or for the deity's highest cleric. West African tribes often have a *smith's throne* within a sacred cave. The smith is both craftsman and priest, playing both social and religious roles.

Totems

A *totem* is an emblem or revered symbol, usually of an animal, which is associated with a particular family or group. This animal is considered to be either a mythical ancestor of the family, or a friend and protector. The term refers to both the physical object (such as a small carving) and the subject it represents. Totems are especially common in cultures which practice ancestor veneration (see *Totemism*, p. 127).

Unguents

Unguents are holy ointments, salves and oils. These sanctified substances, which might be stored in special jars and containers, are used in rites of passage, purification, anointment and healing.

Vestments

Ceremonial clothing and insignia worn by clerics are called vestments. These articles of apparel – tunics, stoles, pendants, hats, scarves, crowns, copes, capes and robes – are worn to indicate both clerical rank and religious affiliation. Vestments may be simple or richly decorated. Style and color varies greatly, depending upon the religion and the rituals involved. Sometimes secular worshipers are required to wear particular articles of clothing. The Amish and Mennonites wear simplistic garb of antique cut; observant male Jews must wear a *yarmulke* covering their hair and a *tallit* (prayer shawl) during morning prayers; Muslim women traditionally wear the *purdah* veils.

Weapons

Some religious traditions forbid the presence of weapons in a place of worship. Others venerate them as symbols of divine power, especially if a particular weapon is associated with a particular god. Some weapons might become symbols of a religious sect because of their similarity with another holy symbol; the Crusader Knights often used their swords as a symbol of their faith because the sword resembles the Christian cross in shape. Holy symbols and invocations might be inscribed on weapons in the hope of obtaining divine favor.

Putting It All Together

When designing a religion, the GM can mix and match many elements, but each should be considered in relation with the others. After determining the nature of divine power, the GM should consider how that power interacts with the world. Symbols are often the means by which divinity is expressed.

Symbols are a vital part of most religions and a GM should choose them carefully, considering that symbol's impact on the culture he is designing. Is the symbol so common that everyone knows what it represents? Or is it used as a secret sign to identify the faithful? If religion is an integral part of everyday life, then religious symbology will likely be overwhelmingly present in that culture. If a religion is persecuted, a subtly carved symbol might indicate a sympathizer, or a place of refuge. Is the symbol seen as inherently holy? If so, anyone who defames it might face religious wrath. Is it merely the symbol of belief, and not of divine power? If so, adherents might wear it proudly, declaring their religious allegiance to all. The young might wear it brazenly, to defy their elders.

A GM might choose symbols whose meanings the players will easily understand, thereby easily conveying a great deal of information. Or a GM might choose more obscure symbols in order to create a more exotic "feel" to the religion. Religions often have many symbols associated with them, some of which they might share with other beliefs. How did this come about? Was it mere coincidence? Or does it indicate an older, common belief that split generations ago, developing into separate religions?

Next, the GM must decide how the symbols are used. They may be venerated in and of themselves, regarded as mere decoration, or used as aids to worship and meditation. They may play a role in the various rituals and ceremonies of that religion – and also play a role in everyday life.

All religions have ceremonies or rituals of some sort. Even a lack of ritual can in itself be a ritual; forbidden actions can carry as much weight as prescribed ones.

Some sects or denominations might support pomp and ceremony while others reject it. Even among individuals, such activity can vary. A priest will probably be involved in more rituals than a lay member. The GM should consider how big a part religion plays in everyday life. Rituals may be relegated to a specific day of the week, or to special festival days. Or adherents may be required to perform certain rituals each day, or each hour. Such rites could be so much a part of daily living that they are performed almost without thinking. An outsider might not even recognize them as religious rites. Or their religious significance may be forgotten, and the ritual is performed by rote – out of habit.

A GM should also remember that symbols play a vital part in religious ceremonies, especially communal services. These worship services begin with an invocation – a formal prayer, a song or chant, or some other action that calls for the attention of the divine. Often a holy symbol is displayed to the worshipers to focus their attention. There may be some indication that the deity (or its divine servant) is present – a chime or gong may ring, a sacred fire might leap higher, candles may flare or go out. Or there might be no sign at all, and the celebrants must take it on faith that the god is present, or at least listening.

After the invocation, a communal service often concerns itself with praising, thanking or petitioning the divine. Celebrants may sing or dance, the priest may lead prayers, sacrifices might be made. Again, symbols often play a key role. An animal holy to the god might be sacrificed, the altar might be decorated with holy objects, special garb might be worn by priest and worshiper alike.

At the end of the service, the priest may announce the god's will, grant boons or pronounce a blessing upon the celebrants. Often a service will end as it began – a reverse procession, or prayers or songs which echo the opening.

Symbols are vital throughout a worship service, evoking common feelings and beliefs. Ceremonies remind believers that they are a community of faithful. Together, symbols and ceremonies both define a religion and strengthen its adherents.

Symbolism of Color

Depending upon the culture, colors will have different associated meanings. This symbolism can be useful when choosing clerical heraldry and garb, adding color to a campaign in every sense of the word. This list includes only the most common associations; it is by no means absolute or complete. (Keep in mind that availability may alter these meanings. If peasants can afford purple cloth, but not orange, for example, the associations of each may be *very* different!)

Black – Death, primordial darkness, the void, shame, destruction, grief, sadness, time, sinister arts, mourning, humiliation, spiritual darkness.

Blue – Truth, revelation, wisdom, loyalty, fidelity, peace, contemplation, the divine feminine principle, the heavens, mercy.

Brown – The earth, spiritual death, renunciation, degradation, penance.

Gold – Divine power, immortality, glory, endurance, light, durability, emotional warmth, truth, enlightenment, the masculine principle.

Green – Life, youth, hope, change, jealousy, abundance, peace, prosperity, immortality, victory.

Gray – Depression, ashes, humility, mourning, penance, wisdom, tribulation.

Orange – Love, happiness, splendor, fire, luxury.

Purple – Royalty, pomp, pride, imperial authority, temperance, truth, justice, penance.

Red – Royalty, truth, love, joy, passion, ferocity, arousal, blood, anger, vengeance, martyrdom, the divine masculine principle, faith, strength, calamity, evil, fertility, fire, creativity.

Silver – Light, purity, the feminine principle, divine power, the moon, virginity.

Violet – Spiritual or religious devotion, humility, intellect, knowledge, sorrow, temperance, grief, mourning, temperance, old age, authority, truth, fasting, penance.

White – Light, sun, perfection, purity, innocence, redemption, salvation, spiritual authority, chastity, mourning, life, love, transformation, virginity, the purified soul, peace, enlightenment, surrender.

Yellow – Intellect, faith, goodness, faithlessness, betrayal, cowardice, treachery, treason, quarantine, secrecy, greed, renunciation, humility, divinity, revealed truth, beauty, life, immortality.

CLERICS

5

Priest, monk, priestess, mullah, shaman – a cleric is one who has dedicated his life to the service of his religion. It is through the efforts and duties of these devoted servants that a religion is sustained, the myths and legends properly told and remembered, the dogmas enforced, the rituals correctly performed. Their duties and responsibilities may vary widely, but in the end their task is the same: to seek the divine and ensure the preservation of their faith, whatever that may be.

Beyond these goals, however, clerics differ as widely as the religions in which they serve. From the wildly tattooed shaman in his bearskin loincloth, to the stately priestess in white robes, to the armor-clad knight of some warrior sect, clerical characters have endless possibility and variation.

Clerical Character Types

Clerics are as varied as the religions they follow, but there are certain accepted stereotypes within history and mythic legend. Most cleric types are likely to have the following:

Advantages: Clerical Investment, Patron: Church.

Disadvantages: Duty, Vows.

Skills: Theology with specialization; Performance/Ritual.

These, of course, are suggestions, not requirements.

Bardic Priest

These clerics who spread tales of the world and the divine through story and song are most commonly found in cultures with strong oral traditions. There is always a vocal ingredient to their spells – usually poetry or song.

Advantages: Appearance, Charisma, Language Talent, Legal Immunity, Musical Ability, Voice.

Disadvantages: Overconfidence, Reputation, Truthfulness.

Skills: Acting, Area Knowledge, Bard, Breath Control, Carousing, Dancing, Detect Lies, Diplomacy, Fast-Talk, Gambling, Heraldry, History, Holdout, Law, Musical Instrument, Performance, Poetry, Riding, Savoir-Faire, Sex Appeal, Scrounging, Singing, Stealth, Survival, Teaching, Theology, any combat/weapon skill, any language.

Healer Priest

These are pacifistic clerics who believe that the divine word is best spread by aiding those in need. They may be associated with proselytizing religions as missionaries, traveling in search of the needy. Or they may work within the bounds of a church which throws its doors open to the general public. They tend to abhor violence, and believe that the divine is benevolent.

Advantages: Blessed, Empathy, Immunity to Disease, Reputation.

Disadvantages: Dependents, Honesty, Pacifism, Sense of Duty.

Skills: Cooking, Diagnosis, Diplomacy, First Aid, Naturalist, Physician, Physiology, Poisons, Surgery, any craft.

Sage Priest

Wise man, crone, sage, hermit – these elder clerics are thought to have a clearer sight of the divine. They may travel in near poverty, isolate themselves from others, or live in comfort, serving as councillors or advisors. They are often sought by students who seek to learn their wisdom.

Advantages: Alertness, Blessed, Eidetic Memory, Intuition, Language Talent, Strong Will.

Disadvantages: Age, Pacifism, Truthfulness, any physical disadvantage.

Skills: Bard, Detect Lies, Diplomacy, Heraldry, History, Holdout, Law, Leadership, Meditation, Poetry, Research, Scrounging, Singing, Stealth, Survival, Teaching, Theology, any craft, any language.

Warrior Priest

Religious warriors may serve as protectors of their religion, or as crusading warriors who make converts by force.

Advantages: Alertness, Ambidexterity, Combat Reflexes, Danger Sense, Peripheral Vision, Strong Will, Toughness.

Disadvantages: Bad Temper, Bloodlust, Code of Honor, Fanaticism, Honesty, Intolerance (Religious), Overconfidence.

Skills: Armory, Carousing, Heraldry, Leadership, Leatherworking, Riding, Strategy, Tactics, any combat/weapon skill.

Resident Clerics

These are clerics who remain in a particular area. Their religious calling might require them to devote themselves to the welfare of a particular group of followers, or they might choose a simple, reclusive lifestyle in which to explore the realities of the divine.

Ascetic Monk

Those who seek the divine through rituals of self-deprivation and physical exertion have rejected the luxuries of society, though they may still feel a duty toward it.

Advantages: Alertness, High Pain Threshold, Strong Will.

Disadvantages: Discipline of Faith (Asceticism), Wealth (Poor), Skinny, Stubbornness.

Skills: Animal Handling, Area Knowledge, Breath Control, Detect Lies, Judo or Karate (or other unarmed combat), Meditation, Naturalist, Scrounging, Survival, any craft skill.

Cloistered Nun/Monk

Those who have chosen a way of strict dedication and devotion to the deity remove themselves from the strictures of normal society.

Advantages: Strong Will.

Disadvantages: Discipline of Faith (Ritualism), Pacifism, Poverty, Shyness, Vows.

Skills: Administration, Artist, Botany, Cooking, First Aid, Herbary, Meditation, Singing, Theology, any craft skill.

Parish Priest

The typical priest has been given the duty of serving the welfare of a particular group of followers. His job is to succor and counsel the faithful, answering questions and providing interpretations of the church's doctrine to the particular situations of life. In times of strife he may be called upon to sacrifice much in protection of his flock, but generally he lives a quiet, retiring life.

Advantages: Charisma, Common Sense, Empathy, Intuition, Literacy.

Disadvantages: Combat Paralysis, Dependents, Gluttony, Honesty, Laziness, Pacifism, Truthfulness.

Skills: Administration, Area Knowledge, Bard, Detect Lies, Diplomacy, Law (Religious), Leadership, Meditation, Politics, Savoir-Faire, Teaching, Theology.

Shaman

Those born within shamanistic societies with the "World Sight" (see *Shamanism,* p. 116).

Advantages: Eidetic Memory, High Pain Threshold, World Sight.

Disadvantages: Addiction, Discipline of Faith (Ecstaticism), Epilepsy.

Skills: Animal Handling, Area Knowledge, Bard, Botany, Breath Control, Climbing, Dancing, Diagnosis, Diplomacy, Fast-Talk, First Aid, Gesture, Heraldry, Herbary, History, Leadership, Leatherworking, Meditation, Musical Instrument, Naturalist, Performance/Ritual, Physiology, Poetry, Savoir-Faire, Singing, Survival, Teaching, Veterinary, Woodworking, any shamanistic spell (see p. 112).

Wandering Clerics

These are clerics whose religious calling sends them to no particular locale, but rather to all people and places, serving those in need. These are generally more pragmatic than those who are able to devote themselves to single-minded contemplation, as they must continually deal with the vagaries of day-to-day existence. Wandering clerics generally make better adventurers than their stay-at-home brethren.

Itinerant Priest

Those who succor and serve the faithful that they meet upon their travels. Some have a set circuit of villages or towns they serve; others will wander wherever their desire (or the will of the gods) takes them.

Advantages: Alertness, Charisma, Common Sense, Empathy, Intuition, Literacy, Voice.

Disadvantages: Code of Honor, Honesty, Impulsive, Overconfident, Stubbornness, Truthfulness.

Skills: Animal Handling, Area Knowledge, Bard, Climbing, Diplomacy, Fast-Talk, Heraldry, History, Jumping, Law, Leadership, Riding, Savoir-Faire, Swimming, Teaching, Teamster, Theology, any combat/weapon skill, any craft skill, any outdoor skill, any language.

Mendicant

These people support themselves by begging, whether because of vows of poverty, or to give opportunities to the faithful to practice charity, or to relieve themselves of any necessity of thinking of anything but the divine.

Advantages: High Pain Threshold, Immunity to Disease.

Disadvantages: Discipline of Faith (Asceticism), Fanaticism, Toughness, Wealth (Poor).

Skills: Meditation, Scrounging, Streetwise, Survival, Theology.

Missionary

These dedicate their lives to spreading their faith in new and often hostile places. They usually attempt to convert by peaceful means, choosing to give aid to those less fortunate than themselves in the hope that their sterling example will win over the populace more surely than violence.

Advantages: Charisma, Danger Sense, Empathy, Immunity to Disease, Literacy, Luck, Pacifism, Strong Will, Voice.

Disadvantages: Fanaticism, Sense of Duty, Stubbornness.

Skills: Administration, Bard, Dancing, Diplomacy, Fast-Talk, Gesture, Law, Leadership, Merchant, Savoir-Faire, Singing, Teaching, any animal skill, any craft skill, any medical skill, any outdoor skill, any science skill, any language.

Missionary Warrior

These missionaries believe in converting by force instead of example.

Advantages: Charisma, Danger Sense, Literacy, Luck, Pacifism, Strong Will, Voice.

Disadvantages: Bloodlust, Fanaticism, Sense of Duty, Stubbornness.

Skills: Area Knowledge, Fast-Talk, Gesture, Leadership, Survival, any animal skill, any combat/weapon skill, any medical skill, any outdoor skill, any language.

Teaching Priest

Those who seek out the secrets of the universe and new people to teach them to may be associated with places of learning, or work as tutors between their travels.

Advantages: Alertness, Blessed, Eidetic Memory, Intuition, Literacy, Strong Will.

Disadvantages: Honesty, Pacifism, Truthfulness.

Skills: Area Knowledge, Bard, Detect Lies, Diplomacy, Heraldry, History, Holdout, Law, Leadership, Literature, Meditation, Research, Scrounging, Stealth, Survival, Teaching, Theology, any science skill, any language.

Wandering Friar

The stereotypical happy friar with a taste for larceny.

Advantages: Alertness, Charisma, Common Sense, Empathy, Intuition, Literacy, Voice.

Disadvantages: Fat, Gluttony, Greed, Lecherousness, Wealth (Poor), Vow of Celibacy.

Skills: Animal Handling, Area Knowledge, Bard, Carousing, Cooking, Diplomacy, Disguise, Fast-Talk, First Aid, Forgery, Gambling, Heraldry, History, Law, Lockpicking, Merchant, Pickpocket, Riding, Savoir-Faire, Staff, Stealth, Teaching, Theology, any craft skill, any outdoor skill, any language.

Other Faithful

Not all religious-minded individuals are clerics. Those of the flock may choose to devote themselves to the tenets of their church even without the investment of clerical status. Indeed, some take great pride in their own sacrifice and dedication, believing it to be a truer indication of their interest in the divinity.

And then there are those who are not particularly religious-minded, but who want others to think they are . . .

Fake

These may simply be hypocrites, who make a display of their piety to impress others. Or they may be con artists, who hope to win material gain by pretending spiritual leanings or attainment. In either case, they will quite possibly be agnostic or atheist in their actual beliefs.

Advantages: Charisma, Voice.

Disadvantages: Gluttony, Greed.

Skills: Acting, Fast-Talk, Performance, Psychology, Public Speaking, Streetwise.

Pilgrim

Pilgrims travel to holy lands or places in an attempt to get closer or better understand the divine. In some cultures pilgrimages are required of all followers. In others it is a rare occurrence, and pilgrims have special stature.

Advantages: Luck, Strong Will.

Disadvantages: Overconfidence, Vows, Wealth (Poor).

Skills: any or none.

Renunciate

Wealthy sybarites who have suddenly reformed and discovered religion. After a life of empty pleasures, they devote most or all of their wealth to the church and dedicate themselves to doing its works in whatever form they can best consider.

Advantages: Empathy, Literacy, Status, Wealth.

Disadvantages: Code of Honor, Dependents.

Skills: History, Law, Merchant, any artistic skill, any craft skill, any social skill, any language.

Retired Nun/Monk

Secular persons who have chosen to live under religious discipline for a specified length of time. They are devoted to the deity and follow the rules of the monastery or convent, but have not taken full religious vows. Some may even still retain their titles and wealth; particularly high-ranking or wealthy individuals may actually be Patrons of the establishment they are living in.

Advantages: Literacy, Status, Strong Will, Wealth.

Disadvantages: Discipline of Faith (Ritualism), Pacifism, Shyness, Vows.

Skills: Administration, Artist, Cooking, First Aid, Herbary, Meditation, Singing, Theology, any craft skill.

Advantages

Advantages may have special effects in campaigns with strong religious influences.

Clerical Investment — 5 points/level of rank; see p. B19

A *must-have* for all clerical characters, Clerical Investment is the social/political advantage of being invested as a cleric of your religion. It represents your status and influence within the church. This advantage does not confer any magical powers. See *Power Investment,* p. 93.

Religions can have one or many ranks of clerics representing levels of investment, forming a hierarchy which determines the levels of rank possible for that church (see *Religious Rank and Hierarchy,* p. 49).

Ranks may have associated prerequisites, such as skills that must be learned, oaths that must be sworn and so forth. Theology and/or Leadership skills are appropriate prerequisites, as are other skills associated with the church. Minimum Attribute scores, certain Advantages or Disadvantages (or lack thereof), race, sex, social status and so on, may also apply. Each rank in the hierarchy will probably bear a title, as determined by the GM, in addition to particular duties and responsibilities within the church (see *Clerical Duty,* p. 98).

Each level of rank confers a +1 reaction bonus from followers of your religion and those who respect your faith. If the person in question is a fanatic believer, or your religion is the primary faith in the area or culture, then all bonuses are doubled.

Patron: Church — Variable; see p. B24

If your church has any material presence or standing in the community, you can claim it as a Patron unless the tenets of the religion expressly forbid giving any assistance or aid to its members.

If the church is your patron, that means that it is willing to claim you and give you personal aid of whatever kind it can. This may be in room and board, living expenses, necessary travel supplies (be it a horse or a plane ticket), medical treatment, or support in times of crisis. A medieval priest could call upon his church for knights to face an enemy of the church, while a 20th-century Methodist minister may receive legal fees or monetary grants. Each has a commitment from his church to support him in times of need.

Frequency of appearance is based on the standing of the church in the community, the likelihood of its being able to respond to any particular request, and the extent of the church's power. (For example, a church which holds considerable power and influence in a small backwater village is not going to be nearly as useful as a less intrusive one with temples in every town.)

Special qualities: Certain aspects of the church can affect its cost as a patron:

Church's clerics have magical abilities: 10 points.

Each Holy Day (see p. 103): 1 point per day.

Each High Holy Day (see p. 103): 2 points per day.

Each Day of Weakness (see p. 103): -1 point per day.

Autotrance — *5 points*

You find it very easy to enter a trance. You may enter a trance state on a successful IQ roll, within the space of a minute. However, your natural affinity for trancing makes it harder for you to awaken. You must make a successful IQ roll whenever you wish to leave a trance. You may only attempt this roll once every 5 minutes. Each additional attempt per hour is at -1 from the previous attempt.

This advantage is useful to shamans and those in meditative disciplines. People with this ability may find that they tend to slip out of awareness of their immediate surroundings quite easily. Netrunners with this advantage receive a +2 bonus on their Cyberdeck Operation skill (see p. 144).

Blessed — *Variable*

The simplest version of this advantage costs 10 points and grants the cleric a limited attunement to his deity. The cleric receives the ability to use any one Divination spell at IQ level (see p. M55). The type of Divination should match the "flavor" of the deity. The cleric also gains a +1 Reaction from any of the deity's followers who know him to be Blessed. For 20 points, the cleric is Very Blessed, which confers a +5 bonus to his Divination skill. Blessed clerics must act in accordance with the rules or values associated with the deity, or the advantage will be lost.

If the GM prefers, he can have the deity grant Blessed characters powers beyond Divination. These powers must match the power or capability of the deity (a goddess of mercy and healing could grant healing gifts, for instance). These abilities come in many different forms, the exact cost of each depending on the ability granted. In addition, many of the standard Advantages can be explained as divine gifts at the GM's discretion. Following are some examples.

Immunity: Your blessing involves an immunity to (or protection from) certain substances, usually those associated with the deity granting the blessing. A fire god might, for example, bless his clerics with an immunity to fire damage. When determining the cost, the GM should keep in mind that these are powerful blessings, and "charge" accordingly. Costs for immunities in ***GURPS Supers*** are a good guide.

Aptitude: Your blessing gives you an added bonus to a particular skill. For Physical skills, the cost for a +1 aptitude is equivalent to the cost (see p. B44) to learn the skill at DX level. The cost for a 2-point aptitude is equal to the cost for DX+1, and so on. For Mental skills, the cost for a +1 aptitude is equal to the cost of learning the skill at IQ level. A 2-point aptitude costs the same as learning it at IQ+1 and so on. The bonus applies to default skill levels as well as to those you have training in.

Magical Knack: Your blessing gives you the innate ability to do a particular magical spell. The cost is 2% of the price of a magic item that would be able to cast the same spell.

Heroic Feats: 10 points. Your blessing gives you the innate ability to perform a particular heroic feat. Once per playing session you may add 1d to either ST, DX, or HT (attribute is specified at the time of the blessing) for up to 3d seconds. At the end of this time, you revert to your normal attribute and must suffer all negatives or penalties amassed during the "heroic" period. (If you raise HT and during this time take more than 5 times your normal HT in damage, then without some sort of healing you will immediately die when the effects wear off.)

Other blessings can be defined at the GM's discretion.

Divine Favor — *Variable*

You are a Holy Person, capable of petitioning your god for miracles (see *Miraculous Magic*, pp. 113-115). This advantage has nothing to do with Clerical Investment, and must be bought separately if an ordained priest wishes to have miraculous powers.

The cost of Divine Favor depends on the power of the deity and the level of favor you have in the god's eyes. The base cost is found by treating the deity as a Patron. Most gods will be 25-point Patrons, while lesser deities will cost 20 points. Modify this by the Frequency of Appearance costs on p. B23 to reflect how capable the deity is of coming to the Holy Person's aid.

The cost is modified again for higher or lower favor in the god's eyes. For every +1 to affect the Reaction roll, add 5 points to the cost of the advantage, up to a maximum of +25 points. For every -1 to the Reaction roll, subtract 5 points from the cost of the advantage.

Legal Immunity — *5, 10, 15 or 20 points*

You are outside the traditional legal structures of your society. You cannot be arrested or charged with a crime by the "temporal authorities" — that is, by the government. Only your own church can try or punish you.

Cost of this advantage depends on how sweeping the immunity is. For 5 points, the cleric is not subject to temporal authority, but his own church regulates his behavior in a strict way, determined by the GM. On the other hand, if the church regulations are less strict than the temporal ones, this is a 10-point advantage. And if a cleric can do pretty much what he pleases as long as he doesn't injure the church itself, that is a 15-point advantage.

For an extra 5 points, the cleric also has "diplomatic pouch" privileges. He can send or receive mail or objects that may not be stopped or examined by the temporal authorities.

Clerics will normally have this advantage only if their churches are so powerful that they have their own religious law outside the bounds of the state. The GM determines this when a religion is created, and may simply add the cost of this advantage to the value of the religion.

Power Investiture — *10 points/level*

You have been invested with the power of your deity, and may cast clerical spells (see *Clerical Magic*, pp. 100-113).

Each level of Investiture confers a +1 bonus to IQ when learning new divine spells. Different levels may represent different states of holiness in regard to a single deity, or may be used to differentiate the clerics of one deity from another. Those deities which have limited ability to transfer power to their followers, or have a small range of possible spell effects, will probably only grant one level of Investiture, while those encompassing a wide range of powers may be more generous. The number of possible levels of Investiture granted should be determined by the GM when creating the religion, and affects the church's value as a Patron.

Note that Power Investiture does not necessarily go hand-in-hand with Clerical Investment. The first is a measure of the cleric's bond with the deity, the second a social/political ranking within the church. Clerics might not be allowed any Power Investiture until reaching the higher ranks of their religion, or the very use of divine magic might be a separate branch of the church, available only to those of one particular order. Or the deity might choose to grant its power when and where it wishes, completely outside the hierarchy of the church.

The exact nature of the Investiture will probably differ with each culture and religion. In some it may be an elaborate ceremony. In others it could be a path of spiritual search and enlightenment, with the cleric himself discovering the secrets necessary to progress through the possible levels. However it is gained, Investiture represents a level of knowledge and attainment that can be made or increased throughout play.

World Sight — *10 points*

You are able to perform shamanistic magics (see pp. 116-125). You have the ability to transcend ordinary human limitations and gain the power to enter the domain of gods and spirits. You may be subject to intermittent visions even if you never receive proper training as a shaman.

Disadvantages

Duty — *Variable; see p. B39*

Most clerics have a duty to preserve and uphold their faith, to support and aid other members of their religion, and, when necessary, to protect it from those who seek to desecrate it. These duties are a very real part of a cleric's "job." The duty and responsibility assigned to each member of the church will, however, vary with his rank and level of commitment. Someone who has devoted the entirety of his life to the church may hold more duties than someone who advises other members of the church on a part-time basis, or is given to purely scholarly pursuits as opposed to dealing directly with the public.

Clerics must determine their desired rank within the church, and the level of commitment they are willing to give, They will be assigned duties and responsibilities accordingly.

Fanaticism — *-15 points; see p. B33*

Fanaticism is a common disadvantage among religious folk. One might say that anyone who devotes his entire life to serving a belief or a faith must be somewhat fanatical, but this is not necessarily true. There are many reasons to join the clergy in most cultures besides depth and truth of faith. However, if your character fully embraces the beliefs and tenets of his church to the exclusion of all else, then you should consider this Disadvantage.

Fanatics react very positively to those who are members of their religion or hold rank in their church. They also tend to react negatively to those who do not follow their faith or, worse yet, actively oppose it. Therefore, a religious fanatic doubles all reaction *bonuses* toward righteous members of his own faith, and doubles all reaction *penalties* toward unbelievers or backsliders.

Fanatics are immune to any doubt or disbelief regarding the church they serve.

Intolerance (Religious) — *-5/-10 points; see p. B34*

Intolerance is another common disadvantage among the religious. Some faiths practically demand it of their followers, teaching that all who do not follow their creed are damned or worse. Others will specifically forbid it, teaching a path of understanding and acceptance to all.

Intolerance of a particular religion (usually one diametrically opposed to your own) is worth -5 points, and causes a -3 reaction to any follower of that religion. Intolerance of *anyone* not of your religion is worth -10 points, and causes a -3 reaction to anyone not of your own faith. (Note that if Fanaticism is also taken, these penalties double to -6.)

Sense of Duty — *Variable; see p. B39*

As true believers of their faith, most clerics are going to have a strong Sense of Duty toward their religion and people of their faith. However, any Sense of Duty which duplicates the responsibilities placed upon them by the church is not worth any additional character points – only a Sense of Duty above and beyond that required of any dutiful cleric at their level of involvement may be used. Keep in mind that a Sense of Duty beyond the church is likely to create conflicts within the character, and may not be allowed by some religions.

Social Status: Excommunicated — *-5/-10 points*

You have been excommunicated from a religion. If the religion is strictly a societal or political power, this is a 5-point disadvantage, and only those directly involved with your excommunication, or who have heard about it via normal means, will know of it. If the religion has true supernatural power, this is a 10-point disadvantage, and all clerics of the religion (and most members) will immediately recognize your shame.

Excommunications usually occur in powerful, widespread, state-backed religions. Small, localized faiths tend to simply exile the offenders.

Once recognized, an excommunicated person has a reaction penalty of -3 from all followers of the religion.

Vow — *Variable; see p. B37*

At times of Investment or other religious significance, it is common for clerics to show their dedication to their faith by swearing vows. Some vows are required by the church: vows of poverty, chastity, truth, etc. are common examples. Other vows may be accepted by the cleric as penance, or as a sign of special devotion.

Trivial Vow: -1 point (a quirk). Tithe some percentage (less than 20%) of income to church; restricted diet; change of name.

Minor Vow: -5 points. Total obedience to the Church; tithe some percentage (21%-90%) of income to the church; chastity; silence of limited duration (during the day, during the night, on holy days, etc.); tell the truth at all times; undertake annual pilgrimage.

Major Vow: -10 points. Total silence; celibacy; complete poverty (tithe all money or property to the church); renounce social rank.

Great Vow: -15 points. Never refuse any request for aid; hunt down and destroy all church enemies; gain all sustenance through begging.

While many religious vows are "for life," some will have definite time periods associated with them (at least a year), or a definite task to be completed to release you from the vow's restrictions. You must buy off a vow's point value whenever it ends. For vows accepted as penance, the points gained by taking the vow may *not* be used to improve the character in other ways. These points remain in holding until you have worked off the penance. At this point you may use them to buy off the vow, or choose to extend the vow and spend the points on other things.

Breaking a religious vow is a serious matter. If the church's power is purely social, any cleric caught in violation of a vow may be stripped of rank and standing, or assigned grave punishments (always worse than the vow that was betrayed). If the church represents a true force or power in the world, then *any* time a vow to that power is broken, there will be severe repercussions (see *Penance*, p. 60).

New Disadvantages

Cursed — *Variable*

You have been cursed by a god. The curse may take whatever form the GM finds appropriate. It may be a continuing commandment such as "you may never sleep at night," or "you must always speak the truth." Or it may be a particularly nasty Disadvantage like Blindness, Epilepsy, or Berserk behavior. The curse may be placed on you in particular, or may have fallen upon you as a member of a cursed family or race. What makes curses distinct from regular Disadvantages is the potential for their removal. Each curse was given for a reason, and the character, through play, has the opportunity to uncover this reason and atone, thereby lifting the curse. The type of curse given should fit the deity in question and the reason for the cursing, as should the eventual terms of atonement.

The cost of the curse is left completely to the GM. The more encompassing or debilitating the curse, the higher the cost. The reason for the cursing, and the ease of atonement should also be considered in the cost – the easier to discover and remove, the lower the cost. The curse should never be for something simple or trivial, and the terms of atonement should always be nearly as bad as the curse itself.

For example, a curse of Berserk rage might be placed upon a certain family whose forefather killed a high-ranking cleric in a fit of rage. To atone, some member of the family must approach the church and seek penance, which may mean becoming a cleric of the church himself, or performing some major service dictated by a cleric of the church. The individual should be given the standard 15 points for the Berserk disadvantage, since the effect on him is the same, though he has the option of roleplaying the atonement and buying it off. A standard disadvantage given as a curse should never exceed the cost of the uncursed Disadvantage. Treat commandments as involuntary oaths.

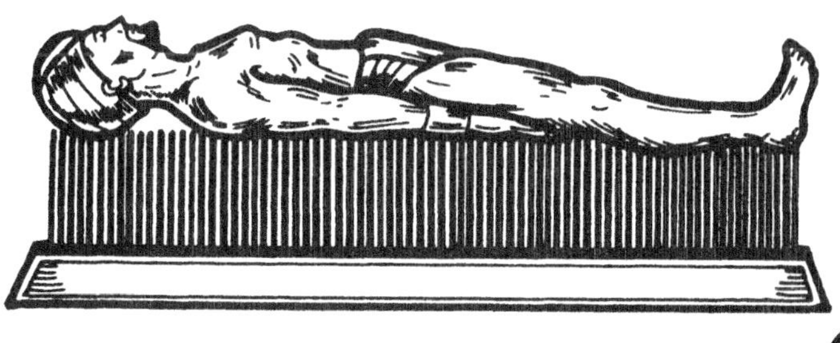

Disciplines of Faith — *Variable*

Similar to Vows, these are fundamental rules that you choose to live your life by, in order to achieve a greater understanding of your faith. Some religions will require one or more of these from their clerics. Others make them optional, adopt lesser or piecemeal methodologies, or forbid such excesses of worship at any time.

These disciplines only apply to religions who share their characteristic worldview, and may be a prerequisite to a greater understanding of the true nature and powers of the divine.

Asceticism: -15 points. The renunciation of all the comforts of society to lead a life of self-denial and self-discipline. May involve sporadic bouts of severe self-punishment to excise the mortal taint of earthly desire. Most often involves some sort of isolation in bleak, austere settings. An ascetic transcends all need for worldly possessions, living in complete and utter poverty. An ascetic may gain no other Status or Wealth modifiers beyond his rank of Clerical Investment.

Iconism: -10 points. Iconists believe that piety accumulates through expenditure of wealth on religious goods: statues, paintings, totems, religious ornamentation of any sort, new and grander temples, etc. They devote their lives to decorating the world with bigger and more beautiful icons of their deity, sure that this will gain them the favor of further truths and understanding.

Many iconists are quite poor beyond the beautiful icons of their deities. A true iconists will spend his last gold piece on a new statue rather than a good, hot meal.

Monasticism: -10 points. A milder form of asceticism, those devoted to monasticism also lead a life separated from worldly concerns, devoting themselves completely to religious pursuits often involving the denial of ego and self. This discipline is more contemplative than restrictive, and is most often used by those trying to obtain a purity of mind and body that they expect to bring them closer to their deity or ruling force. One practicing monasticism may gain no other Status or Wealth modifiers except Clerical Investment, and must spend at least 75% of his time sequestered from the world.

Mysticism: -10 points. A discipline of deep meditation and trance-like contemplation aimed at obtaining a closer union with the divine. The cleric spends a majority of his time engaged in rituals of meditation, complete with chanting and whatever other trappings are necessary. Mystics are often considered a bit mad, and receive a -2 reaction penalty from anyone except devout followers of the religion.

Ritualism: -5 points. The strict adherence to elaborate rituals regarding every aspect of life – from waking to eating to bathing to sex. Each ritual has its proper place, time, words, trappings and ceremony. The fundamental belief of a ritualist is that through the perfect performance of each ritual, they bring each aspect of their life closer to the divine.

Skills

Craft Skills

Many churches support themselves by selling goods or services to the community. Thus, clerics who spend any length of time at retreats, monasteries, or smaller shrines or temples may end up learning craft skills such as brewing, glassblowing, carpentry, leatherworking, illumination, calligraphy, pottery, woodworking, and so on. In extremely remote places, such skills may be required for the sustenance of the community. Or the church may choose to separate itself completely, forming independent communities which require such skills to survive.

Medical Skills

Physician/TL (Mental/Hard) — *see p. B56*

At tech levels under TL3, this skill is the equivalent of Botany plus Herbary.

Professional Skills

Law (Mental/Hard) — *see p. B58*

In places and times where the church is considered either beyond, or one and the same as, the law of the state, clerics may be required to specialize in the particular laws and legal structure of the church.

Clerics who act as judges will require a Law skill of 17 or above.

Theology (Mental/Hard) — *see p. B62*

The study of religions, their history, development, basic tenets and interrelations. Specializations give in-depth knowledge of a particular religion, including knowledge of religious doctrine, dogma and rituals, as well as mysterious or hidden knowledge unavailable to the general populace. GMs may limit skill levels in such a specialization based on the cleric's rank. Promotions within the church may have this skill as a prerequisite.

Science Skills

Botany — *see p. B60*

This skill includes a working knowledge of herbs and their properties. If the skilled character also has Herbary, it is possible to prepare herbal remedies.

Social Skills

Bard (Mental/Average) — *see p. B47*

The ability to speak well in public can serve a cleric well, to convert new followers or maintain the faith of those who question. Few, however, will have any formal training in this skill, though certain religions may find bardic priests quite useful.

Diplomacy (Mental/Hard) — *see p. B63*

The skill of negotiating compromises and getting along with others. As any major church defines a community and social hierarchy in and of itself, and may often be called upon to render judgments and answer complaints in the society as a whole, this skill is quite important to ranking clerics.

Fast-Talk (Mental/Average) — *see p. B63*

The ability to talk others into doing things against their better judgment. Constructed, "flash" religions may depend on clerics with high levels of this skill to sell their message to a skeptical public. Members of proselytizing religions may find it useful as well.

Leadership (Mental/Average) *see p. B63*

A very important skill for high-ranking clerics. Absolutely essential for church leaders. A successful Leadership roll is required to make NPC clerics follow your orders in any stressful situation.

Politics (Mental/Average) *see p. B64*

In churches based on secular power and social status, skill in Politics might be necessary to progress beyond the lowest clerical levels. This skill can only be learned by experience, or by closely watching others "at work." In a church of this type, advancement in the church is likely to be tied to levels of this skill.

Teaching (Mental/Average) *see p. B64*

Teaching is an important skill for those clerics who are called upon to explain the word of god to their followers, or who must train the younger clergy in their duties and responsibilities with the church. Sages and wisemen are often noted for their teaching ability.

New Skills

Herbary (Mental/Average) *see p. BB38*

Herbary is a venerable English word meaning, among other things, the science of herbs. This skill is the knowledge of herbal concoctions from harvesting, to storage, to effects, to delivery, to potency. Once a herbalist has correctly identified a plant with Botany skill, he then must roll against Herbary skill to successfully transmute the raw material to an active herbal concoction.

Herbary skill level determines the *number* of prepared herbs a beginning herbalist starts with. These concoctions *must* be chosen from plants he is familiar with – see Botany, above.

Note: At TL2 or below, Herbary is the equivalent of the Physician skill; players in such campaigns should not take both.

Meditation (Mental/Hard) *Defaults to IQ-5*

This is the ability to enter a trance-like state which may then be maintained for several hours. A meditative trance may be required for certain rituals, as well as being a common preparation for prayer. While in a such a trance, fatigue is regained at twice normal rate.

Performance/Ritual (Mental/Average) *Defaults to IQ-5, Acting-2, Bard-2*

The ability to perform a particular religion's rituals (holiday celebration, wedding, funeral, etc.) before a congregation. It includes precise knowledge of the appropriate trappings, motions and prayers, etc., as well as the performance skill necessary to capture and hold the attention of those participating. A particular ritual may have a Theology specialization as a prerequisite.

Money and Equipment

When designing clerical characters, it is important to consider their position and relationship with the church. Will the church provide most of their equipment from general stock, or none? Are clerics allowed to own personal or private items? What religious equipment and regalia will they have? How much money are they likely to keep with them? How much of the monies they acquire "belong" to their church?

The GM should prepare a list of common regalia and equipment available to clerical PCs, especially if the church denies its clerics the right of private property.

Clothing

Garb, both for daily wear and for special ceremony, should be clearly defined, as well as the common religious symbols worn. Cost is not generally an issue, but rank often is – certain trappings may be appropriate only to clerics of certain ranks; a church leader usually dresses very differently from a simple monk. Alternatively, the church may provide no special clothing at all, preferring its clerics to be seen as ordinary members of their congregation. In other cases, the church may limit the cleric to sackcloth, the work of his own hands, or whatever others are willing to give him. Anything is possible. See p. 85 for description.

Religious Items

Clerics often carry certain mementos of their faith: holy symbols, books of scripture, small relics, various trappings necessary for common rituals, icons of their god, and so forth. Some may be necessary for their work, or the casting of spells. Others are but familiar reminders of their faith. Both players and GMs should give thought to what is appropriate to the culture and the religion and equip each cleric accordingly. See pp. 80-84 for a list of possibilities.

The Role of the Church

When equipping a cleric, the role the church plays in his life must be considered. In some cases the cleric is responsible to himself alone and may equip himself as he sees fit. Or the cleric might be considered an extension of the church, with no real property of his own, gaining whatever home, clothing and supplies he gets directly from the church. Some are forbidden to have anything but what they get from the charity of their worshipers. Other religions vary between these extremes, providing or forbidding only certain items, while leaving the rest to the cleric's discretion.

This is particularly important if the cleric finds himself at odds with the church for any reason, or if the church's resources become scarce. For, as the church gives, so it can take.

❁ Clerical Duty ❁

The first responsibility of any cleric is to serve his deity. In most cases, the second is to serve, support, lead and succor the followers of his faith. Very few religions can exist without the faithful; those that do tend to represent some archetypal force or aspect of the world which cannot be denied (such as death). For the rest, power and status come from the conviction of their followers – conviction that often rises and falls with the material and spiritual benefits gained.

The exact nature of a cleric's service to his followers will depend upon the nature of the deity he serves. However, certain common duties cross almost all religions. They speak the religion's message to the faithful in daily prayers. They teach the young (and indoctrinate them into the religion). They perform the ceremonies and rituals important to holy times and places. They collect holy scripture and the truths contained within. They arbitrate in matters of religious law or tradition, and so on. It is the cleric's task to see that all customs of the religion are upheld by all followers, and that none who worship forget the true purpose and intent of the deity.

Protection of Church Members/Property

Protection of those under their care is an important duty for most clerics, especially those of knightly orders. The well-being of the worshipers and the protection of church property (especially Holy Objects, relics, scriptures, vestments and other components of the faith) are of utmost importance. If the church is considered sacred and untouchable, then this task will be easy. But if there is a strong and militant population of nonbelievers nearby, or a strong opposing deity exists, then the task may be a bit more challenging. If threatened often enough (and in ways that the deity's power cannot fully protect against), the church may seek pacifistic solutions, or develop military orders to deal with the problem.

In some cases the church, vestment, scriptures and other trappings are not only considered the property of the deity, but an extension of the deity itself. To steal from the church is to defame the deity, and will be treated harshly.

Recruitment

Every church requires fresh recruits to carry on. While some deities may do their own recruiting, most leave this task to their clerics. They will be required to keep an eye out for promising young talent to indoctrinate in the ways of the church. In some cases force might even be an acceptable option.

Depending on the hierarchy of the church, a cleric may be called upon to aid in teaching or testing of the younger clergy.

In some religions, recruitment may follow custom; a family might be encouraged, or even required, to dedicate a certain child (or number of children) to the church. This might be a permanent duty (every third son becomes a priest) or a temporary one (all daughters receive two years of religious training, after which time they may leave the church if they wish).

DIVINE MAGIC

6

Do deities shake the world with their powers? Bestow miracles upon the worthy? Grant their faithful servants smaller aspects of their powers to call upon at will? Answer calls from their followers?

In certain game worlds, the power of the gods manifests in very concrete forms, easily perceived by all. In these worlds, clerics will be powerful figures, respected by all, able to draw upon the supernatural power or force personified by their particular deity or faith.

How true divine magic works is closely tied to the design of the cosmos, and the interaction of the divine forces within it. Prior to play, the GM must fully design this magic for each religion in the game world which manifests it.

To this end, a series of different approaches to divine magic is presented in this chapter. GMs should use whichever one best suits their campaign, modifying or expanding upon the basic guidelines as needed.

Clerical Magic

Clerics draw upon the supernatural power or force personified by their particular deity in order to create predictable, reoccurring effects known as spells. Unlike "pure" magic, clerical magic is not at all affected by the mana rating of an area. It may, however, be affected by the strength of the deity in a given location, the time of the year, the number of faithful present, the strength of the cleric's devotion to the deity, and so forth.

Power Investiture

Before a cleric can cast a spell, he must undergo a special rite known as a Power Investiture in which he is imbued with the deity's power (see *Advantages,* pp. 93-94). This ceremony is designed to attune the cleric to the power of the deity, allowing him to draw upon that power in specialized rituals, and focus it into spells. Thus while the cleric initiates the spell, it is, in truth, the deity which powers it. Therefore it is *always* the prerogative of the deity to deny this power, or to manipulate it in unexpected ways. Clerical magic is highly prone (much more so than "pure" magic) to variant effects due to circumstances. Clerics who break faith with their deity (as opposed to the church – it is possible to do one without the other) may find that all their spells fail until they make atonement in one way or another.

The investiture is a two-way link: as the cleric may draw upon the deity, the deity may also draw upon the life-energies of the cleric (in terms of Fatigue, or in dire cases, directly upon HT), or may use the cleric as a channel through which to draw in the willingly-given energies of the faithful. This is the mechanism through which some deities gain power from their followers. Some deities might never do this, while others may consider this sort of "sacrifice" commonplace.

Spells

Clerics use the same spell list as mages. However, clerical spells draw their power from a different source, and vary from their magical equivalents in a number of other ways.

The Nature of the Spell

Clerical magics are an appeal to the divine, an expression of faith and belief. In this, though the end effect may be the same, they differ greatly from their pure magical counterparts.

Clerical Terms

Ceremony: A gathering of clerics and worshipers for religious purpose, often including the casting of a clerical spell.

Clerical Ranking: The cleric's rank in the hierarchy of the church. The cleric's level of Clerical Investment.

Clerical Investment: The social/political advantage of being a cleric within a religion. Represents status and influence within the church and is measured in levels, or ranks, depending on the religion.

Consecrate: To dedicate an object or area to the divine. To focus the power of the deity within an object or area. The clerical equivalent of enchantment.

Consecrated Objects: Sacred Objects (see below) which have been cleansed or blessed by the deity's power for use in various clerical magics.

Divine Intervention: Direct intervention of the deity or its associated powers within the world.

Holy Object: Sacred Object (see below) with the ability to cast one or more spells common to the deity. Clerical magic item.

Investiture: see Power Investiture, below.

Investiture Link: Spiritual link with the divine created during the Power Investiture.

Object of Power: Holy Object (see above) which creates an area of High or Very High Sanctity (see p. 102) around it.

Power Investiture or *Investiture:* Rite which imparts the power of the divine to the cleric, allowing magical spells and abilities. Clerical equivalent to Magical Aptitude.

Ritual: Formal symbolic act associated with the casting of a spell or the petitioning of the deity. Sometimes used interchangeably with the word "spell."

Sacred Object: Any object consecrated to a deity.

Sacred Vessel: Personal Sacred Object used to store the combined power of the deity and the cleric.

Sanctity: The measure of the deity's power in a given locale.

Many spells will take the form of prayer: a gently-worded plea to draw the deity's attention, as the cleric calls upon whatever power might be necessary. The prayer is a focus, a mantra for the casting of the spell. In some cases it might be absolutely necessary to the spell to work; in others it may simply be an expected component (see *Magical Rituals*, below). The GM (or player) should feel free to invent small rituals or prayers to go with the spells to add flavor (see sidebar, p. 106).

Faith: Faith is an absolutely essential component to any divine spell. If the cleric doubts himself, his deity, or the truth and reality of the deity's power, then the spell can be hopeless even before it has begun. Thus any occurrence which temporarily shakes the foundation of a cleric's faith may have disastrous effects on his ability to cast spells. Mind-control spells such as Suggestion may be used to cause the cleric to doubt, and thereby weaken his spellcasting.

Casting the Spell

To cast a clerical spell the cleric must first know the spell, having been invested with the power of the deity. He must also learn the necessary steps to focus the power into this particular effect (by spending character points to learn the spell). He must then spend one or more turns in *concentration*, performing whatever prayer and ritual motions are appropriate. At the beginning of the turn *after* the last turn of concentration, the cleric makes a skill roll for the spell. He may then do some other action on that turn (use a weapon, start concentrating again, etc.).

Casting a spell works just like the use of any other skill. The cleric rolls three dice and compares the result with his skill level in that spell combined with any circumstantial modifiers. If the roll is less than or equal to the modified skill, then the spell works. If the roll is greater than the skill, then the spell fails.

Like pure magical spells, clerical spells are subject to critical successes and failures, corresponding to instances of divine favor, disfavor, or whim. The GM determines the exact effect of a critical success or failure. He should base his decision on the nature of the deity in question.

Magical Rituals

All clerical spells require concentration and focus. Clerics gain no bonuses in casting time for increased skill, and all clerical magics take a minimum of one round of concentration to cast (defensive or blocking spells, if used, are an exception to this rule).

Since all clerical spells involve a plea to the deity, the more elaborate or grand the request, the better chance there is that the spell will succeed. Each spell will have a standard ritual associated with it. This may include a verbal chant or prayer, gestures and motions of the hands or feet, a position or posture to assume (kneeling or bowing is common), or possibly even an ingredient prepared previously (for example, incense or holy water). For each part of the ritual that is omitted, there is a penalty to the spell's chance of success. For each part of the ritual that is prolonged or extended, there is a bonus to the spell's chance of success. These bonuses or penalties are cumulative:

-2 for soft speech, or -4 for no speech.

-2 if gestures are made with only one hand, or -4 if no gestures are used.

-2 if the proper foot movements and/or position is not used.

-4 if the proper ingredient is not used.

Pure Magic vs. Clerical Magic

Though the sources that power divine magic and "pure" magic differ greatly, the worldly effects of the powers are essentially equivalent. A magic spell can attack and resist a clerical spell as easily as any other, just as clerical magic can protect against magical effects. Wards, Counterspell, and all other defensive or protective magics work interchangeably between clerics and mages.

As to whether or not a single individual may combine magery and clerical magic, the GM has two choices.

In the first case, magery and clerical magic may not be mixed within a particular individual. The divine link will override any natural magery the character might have, hopelessly interfering with his ability to cast pure magic spells. If the individual knew pure magic prior to his Power Investiture, he will not lose this skill, but neither may he use it in any way as long as the connection exists. If, however, the link is broken for some reason, then the person's natural magery will reassert itself and he may once again practice his rusty magic skills.

In the second case, the two may occur without interference within a single character, but they remain completely separate abilities and powers. Consider this the default case, unless otherwise decided by the GM. Clerical spells learned do *not* count as prerequisites for magic spells – the manner of casting and the source of power is simply too different. Indeed, it is quite possible for someone to know the *same* spell – one as a channel of the deity's power, the other as a skill which draws upon mana – at separate skill levels. Although these spells will have the same effect when cast, the manner of their casting and the sources of their power are so different that the knowledge of one could not possibly affect the other. The existence of mage talent within an individual does not in any way affect the Power Investiture or the investiture link created with the deity.

Mana

Magical mana need not affect the workings of clerical magics or Holy Objects. Sanctity and mana are two completely different things, and may coexist peacefully – or not, as the GM decides.

+1 for each additional round spent concentrating on a spell, to a total of +4.

+1 for each additional hour spent in ceremonial magics (see p. 104), to a total of +6.

Energy Cost

Clerical spells, like magical ones, have an associated energy cost. The higher the ability with the spell, the less energy is required to cast it. Higher levels of Power Investiture (conferring larger learning bonuses) allow the cleric to draw more of the spell's cost from the deity, rather than himself. At a skill of 15, the spell's cost to the cleric is reduced by 1; at 20 it is reduced by 2; and at 25 it is reduced by 3.

The Sanctity level of an area also affects the cost, as does the time of year. These costs are additive. For example, a cleric casting a spell in a place of High Sanctity on a holy day (see below) will only pay one-fourth the normal cost, and will regain fatigue four times as fast as usual. However, a spell cast in a place of Low Sanctity on a day of weakness will cost *four* times as much, and the cleric will have to wait four times longer than usual to recover lost fatigue.

Sanctity

Sanctity is a measure of the deity's power in a given locale. The Sanctity of an area affects the cost and overall effect of a clerical spell.

Very High Sanctity: The area directly surrounding the presence of the deity, a shrine, a temple, a church, or any holy place consecrated to the deity, particular to the religion. These places are the seat of the deity's power. Spells cast here have *no* energy cost (unless they can *only* be cast in a place of Very High Sanctity, in which case normal costs apply). Fatigue spent through the casting of clerical magics is immediately renewed at the end of each turn. This is a No-Sanctity area for all non-allied deities.

High Sanctity: The area directly surrounding a shrine, a temple, or a church; any non-consecrated place where worshipers regularly gather for prayer (it takes at least five years of constant activity for a given locale to be so imprinted); any place special to the deity, but not considered to be specifically sacred. The deity is strong in such areas, though not as strong as in its immediate shrines. Spells cast here have half the normal energy cost, and clerics regain fatigue at twice ordinary rate.

Normal Sanctity: Any area (town, city, country) in which the deity would normally hold sway. The deity's power is available in these areas, but at no special benefit or cost.

Low Sanctity: Any area (town, city, country) where the deity's power would not normally extend. The deity is weak in these places. Spells cast here have twice the normal energy cost, and clerics regain fatigue at only half the normal rate.

No Sanctity: Any area in which the deity holds absolutely no power, and whose very nature is contrary to that of the deity. The deity's power is essentially

Power Investiture as a Gift

As described on p. 100, the Power Investiture is a ritual anointing or initiation that a cleric undergoes to gain access to the power of the deity. It could just as easily be played as an inborn trait or quality, much like Magical Aptitude. In this case, it would indicate a particular affinity for the power of a specific deity, or a natural "holiness." Levels of investiture will be completely independent of Clerical Investment, and may in fact occur in those who have little interest in becoming clerics.

Note that having an Investiture link does not confer the knowledge of spells. The person must still find some training in order to focus his gift. This training must teach him the clerical version of the spell – magery training will avail him little unless he also has Magical Aptitude.

Religions may seek out those with particular insight (sometimes called a *vocation*) to be clerics. It may be a prerequisite for certain clerical rankings (thereby reestablishing the link between rank and investiture), or for certain religious orders. Whatever the case, the church will probably not provide training for talented folk without indoctrinating them into the structure of the religion in some way.

nonexistent here. Spells will generally not work (except Divine Intervention, p. 113), and a cleric will regain no fatigue spent on clerical magics.

Areas of High or Very High Sanctity for one deity will usually lower the Sanctity level of any other deity in that area by 1, unless their powers are allied. Allied powers may coexist at higher than normal sanctity levels. For example, though all the Lands of Bethany (see pp. 156-166) are usually of Normal Sanctity, clerics of Volt will find temples of Dorn to be areas of Low Sanctity. Clerics of Keldan have no such penalty, and may find the temple to be an area of High Sanctity for them as well.

Anyone with an Investiture link may roll IQ + Investiture level to determine the Sanctity level of his current location.

Holy Days

A deity's power may also vary according to the time of year. Certain days may be considered holy times when the deity's power is at its strongest, while others may mark times of weakness.

Days of Strength: On holy days particular to a given deity, the energy cost of all clerical spells powered by that deity will be halved, and clerics will regain fatigue lost due to spellcasting at twice the ordinary rate. A special high holy day may be defined, when the deity is particularly strong. On this day all areas of High Sanctity will act as areas of Very High Sanctity, and areas of Normal Sanctity will act as areas of High Sanctity. These days should be quite rare.

Each Holy Day will add 1 point to the cost of the church as a patron. High Holy Days add 2 points each to the cost of church patronage.

Days of Weakness: A deity may also be particularly weak on certain days or times of the year. On these days, the energy cost of all clerical spells powered by that deity will be doubled, and clerics will regain lost fatigue at half the usual rate. A special day of weakness, when the deity is especially weak, may be designated on which areas of Very High Sanctity act like areas of High Sanctity, areas of High Sanctity act as areas of Normal Sanctity, and so on.

Each Day of Weakness will subtract 1 point from the cost of the church as a patron.

Divine Power

All deities who are actively worshipped will have the power to sustain the number of clerics who are Invested. This power may be drawn from the worship of its followers, or may be integral to the deity.

If there is a sudden decrease in the number of followers through war, calamity, or some other great disaster, then the balance of things must

Sanctifying an Area

There are three ways that an area can be Sanctified to a deity, depending on the relative power of the deity on the world. First, if the deity is able to manifest at will within the material world, it may simply select an area and claim it. Any area in which a deity manifests will become Sanctified to some extent, though only if the deity manifests repeatedly in the same area will the locale retain its Sanctity rating over time.

Secondly, an existing deity may extend its areas of Sanctity into new areas by converting new worshipers to its faith. Over time, as their energies are continually given to the deity, the area will gain a higher level of Sanctity.

Finally, the quick and dirty method is for a cleric to go to the area he wishes to Sanctify, and perform a Divine Intervention to manifest the power of the deity in the locale. As long as the power is exhibited, the area is considered to have a Very High Sanctity rating. The cleric then Consecrates the area to focus the power displayed. If the ritual succeeds, then the area will become one of High Sanctity. Repeated worship to the deity held within the area may eventually elevate its Sanctity to the level of Very High.

Altering the Sanctity of an Area

Sanctity levels can be modified both up and down. Generally, the most common way of altering the Sanctity of an area is to change the deity most commonly worshiped in that area. A shrine which is left vacant for decades will begin to lose its affinity for the divine (unless the deity takes pains to see that this does not occur). A Low Sanctity area can be gradually transformed into a higher level by continual prayers and sacrifices of power (and other things) to the deity.

More expedient methods use the Desecrate and Consecrate spells to lessen or increase the rating of an area (see p. 110).

be re-evaluated. If the deity does, indeed, draw power from its followers, then the GM must determine if there is still enough to supply the deity and maintain what power the clerics require. There are no mechanics to this decision – it is at the discretion of the GM. If not, then the deity may refuse to provide the raw power for spells, or cut off certain clerics, until some sort of balance is restored. Should restoration be impossible, the deity may fade, leaving its clerics with little purpose except the restoration of the deity.

Sudden increases in followers are never a problem – a deity can never have too *much* power, except from the point of view of its enemies.

Other Modifying Circumstances

Other circumstances that may affect the casting of a clerical spell include:

Fanaticism: If the cleric is fanatical about his religion, he gains a +1 modifier to all clerical spell rolls.

Divine Favor: If the cleric is engaging in an activity that the deity particularly approves of, or for whatever reason enjoys extreme divine favor, the god may grant a bonus up to +5! This is rare, and should only be used in extreme cases.

Divine Disfavor: If the cleric is engaging in an activity that the deity disapproves of, then it is most likely that the spell's effect will be muted, or will not occur at all.

All normal magical modifiers for area of effect and range still apply.

Ceremonial Magic

Ceremonial Magic (see p. M14) is quite common among clerics. Very powerful effects can be created when several clerics gather together, supported by the energies of an entire congregation. All "spectators" must be actively engaged in worshipping the deity in some prescribed fashion – dancing, singing, praying, etc. There is no upper limit on the number of total points the congregation can add to the spell, though each may still only contribute a single point.

For those deities who receive their power from their followers, each act of worship is in fact the casting of a Ceremonial Magic designed to transfer power to the deity. The cleric leading the worship casts the equivalent of a Recover Strength spell, but instead of recovering the fatigue from the effects of the spell, he gathers it from the energies devoted by the "spectators" (or worshipers). Each point they donate to the spell is then transferred to the deity through the Investiture link. For this purpose (and this purpose *only*) members of the congregation may provide more than a single spell point to the ceremony. Such energies must be given willingly in the name of the deity.

Sacred Objects

Clerics do not make magical items as mages do. As ever, the exercise of their power is limited to that dictated by the deity. However, holy or sacred objects with magical powers will almost certainly be found in any world where magic exists.

Consecrated Objects

These are normal objects or materials which have been made holy or sacred through a ceremony of consecration (see p. 110). Examples are holy water, special oils used for certain rituals, and religious symbols worn by the cleric.

Ritualized Magic

As described on pp. 100-104, clerical magics can be cast with all the speed and alacrity of pure magics. This better balances the two different power bases, but may not be the way in which a GM wants divine magics to occur on his world. Another option is to force all clerical magics to be ritualized in nature – that is, they must all be accompanied by great fanfare, ceremony and ritual. This takes clerical magics out of the realm of combat or immediate action, and relegates it to those feats worthy of a long, protracted service.

Ritualizing magic can be accomplished by applying a modifier to the spell casting times, forcing them to take, say, three times longer than their magical equivalents. This accounts for the additional time of prayer and supplication to the deity, but still allows the clerics some flexibility.

The other option is to require all clerical magics to be cast in their ceremonial forms.

Spheres of Influence

The ease with which clerics can cast certain spells is based on their deity's sphere of influence. The elements or powers in which the deity is strong will be easier for their clerics to manipulate than those over which it has only incidental power. Those spells which the GM decides are within the deity's sway can be cast as written. However, other spells, which the cleric cannot cast as simply or quickly, may be learned from allied deities.

Spells gained from allied powers may only be cast in their full ceremonial form.

Ceremonies of consecration can only be performed in areas of Very High Sanctity, by clerics of the deity. Consecration is not particularly difficult, and thus consecrated objects are not terribly rare. Anything that is appropriate to the deity may be consecrated, for varying effects. For example, a warrior deity might consecrate the blades of swords used by his followers, giving them a +1 to skill when used against a follower of an enemy faith for a particular conflict. (The GM should be careful when assigning these bonuses, and always remember that any gain must be relative to the difficulty of the ritual in question.) In no case should a simple consecration endow an object with a power equivalent to a spell effect – those are Holy Objects, discussed below. Consecration purifies and "blesses" an object . . . it does not endow it with the power of the deity.

Consecrated objects are most commonly used to aid clerical spells.

Sacred Vessels

Sacred Vessels are objects used to store a combination of the cleric's and the deity's power. The cleric who creates the vessel may use its stored power in place of his own to cast any clerical spell. Such a vessel may *only* be used by the cleric who created it, and he must be within 6 feet of it. Any consecrated object of special meaning to the religion (most often some sort of holy symbol) may be used. There is no restriction on the total number of power points stored in the Sacred Vessel (its strength), but once set, it may not be increased later. Only one such Sacred Vessel may be used per round by a cleric.

To create a Sacred Vessel, a cleric must first find the object he wishes to use and consecrate it. Then he must prepare it with an elaborate ritual in a place of High or Very High Sanctity, spending a full 12 hours per day for each point of power he wishes it to eventually contain. These days must be consecutive, and must end on a day considered particularly holy to the religion. During this holy day, in a place of Very High Sanctity, the cleric casts the Consecrate spell (see p. 110) continuously, once for each point of strength that he wishes the vessel to have. The skill roll is made, once for each casting of the spell. A success adds that potential point of power to the vessel.

A failure may not be repeated, meaning the vessel will have less total strength – the will of the god. A roll of 17 ends the casting; no more points may be added. A roll of 18 destroys the vessel, and the cleric's hopes. He must begin anew.

Few clerics keep more than one Sacred Vessel with them at a time, and for many the vessel represents an important personal link with the deity. Most create their vessel soon after their Power Investiture.

A Sacred Vessel "recharges" itself after use, by absorbing power from the deity through the cleric's Investiture link. It must be within 6 feet of the cleric in order to recharge. The speed varies according to the Sanctity of the area:

No Sanctity: No recharge.

Low Sanctity: 1 point per week.

Normal Sanctity: 1 point per day.

High Sanctity: 1 point per 12 hours.

Very High Sanctity: 1 point per 6 hours.

Holy or Blessed Objects

These objects are the clerical equivalents of magical items. They have the ability to cast one or more spells appropriate to the deity. They may *only* be used by clerics of that deity, and each use of a Holy Object requires a preparatory ritual done by one or more clerics. These clerics need not know the spell stored in the item, but they do need to know the precise ritual which activates it. Any element of the ritual which is left out or done improperly (the cleric must make a successful Performance/Ritual roll) will abort the spell. If the object can cast multiple spells, then the ritual for each different effect will vary slightly. The length of time for the ritual is specified at the creation of the object and can never be less than that normally required to cast the spell.

There is never an energy cost associated with the use of a Holy Object. The spell's success (assuming the ritual has first been successfully completed) is determined normally, using the item's Power as the caster's skill and applying all normal modifiers. As there is no cost associated with using the object, the Sanctity and time of year do not affect it. Holy Objects work *no matter where* they are, even in the temples of other deities!

To create a Holy Object, the cleric first needs the cooperation of the deity. The deity will not invest its power into material objects lightly – in general, such objects are made for a particular quest or purpose important to the deity and the church as a whole (although once the quest is finished, the object may continue to exist). The cleric must then consecrate the object to be used, in the usual fashion, and decide exactly what he wishes it to be able to do (like Sacred Vessels, Holy Objects are forged in a single, continuous casting – once created, no further effects may be added). Costs are determined exactly as for magic items (see pp. 110-112). Then the object must be "prepared." This preparation is done by the cleric in an area of either High Sanctity or Very High Sanctity, and takes a day for each point of energy required in the final result. There is *no* shortcut to this process. If the desired result has an energy cost of 100, then it will take the cleric 100 days of continuous preparation. This is a full-time process, requiring 12 hours of arduous ritual. The cleric may do nothing but eat, sleep and prepare the object. If the preparation is disturbed in any way, the cleric must make a Performance/Ritual skill roll at -5 for each day of ritual lost in order to continue, and must make up lost time with sleepless nights (this may only be done once; a second break means the project is lost). If the roll fails, then the cleric must begin again. No other cleric may continue the preparation – if something should happen to the original cleric, then the preparation must begin anew.

Prayer

Almost all clerical spells will have a vocal element–a prayer or incantation of some sort that focuses the cleric's mind and attracts the attention of the deity (see *Prayer*, p. 74). Either the GM or the player can come up with short prayers for each spell that the player can read, shout, or mutter as the occasion requires. Players or GMs who object to verbalizing a prayer to an imaginary deity may omit this, of course!

Prayer tends to follow one of a general set of forms, depending on whether the prayer is meant to be spontaneous or ceremonial in nature.

Spontaneous, or simple, prayer tends to be just that – simple. Liturgical prayer commonly begins with invoking the name(s) of the god, continues on to the justification for fulfillment, and concludes by formulating the result desired. Other prayers are litanies, simply repeating the name of the god, or some other key element or formula, over and over and over again. There may be a bargaining aspect – "I'll do this for you if you do that for me" – or it may be a simple cry or plea for aid – "Come . . . hear me . . . have pity." Still others are completely freeform, finding more value in the inspiration of the moment than in memorized formula. Some do little more than offer praise and glory to the deity, obviously hoping it will bestow its favor in return.

Ceremonial prayers follow more ritualized patterns, often requiring gestures and symbolic motions such as washing the hands or drinking or eating particular substances. Some ceremonies use formalized dialogues of question and answer, demonstrating tests passed and knowledge learned.

Players and GMs should be imaginative and do their best to make the prayers reflect the nature of the religion followed.

The final day of preparation must fall on a holy day. On this day, the cleric performs the final casting which will create the object. It *must* be done in a place of Very High Sanctity. The final casting requires one hour for each 100 points of energy required (round up). At the end of each hour, a Consecrate roll is made. If the roll succeeds, the ceremony progresses; if it fails, the cleric may choose to extend the ritual to try again (repeat the work of the last hour, including an additional 100 points of energy that must be spent), lessen the object's final ability by deducting the 100 points from the cost, or abort the ritual altogether. A critical failure (a roll of 18) leaves no choice but to abort. A critical success (a roll of 3) means that no further rolls need be made – the ceremony will be completely successful.

A lone cleric is limited to the energy provided by his own HT and ST and one Sacred Vessel. But in this final stage, the cleric may have assistants. Each of these may use his own Sacred Vessel, so assistants may dramatically multiply available energy. There is no limit to the number of assistants, or to the amount of extra energy they may supply. "Spectators" may also be present and through prayer and devotion lend their own assistance to the casting by providing 1 extra power point each.

Thus a grand ceremony bringing in all the clerics of the church, along with a large congregation, can generate a massive amount of power for this final casting, allowing the forging of very powerful objects. It is also possible to channel this energy into a higher Power for the object.

An object's Power is normally 15, no matter what the skill of the cleric making it. Extra energy in the final ceremony may add to this: +1 for energies exceeding those required by 20%, +2 for an additional 40%, +3 for an additional 60%, +4 for an additional 100%, and an extra +1 for each additional 100% of the required energy.

Special Enchantments such as Accuracy, Puissance, Quick-Draw, Loyal Sword, etc., are considered modifications of the Consecrate spell. While they add the costs listed in ***GURPS Magic,*** they do not need to be learned as separate spells.

Objects of Power

Objects of Power are Holy Objects with a special difference: they create an area of High or Very High Sanctity about themselves, with all attendant benefits for the cleric. They represent the presence of the deity itself. They are *exceedingly* rare.

Miracles

A miracle is an extraordinary event which is a manifest example of divine intervention. These events are often seen as proof of a god's interest in his followers, and a few well-placed miracles can do wonders for faith and recruitment. True miracles *always* greatly exceed what might be accomplished by a cleric or other divine representative.

Places where miracles occur often become shrines or other holy sites.

Miracles are also associated with new teachers and prophets. In this context, miracles act as proof of the prophet's authority and wisdom. New religions and sects might develop on the basis of such miracles.

Divine Will and the Dice

What happens when an all-important consecration fails? Whenever dice are used, there's a possibility of failure, even when it seems almost a given that the spell should succeed.

There are two different options. First, modify the roll into acceptance. If the priest only has Consecrate at 15-, and he rolls a 16, apply the "Divine Favor" modifier to make the roll succeed. Dice are useful for randomizing the events of a game session, but the final ceremony roll for an effect that's required months and months of hard work and preparation might deserve a little GM tweaking.

But the GM might just consider the roll to be a portent of the divine will. Perhaps there's a reason this particular ceremony should fail. Chaotic or temperamental deities are particularly prone to such vagaries, but even the forthright types might choose to withhold their power for some undiscovered cause.

Minor Objects of Power will create an area of High Sanctity within a given radius, no matter the true Sanctity of the area. Major Objects of Power will create an area of Very High Sanctity within a given radius, affecting the area so strongly that even after the object has moved on, the location will remain an area of High Sanctity for 1 week per day the object was in the location. This special area of effect is "always on." The default area is a 5-hex radius.

Objects of Power are made in two ways. The first is exactly the same as the making of a Holy Object, but during the final hour of the final ceremony the cleric requests Divine Intervention, thereby endowing the object with the true touch of the deity. The success of the request, and the deity's own whim, will decide the power of the resulting object. In these cases, the Object of Power will have both the "area of effect" bonus and whatever spells were consecrated into it. If the request fails, then the object will still be a Holy Object, but not an Object of Power. The radius of effect is set during the ritual, for the cost associated with enchanting an object.

The second method is through some direct intervention of the deity. In these cases the object will have whatever powers and area of effect the GM decides. Objects empowered by the deity in this way will always have some other important religious significance, be they the remains of a true martyr or some other item of symbolic importance. No cleric may request this sort of empowerment. It is, as they say, in the hands of the god.

Objects of Power have a base Power of 25.

Modified Magic

The effects of most spells translate directly from the rules given in ***GURPS Magic***. A few requiring special attention are detailed below. Only a small selection of the possible magic spells will be available to the clerics of each religion, depending on the deity's spheres of influence.

Prerequisites can be considered as only guidelines for the purposes of clerical magics. Many religions will define their own path of "prerequisites" that the clerics of that faith will follow, so no general rule applies.

Aura

This spell will identify clerics along with the deity they follow (as long as the mage or cleric casting the spell is familiar with that deity) and the level of Power Investiture the cleric has undergone. This is true whether the spell is cast by a mage or a cleric.

Divination

Divination is a common clerical ability. Most religions should have access to this spell in one form or another at the higher levels. The form of the divination, however, will vary widely, and should reflect the nature of the deity or the driving force of the religion. Consider those methods listed in ***GURPS Magic*** or ***GURPS Grimoire*** as a starting point and feel free to extrapolate other methods that seem appropriate.

Lead Worship

Clerics may not use the Recover Strength spell as described in ***GURPS Magic***. They have their own version which allows them to gather strength from the worship or prayer of devout followers of their deity. This gathered strength may restore their own fatigue, but at least half must be given to the deity through the Investiture link. These energies must be willingly given by the worshipers, and can never exceed their own ST. Energy gathered through use of this spell may never increase the cleric's ST – all extra points automatically transfer directly to the deity. For example, a cleric leading a congregation of 20 may receive up to an average of 200 fatigue points from them. If his own ST is 12, then the additional 188 points go to the deity.

It is rare, however, for a congregation to drain itself completely. For a normal service, assume 1 point per worshiper. For an intense, involving ceremony, assume half of each worshiper's available ST is given. Only the extremely fanatical are likely to devote more than half of their available ST.

Remember that the cleric has no control over how much is given – it is strictly up to the worshiper. Thus it is more likely that the aforementioned cleric will only receive 20 fatigue points from his congregation through the use of the spell, 10 of which must go to the deity, leaving him only 10 fatigue points to bolster his own.

The spell is commonly used by deities who gather their power directly from their followers. Clerics of deities who do not depend upon their followers for power may not have access to this spell at all.

Cost: None.

Item: This spell may *not* be consecrated into a Holy Object.

Steal Strength/Health

In addition to restoring the cleric, these spells can be used to perform sacrifices to the deity. Strength or Health stolen can be transferred to the deity through the Investiture link.

In special cases where the victim is ceremonially drained, and then killed, power equivalent to the victims (ST+HT)×3 can be generated, half of which must be given directly to the deity. The other half can be used to power ceremonial spells or added to the total energy for the creation of Holy Objects (see p. 106).

Some deities will refuse to accept energy taken in this manner.

Clerical Magic Spells

The following are spells for use by clerics only. Not all religions will use all of these spells. The GM should feel free to add more spells, or modify these to suit his purposes.

Divination

The ancient world used many different techniques in attempts to foresee events of the future. Predicting fate or destiny has long captured the human imagination. It is up to the GM whether any given technique has true validity, or is a convenient front for more common intuition and tricks of charlatanry. Any of these methods may also be combined into the clerical spell Divination, as a technique for focusing the mind of the cleric and the power of the god. (Both ***GURPS Magic*** and ***GURPS Grimoire*** contain ideas for other methods, as well.)

Astrology and Astronomy

The science of the stars, called *natural astrology* in more ancient times, was once used to predict natural celestial events such as eclipses and other meteorological phenomena. More recently, *astrology* has come to refer to the study of the movement of celestial bodies and their resultant effects upon the course of human life. This form of star-divination, also called *astromancy*, studies the configurations of the heavens at times of critical events and attempts to determine the outcome of future events. It become very popular in Rome at the beginning of the Christian Era, where astrologers were called "mathematicians" and Chaldeans.

Modern astrology commonly focuses upon the movements of the sun, moon and planets, as well as certain constellations. Based on the time of year and the hour of the day of birth, a precise "star chart" is compiled which locates each of the major celestial bodies and defines their relations to one another. The results form a unique pattern which, some believe, will influence the personality and life events of the individual. True believers will ensure that important events such as marriages and births occur at auspicious times.

Chaldean astrology believed in the concept of universal solidarity. The universe was, to them, a great organism governed by celestial deities. The events of their world were determined by relationships between these deities, echoed by the movements of the stars and planets. Still others saw the heavens as a whole other realm peopled with heroes and monsters whose actions echoed into our world. By studying their interrelations, insights could be gained into our future.

Continued on next page . . .

Consecrate *Enchantment*

The Enchantment spell for clerics. In its simplest form it purifies a given object, cleansing it with the deity's power. In combination with complex ritual preparations it allows the creation of Sacred Vessels, Holy Objects, and Objects of Power. Most religions will teach this spell to all invested clerics.

The spell may only be cast in areas of Very High Sanctity, though all costs will be computed as if it were cast in a place of Normal Sanctity, and the cleric will regain fatigue spent on this spell at normal rates.

Duration: All sacred objects are permanent until destroyed. Use of the Desecrate spell may render them temporarily unusable.

Cost: The simplest form of this spell (and the one used in the creation of Sacred Vessels) costs 10 points. For the making of Holy Objects the cost will vary with the effect desired.

This may be cast as an area spell to raise the sanctity of a given area or restore lost Sanctity after a desecration. Each casting raises the area's Sanctity by one level, to a possible maximum of High Sanctity – unless the area was previously of Very High Sanctity, in which case it may be once again be raised to that level. To create an area of Very High Sanctity, a successful request for Divine Intervention must be performed in tandem with the Consecrate spell.

Duration: Permanent as long as the deity remains active.

Cost: 10 for a single item; 100 per hex for an area.

Time to cast: This spell is always done as a ceremony. Minimum casting time is 5 minutes for a single item, or 1 hour per hex for an area.

Item: This spell may not be consecrated into an item.

Desecrate *Special*

Desecrates a consecrated object, rendering it impure and unclean. *None* of its magical effects will work until it has been repurified with the Consecrate spell. There is a 10% chance that a desecration will destroy the object. Objects of Power may never be desecrated.

May be cast as an area spell, to lessen the Sanctity rating of a given locale. Each casting reduces the area's Sanctity by one level, to a possible minimum of No Sanctity.

Duration: Lasts until repurification is done.

Cost: 10 for single item; 100 per hex for an area.

Divination (Continued)

To facilitate their studies, ancient astrologers built temples, monuments, and other strategically located edifices by which they measured the movements of the heavenly bodies. Stonehenge is believed by many to be the most famous example. These observations also helped them predict eclipses and other solar events, as well as a primitive ability to predict the weather.

Heptascopy

Heptascopy, or the art of divination through the study of animal livers, particular those of sheep, was common in Mesopotamia, and many other ancient cultures, including Rome. The liver was believed to be the seat of baser desires, separated from the intellect, and thus closer to the spiritual realm. Animals, in particular, were open to these influences, having simpler minds. Thus the patterns of future events could be found imprinted upon their livers. In humans, livers were thought to be the organ of consciousness and dreams.

Augury

Some philosophers believed that the world is an interconnected cosmos, and that indications of its current state could be found by studying patterns of nature. Simple things, such as ripples upon water, the flight path of bees, the songs of birds, the shape and movements of animals . . . each gave clues that a wise man could read. Much of what is now dismissed as superstition was once the keystone of the augerer's art – an owl's hoot, the path of a black cat, the meanings of sneezes are common examples.

People who became obsessed with such observations were often considered more than a little mad. But since madness was often associated with the divine, the ramblings of lunatics were given long consideration lest they conceal wisdom.

Tarot

Other forms of divination use well-known symbols chosen or laid out in seemingly random order to form patterns which the seer can study. One of the most common techniques is card reading, or tarot.

Continued on next page . . .

Time to cast: 1 minute for a single item, or 30 minutes per hex for an area.

Item: This spell may not be consecrated into an item.

Excommunicate — *Regular*

Excommunicates a single follower of a religion (see *Excommunication*, p. 117). This spell confers the Excommunicated disadvantage on the recipient and as such is never "rolled." If the deity deems the Excommunication just, then it occurs. Otherwise it does not. The cleric receives a clear sign of the outcome, and if successful, will brand the individual in some way that will be evident to all followers of the religion.

Revocation of an excommunication can be done only with a successful request for Divine Intervention.

Duration: Permanent, until revoked by another cleric of the same religion.

Cost: 15.

Time to cast: Minimum 10 minutes. This spell is always done as a ceremony.

Item: This spell may not be consecrated into an item.

Final Rest — *Regular*

Escorts the soul of a dead person into the presence of the deity. This assures that the soul will rest in peace, and may not be summoned, animated, or resurrected. It has no physical effect on the body. Commonly used for funeral rites.

This spell can be done at any time after the subject dies, though there is a cumulative -1 point penalty for each month that the person has been dead, up to a total of -10. Each caster may attempt the spell only once per subject.

This spell has absolutely no effect on a living person.

Duration: Permanent.

Cost: 20.

Time to cast: Minimum 10 minutes. This spell is always done as a ceremony.

Item: This spell may be consecrated into funerary regalia. Energy cost: 1,200.

Oath — *Regular*

Binds a willing subject to a promise. The caster speaks the spell, but the subject must speak the oath. This spell is used to bind vows in many religions, as well as being a respected means of bonding an agreement among followers of the deity. Actions taken to ensure that the terms of the oath remain unbroken are assured of the deity's favor (this may, at the GM's discretion, gain the subject +1 to all such skill rolls, as described for the *Blessed* advantage). Breaking the oath is a sure way of gaining the deity's *disfavor.*

In addition, if the oath is broken by conscious action of the swearer, he will immediately take 1d of damage for each 10 points of energy put into the casting of this spell.

Duration: The oath is permanent, unless specifically sworn for a limited duration.

Cost: Variable (see above).

Time to cast: Minimum 10 minutes. This spell is always done as a ceremony.

Item: The ability to cast this spell is commonly consecrated into Holy Objects of all sorts. Energy cost: 1,000.

Divination (Continued)

A tarot deck consists of 78 cards, divided into Minor and Major Arcana. The Minor Arcana is made of four suits – cups (water), wands (fire), pentacles (earth) and swords (air) – with cards for King, Queen, Knight, Page and the numbers 1 through 10 in each. Each numbered and face card has a particular association modified by the general meaning of each suit, to give it a divinatory meaning. The Major Arcana consists of 22 picture cards said to be derived from a book written by a councillor of Osiris, King of Egypt. These are the Fool, the Magician, the High Priestess, the Empress, the Emperor, the Hierophant, the Lovers, the Chariot, Strength, the Hermit, the Wheel of Fortune, Justice, the Hanged Man, Death, Temperance, the Devil, the Tower, the Star, the Moon, the Sun, Judgment, and the World. When laid out in patterns, the cards reflect states of the greater cosmos, giving the reader insight.

One of the more common spreads for divination is known as the Celtic Cross. The reader places a *significator*, a card representing the questioner (usually a face card or Major Arcana), in the center. Then while the questioner concentrates on his question, the reader shuffles the deck. The questioner then cuts the deck into three piles, from left to right, using his left hand. The reader gathers the cards and lays them out. He places a second card over the significator, representing that which surrounds the questioner. A third card crosses the other two, being that which provides impediment, obstacle or challenge. The next four are placed below, to the left, above, and to the right of the pile. They represent, in turn, the foundations of the question, the past, the present and the possible future. Finally, to the right, a line of four cards is made, one above the other. The first represents the questioner's fears, the second family or world opinion, the third his hopes, and the last the final outcome. Relationships between the cards are as important as which card falls in which position.

Summon Allied Entity — *Special*

Summons an available allied entity or demigod (see *Demigods*, p. 42) of the deity to perform a particular task. Availability and type of agent must be previously decided by the GM. If the spell is cast successfully, then the GM makes the availability roll. The more available a demigod is, the more power it takes to draw it into any particular service. Example entities could be animalistic, like wolves or birds with preternatural intelligence and power, elementals, or something as unearthly as an angel, ghost, or demon.

Once summoned, the allied entity will obey a single command. Usually these commands are given in the form of ceremonial rituals, often preordained by the deity. In some cases an allied entity may *only* perform those tasks previously arranged by the deity. In any case, the cleric must make a Performance/Ritual roll to bind the entity to the task – if the roll fails, then the entity appears, but is not enticed into staying.

Typical tasks for these entities might be to deliver retribution against an enemy of the church, to guard a place or object of religious import, or to guide the cleric toward an important bit of wisdom.

If allied entities appear without being summoned, they have been sent by the god. Their purpose may or may not be known by the cleric, who can in no way alter it.

Allied entities will generally not harm a cleric of the deity. If angered they will simply leave. There are exceptions, however, especially in religions with maltheistic or uncaring deities.

Duration: Until the task is complete.

Cost: Depends on the availability of the entity. If the entity will appear only on a roll of 6 or less, the cost of the spell is 15; if it will appear on a roll of 9 or less, it costs 20; on a roll of 12 or less, it costs 25; and if the entity will appear on a roll of 15 or less, the spell costs 30 points.

Time to cast: Minimum 5 minutes. This spell is always done as a ceremony.

Item: This spell may be consecrated into an item for 100 times the base cost.

Magical Clerics

It is also possible that there is truly *no* difference between magicians and clerics. In a "rational" cosmology where deities do not exist, religions might be little more than clever facades propagated by magicians for their own edification. In this system, religion and beliefs are made up by the founding magicians out of whole cloth. "Clerics" would be taught "rituals" which were nothing more than the incantations any mage might make to engender the same effect. Thus, the rules for such magics would differ in no way from those presented in ***GURPS Magic.***

It is also quite likely that those who promulgate such a system would fiercely hunt any who practice "foul" and "perverted" magics, as they would not want it known that their powers come from one and the same source. As the generations pass, it is even possible that the initial foundations of the church might be forgotten, until even the highest of "clerics" are unaware that the rituals they undertake call upon no gods at all, but rather draw upon the essential manas of the world.

Alternatively, the presiding religion might believe that magic ability is a true gift of the gods, and press those with such talents to join the church. In this case it might have no prejudice against "wild" mages, though it will probably always encourage them to recognize their true calling to serve the gods.

Divine Intervention

Divine Intervention is a plea to the deity for direct intervention in the affairs of the world. The plea must come in the form of a specific request which the deity interprets. A cleric may ask for anything at all, but it must be in the best interest of the deity, and the faith as a whole, and in all cases the request will be interpreted conservatively. Clerics who request such intervention for trivial matters will earn their deity's instant disfavor, and risk more dramatic action.

Divine Intervention costs character points. The cleric declares how many points he will spend (at least 3 points must be spent to have any possibility of effect). These points are spent whether the Intervention is granted or not. If the cleric does not currently have the points available, then he must instantly accept a new Disadvantage (chosen by the cleric, but approved by the deity, or GM) to offset the cost of the call. He will continue to suffer from this Disadvantage (most often a new vow of some sort) until he buys it off in the usual manner. The GM then secretly rolls 3 dice. If the result is less than or equal to the number of points spent, and the cleric has remained true to the precepts of his faith, then the Intervention will be granted.

If the Intervention is a critical success (roll of 3 or 4), the request is granted in an immediate, "miraculous" way, obvious to all who see it. If it is a standard success, then the request will be granted in a way convenient to the deity. There may be no immediate effect, and when it does occur, it may not even be obvious that it was an act of the deity. If the Intervention roll is an 18, the Intervention will work, but the cleric is immediately drawn into service by the deity as payment for the call. In other words – he dies. This death should be related in some way to the request being answered; the cleric will not just drop dead.

When interpreting the effects of a successful Divine Intervention, the GM must take into account the circumstance, the exact wording of the cleric's request, and the nature and temperament of the deity. Given the potential cost, a Divine Intervention should never be futile or used for comic effect (though certainly it may have certain comical aspects). But neither should a single Divine Intervention be used to destroy entire nations. Remember, also, that a deity cannot act outside of its own particular spheres of influence. A goddess of healing and mercy would refuse to kill a hated enemy, and a god of fire cannot make it rain.

In addition to answering specific requests, Divine Interventions create Objects of Power (see p. 107) and Areas of High Sanctity (see p. 102).

Miraculous Magic

Clerics can request the favor of their patron deity to perform "miracles." The effects of their appeal depend entirely upon the interest and whim of the god. These effects are not at all predictable, and often impossible to recreate.

This sort of divine magic is particularly applicable to meddlesome deities who find it easy to manifest powers, and who like to interest themselves in the day-to-day lives of their followers.

False Prophets

In a world where magic can easily duplicate miracles, it is possible that a charlatan might attempt to impersonate a cleric, or even start a new religion.

As long as the false cleric keeps his facts straight and tosses out a "miracle" or two, he might make a very good living for himself – unless the deity is offended and decides to do something about it, that is! In a game world where the deities are both active and real, the imposter must be *very* certain of his scheme before starting.

Runic Powers

Rather than manifesting directly, the power of a deity can be represented by symbols or *runes*. Clerics may use runes to focus and manipulate the abstract will of the god into particular invocations of power. This sort of magic is particularly appropriate for abstract forces, or deities who are normally indifferent or oblivious to the desires of their followers.

The rules on Rune Magic contained in ***GURPS Magic*** (see pp. M90-93) will work as well for divinely-inspired castings as magically-empowered ones.

Special Advantages

Divine Favor

An individual with the Divine Favor advantage (see p. 93) is called a Holy Person. This person has the ability to petition his deity for a miracle with some chance of being heard!

To determine whether a particular miracle will occur, the GM rolls against the Frequency of Appearance number to see if the god hears the plea. If the Holy Person has the deity's attention, the GM then rolls on the NPC Reaction Table, Requests for Aid (pp. B204-205), to see if the miracle is performed. Reaction bonuses specified as a part of the Divine Favor advantage modify this roll.

Miracles

Miracles are small, personalized instances of Divine Intervention. In most cases, these interventions will center about a Holy Person. Miracles can take several forms, depending on the degree of favor, and the deity's preferred mode of intervention. They can be subtle or blatant. They can appear coincidental, or be marked by omens, prophecy, or visions.

A miraculous effect can be played as a straight spell, though no skill roll, fatigue cost, or casting time is necessary. The GM has a lot of leeway. Suppose, for example, that the god chooses to put a 10-die Explosive Fireball in his supplicant's hand. Will the PC have to roll vs. IQ to realize what that glowing red ball is? Or will the deity supply the knowledge, and maybe even a temporary boost in Throwing skill?

Requests for Aid

Holy Persons may call on the power of their god for help. The GM may adjudicate the effects of the request by pure fiat, or using the following guidelines.

To see if the god notices the petition, the GM rolls against the god's Frequency of Appearance (as given in the Divine Favor advantage), modified by:

Interest of the god in the goal furthered by the character's action: up to +5.

Appropriateness of the expected miracle to the god's sphere of influence: from -10 to 0. (Requesting a fireball from Agni, the Hindu god of fire, is at 0. Requesting a flood is at -10.)

Once the god is listening to the petition, the GM rolls against the NPC Reaction Table, checking under the Requests for Aid section (see pp. B204-205). He adjusts this roll by the reaction modifiers in the Holy Person's Divine Favor advantage, and by:

Number of times the god has been called upon since the beginning of the adventure: -1 for each time.

Esteem of the PC in his god's eyes, based on recent behavior and achievements: from -5 to +5.

Consult the Reaction Table to see whether or not the miracle occurs.

The PC may improve the chance of a successful miracle by sacrifice. He may sacrifice character points, either by taking on a Vow or Duty or some other "instant" Disadvantage, or by forfeiting unspent points. Material sacrifices translate into character points at the rate of one point per month of character job earnings (see the sidebar on p. B16). The GM adds the number of character points sacrificed to the reaction roll. The points are spent whether the miracle is successful or not.

Other factors may intervene. In the Greek pantheon, for example, it was not uncommon for two gods to oppose each other's intervention; thus even if the PC's god is very inclined to grant aid, some other god may prevent it. In other words, the GM is free to ignore the dice.

Luck cannot be applied to the roll. The gods are powers too lofty to be subject to that! Also note that the supplicant's success roll does not depend on his ranking in the church or his IQ. Rank within the temple might be held solely because of one's Diplomacy, Administration or Politics skills. Neither do any of the petitioner's attributes modify the die roll. All are equal in a god's eyes; if the GM wants some characters to be "more blessed" than others, he may do so by increasing their points in the Divine Favor advantage.

Divine Whim

Alternatively, miracles can just occur. They might go completely unnoticed, or be accompanied by omens, visions, or other signs – this is completely up to the GM.

Sacred Objects

In a system of miraculous magic, sacred objects are created completely and solely by the god. A Holy Person may request that an object be made, but positive results are unlikely. Most often such objects are simply given to favored individuals at the wish of the deity.

Sacred objects may be treated like magical items that can cast one or more spells particular to the god. They aren't *really* magical items – out of the cleric's hands, they are perfectly ordinary items – but when wielded by one with true divine favor, they behave like magical items.

Relics

Bones and other relics of those with the Divine Favor advantage are often thought to interest the deity even after the individual's death. Remains of such Holy Persons are gathered into reliquaries and used in invocations of the deity's power. The GM can decide how real this power is, and whether the artifacts have a chance of gaining further miracles from the god.

Runic Divination

Runic inscriptions and castings are a way of invoking the power invested within the runes to a set purpose or task. Alternatively, the power inherent in the symbols can reflect the current state of the world, answering questions important to the cleric.

Runes used for this purpose must be specially prepared, and then destroyed afterward, for the reading to have any true meaning. The patterns that lead to the proper answers are instilled in the making as much as in the actual reading itself. Since an entire alphabet must be created, each divination is a major undertaking. The exact response or effect of the divination is, of course, completely up to the GM. In most cases, it should contain some real information veiled in ways that are not necessarily immediately evident to the characters.

Two different methods of runic divination are described below.

Rune Wands

Divination by rune wands is the most common traditional method. It is also the most time-consuming, but when done properly, it yields the best results.

The period of preparation is nine days and nights. During this time the cleric undergoes moderate fasting and ritual purification to focus his mind on the question. On the morning of the 10th day, the cleric goes to a nearby wood and selects a tree – oak, apple, cherry, and chestnut are the most advantageous. At the moment of sunrise, he strikes off a branch with a knife that has been sprinkled with water and exposed to open flame, and then offered in prayer to the service of the rune gods. Using the same knife, the cleric then makes a cut in the palm of his right hand and applies it to the tree stump – sacrifice given for the taking of the branch. The branch is then cut into wands, a single wand for each rune in the alphabet. Then the runes are inscribed (check against the cleric's skill with the rune if using Rune Magic, p. M90), one per wand, while the cleric meditates upon the meaning of each. The runes are then stained with the cleric's own blood.

Continued on next page . . .

Runic Divination (Continued)

Once the wands are prepared, the actual divination can occur. First a clean cloth is laid out upon the ground, symbolizing a holy altar. The wands are gathered into one hand, and the hand held out over the cloth. Ritual gestures are appropriate here, as well as prayer to the gods for a true divination. In game terms, the cleric casts the Divination spell (or Activate Runes, if Rune Magic is used; see p. M92), and then lets the wands fall so that they scatter all over the cloth. With his eyes closed, he then chooses three wands at random.

The runes are read in the order of selection. The first represents past, or the circumstances that gave rise to the question. The second gives insight into the current situation. The third indicates the course of future events, or comments upon the potential outcome.

Rune Cards

Rune cards are made by applying each rune to a single card, usually made from cardboard or some other sturdy paper-like substance. Each rune is inscribed (using the skill for the rune if Rune Magic is used, see p. M90), and then the card is varnished. Once completed, the cards are prayed over, and a Consecrate spell is cast.

Rune cards are read much like the tarot. The questioner holds the cards while concentrating on his question. Then the cleric takes the deck, shuffles it thoroughly and lays the cards out in a spread. This is the ritual of casting the Divination spell (or Activate Runes if Rune Magic is used; see p. M92).

The simplest spread is a run of three, exactly like that used in the Rune Wand reading. The first card represents the past, the second the present, and the third the future. Reversed cards have negative interpretations.

A more in-depth reading may be done by using a more complicated spread. The *Five Elements* spread is another one commonly used. Here five cards are laid out, the first four in a square cross, with the vertical arm from top to bottom laid first, and then the horizontal from left to right. The fifth card goes in the center. The first card (top, center) represents the intellect, and marks the element of air. The second card (bottom, center) is desire and marks the element of fire. The third card (left) is strength and marks the element of earth. The fourth card (right) is love, and marks the element of water. The fifth card is balance; from it the others are born and to it they return. With this spread, a detailed analysis of the life and character of a person can be obtained.

Shamanism

Clerics communicate with spirits of this and other realms, which grant them visions of the past, present and future, and the ability to command, entrap and banish their spiritual allies. Such manipulations bring great potential dangers for the cleric and those associated with him, and often have unpredictable results.

Shamanistic magic is only appropriate for a cosmos inhabited by meddlesome spirits who interfere frequently with the daily affairs of people. Major deities may exist, but they are either unable or unwilling to grant such power to their followers. Shamanism is a lower-powered, less-predictable version of divine magics than the others discussed in this chapter.

World View

The shaman is commonly found in tribal or totemic cultures having a strong spiritualistic worldview. Their world is one filled with spirits of varying natures – from the helpful to the malign, each having its own particular place and function. Shamans do not gain their powers directly from the divine, (except, perhaps, for the original gift of the ability that grants them their power – the *World Sight,*below). Rather they are born marked, or gifted, with a special talent that manifests itself around the time of puberty, frequently in the form of an illness or near-death experience.

One should not assume, however, that shamans and their associated worldview can only exist in primitive or tribal societies. Modern-day channeling and attempts to rediscover past-life experiences borrow a lot from the shamanistic worldview and methodology. Trancing techniques are used by many "New Age" religions. It is quite possible to envision a future where experimentation with the mind has lead to the rediscovery of the spiritualistic worldview, and provided new techniques for people to reach beyond this world into a different plane of existence.

World Sight

A shaman is one with the ability to voluntarily enter into a state of ecstasy from which he can enter the domain of gods and spirits. This advantage is called World Sight (see p. 94). Using this ability, the shaman can interact freely with all sorts of spirits, perform acts of diagnosis and healing, determine future events, initiate spirit-related attacks, escort the souls of the dead to their proper resting place, and so forth.

Each use of the World Sight ability is ritualistic in nature, requiring the shaman to voluntarily enter an ecstatic trance state and link with the spiritual entities that aid him in his tasks. Often a shaman will have one or more particular spirits which will accompany him time and time again. At times these spirits may possess his body, using him as a mouthpiece or agent in their works. But it is the shaman who controls the interaction with the spirits. It is his willing sacrifice which allows the spirits to enter his body, and it is at his behest that they leave.

Spirits

Spirits are disembodied creatures made up entirely of mana. As such, they have numerous powers, the magnitude of which varies greatly from spirit to spirit. Spirits have IQ and ST attributes which determine their relative intelligence, Will and Fatigue. Most have the ability to possess the bodies of living persons, thereby gaining the HT and DX attributes of the body, while retaining their own IQ and ST. They are generally willful and capricious creatures, but a shaman can bargain with them on an individual basis. They are usually quite loyal to those who aid them.

Shamans have limited means of controlling or befriending spirits. He can then consult these spirits for information, or ask them to aid in some other way. Powerful evil spirits are called demons.

Spirit Combat

Spirit combat is a Contest of Will between the spirit and the shaman. If the spirit wins, it may either choose to possess the shaman, or escape his immediate area. If the shaman wins, the spirit must perform one task (of limited duration, subject to the GM's approval) for the shaman – usually this will be to divulge some bit of information, or to remove itself from the vicinity.

Once beaten, the spirit will be respectful toward the shaman, and is unlikely to initiate such combat again.

Excommunication

The expulsion of a believer from a religious fellowship or church is called excommunication. This rite is done only under the most dire circumstances. Its intent, however, is not to exile the sinner permanently, but to bring about his repentance. Most excommunications are decreed after a *Canon* trial.

Canon law regulates the internal workings of a religious organization. It is a set of rules regarding worship, sacraments and other matters of religious living. An excommunicant is forbidden to participate in (or receive benefit from) holy rites and ceremonies – in effect, he is cut off from his god. No longer will a priest intercede in his behalf. In game terms, an excommunicant PC will not benefit from any clerical magic.

Any high-ranking cleric can perform the rite of excommunication. In magical religions, this takes the form of a spell. If it succeeds, then the god approves. A ban of excommunication can only be lifted by divine intervention. It is possible that the church may *still* consider the offender officially excommunicated even if the spell did not work. In such a case, should the PC find a cleric willing to disobey a superior, the PC could still benefit from divine magic.

Excommunication can be a dangerous tool. Historically, fear of excommunication has been one of the Roman Catholic Church's most potent political weapons. Often if a noble or royal personage was excommunicated the ban extended to his vassals. Pressure from fearful peasants who were denied the sacraments of the church would often cause a noble to back down, or at least to pretend repentance.

This can backfire, however, if it is aimed at an overly powerful person. Henry VIII of England ignored the ban of excommunication that the Pope placed on him and went on to create his own church – the Church of England – with himself as its spiritual and temporal head.

The Cost of Favor

In the worldview of *Miraculous Magic*, the recipient of Divine Favor need not be a cleric or associated with the official religion in any way. He may be born to a particular purpose or task that the god desires (and will, no doubt, inform him of, somewhere along the line). He may have a simple affinity for the power of the divine, or have performed some action that attracts the interest and favor of the deity. It is possible that the person does not even "believe" in the deity, though this will likely change quite quickly.

Holy People can fill many different roles. They can be wise elders, or young miracle workers who capture the imagination of all who see them. They can be prophets, saviors, or simple folk with a talent or calling. They should be quite rare. PCs with this advantage may find they have a duty or obligation to the deity that has little to do with clerical rank or responsibility. It may even be that the individual is fated to "correct" a corrupt or misguided church.

The GM must also decide how much direct contact the Holy Person has with the deity who favors him. The deity might speak to him silently, when he is alone, providing guidance or plans. It may simply ensure that the individual "knows" what is right and/or wrong. Or the deity might send divine messengers to deliver instructions. Alternatively, the deity might not speak to the person at all, responding in terms of "miracles," with the assumption that the Holy Person will figure out how to make the best use of that which is given.

Given the dangers of spirit combat, most shamans prefer to use spells to deal with spirits (see pp. 122-125). However, an unprepared shaman may find spirit combat an acceptable means of improvisation.

People without the World Sight advantage may be possessed through spirit combat. Should they happen to win, they accomplish nothing, but avoid an unhappy fate.

Possession

A possessed individual is subject to the whim of the possessing spirit. The spirit will probably control the person a great deal of the time, only granting control to the usual personality when the spirit is fatigued or feels threatened in some way. The person will have no idea what is occurring, and will most likely be quite disoriented by the lapses of time when the spirit is in control. Most possessing spirits are malicious, and will force the victim to act in violent and degrading ways. Once the spirit is banished, the usual personality will reassert control.

Those with the World Sight advantage are particularly likely targets for such attacks. Such a person with no training may get his first clue about the nature of the spirit world by surviving a demon's attack!

Shamanistic Methods

Trancing

The trance is the shaman's primary method of contacting the spirit world. Most shamanistic spells can only be cast while in a trace state, and trancing is an important method of gathering information. While in the trance state, a shaman can see spirits that are normally invisible to humans. He may travel to other realms and places. He may also see visions of animals, people and places – even ones he has never seen in waking life. The interpretation of these visions provides the shaman with information. Correct interpretation is aided by a successful roll against his Theology skill, with whatever modifiers the GM thinks appropriate.

Note: Trance visions are not intended to replace the Divination spell. Unlike the spell, visions may bear no relation to the questions or problems of the tranced person. These visions are primarily a method by which the GM can offer information to the characters, or a desperate long shot for a shaman who is completely stumped during the course of an adventure. Shamans usually have more reliable means of getting information.

For game purposes, the trance is treated as an extended period of concentration. The depth of the trance (the shaman's awareness of his surroundings, and the ease with which the trance can be broken) as well as the length of the trance, depend on the method used.

Meditation: The simplest way to enter a trance is through use of the Meditation skill (see p. 97). The shaman secludes himself and concentrates. He may use chanting or breathing exercises to enhance his concentration, or have an assistant beat a drum. On a successful roll, the shaman will achieve a trance in about 10 minutes, and can maintain it as long as he wishes. The advantage of this method is that the shaman remains aware of his surroundings. The disadvantage is that the trance is easy to disturb. Any loud noise or physical contact outside of the usual trancing ritual will break the trance unless the shaman makes a Will-3 roll (see pp. B93 and B148). If he is injured, an additional -1 is added for every hit taken! Once the trance is broken, the shaman must begin again.

Shamans with the Autotrance advantage (see p. 93) may enter a trance whenever they desire on a successful IQ roll, though they will find it more difficult to break away from. Distractions only affect them on a failed Will roll (though modifiers for injuries taken still apply), and they must make another successful IQ roll to awaken.

Hallucinogens: Another common way of reaching the trance state is through the ingestion of hallucinogenic drugs, usually made from plants. The trance will begin within a short period, determined by the strength of the drug and how it is taken (see *Herbalism,* below). In any case, less than half an hour is required, during which time the shaman is fully alert. When the drug takes effect, however, the shaman is only vaguely aware of what is happening around him. Duration and other details vary with the drug being used. It is the drug, however, not the shaman, which controls the length of the trance, and a recovery period is almost always necessary once the drug wears off. This method of trancing provides the most numerous and vivid visions, but is limited by the availability of the hallucinogen and the skill to prepare it for use.

Fasting and Sleep Deprivation: The shaman forgoes all food, water and sleep until physical exhaustion brings on the trance and its visions. The theory is that by denying physical needs, one's soul is freed to leave the body and enter the spirit world. It will require 24-48 hours for this method to work, and the trance which ensues is very deep. The trance will last until the shaman is brought out of it by someone else, or he becomes unconscious from fatigue. Only extreme pain or the administration of an herbal stimulant will bring the shaman out of it, and only on a successful roll vs. HT-3. When the trance has ended, the shaman will be unconscious for 2d×6 hours, and will have a ST of 1 upon awakening. The problem with this method is that it saps the shaman's strength for spellcasting. The advantage is that no special training or drug is necessary, making it the most common method for training new shamans.

Gifts of the Gods

In some worlds, the gods might choose to grant each individual person gifts or abilities which indicate divine favor, rather than granting their power only to those who choose to serve them. These gifts might be in addition to those given to their clerics, often marking a person as being particularly holy or blessed. Or they might be the sole way in which the deity directly grants powers to a person.

Generally it is thought that these people are special and holy to whatever deity is responsible for the gift (usually easily discerned by the nature of the gift itself). Often they will be marked for the service of the deity from a young age, whether they will it or not! In those cases where the only manifestation of the deity's power is through these gifts, a religion's clerics might be chosen only from those who manifest the gifts. However, it is more likely that a fundamental core of clerics without the gifts will support the day-to-day workings of the church, while those *with* the gifts work on those tasks directly applicable to their gift. In some cases, those so gifted will be fated to perform certain functions or tasks for the deity, with the rest existing so that the fated one will have the time and ability to do what is needed.

It is even possible that such gifts are *not* divinely inspired, but are viewed as being such by the local church. Alternatively, the "gifts" might be seen as curses, marking a particular person as being foul or unclean, aligned with some malign force.

There are generally three different types of gifts that can be given: Psionics (as described in the ***GURPS Basic Set***, ***GURPS Psionics***, or ***GURPS Supers***), Magical Knacks (p. M96), and Blessings (see p. 93). Whichever the case, in order to be considered the gift of the divine, the powers and abilities must be in line with the nature of the deity in question. It is also possible that these gifts might be hereditary, the result of a bloodline considered particularly holy or divine. In this case all members of the family would be naturally accepted into the priesthood as a matter of course. Indeed, they might be the only ones *allowed* in.

GMing Shamanism

When GMing the shamanistic worldview, the GM will often be called upon to improvise, describing visions of spirits and the spirit world. Shamans may interact with these spirits to achieve things impossible for normal men. Good players will come up with unexpected uses for the spells listed, and ideas for new spells.

A GM is not required, however, to use the magic system just because he wants to have shamanism in his campaign. With only one or two exceptions, the spells listed are of an inherently ambiguous nature. The characters could conceivably use them without ever knowing if they really work. The GM need merely make all the die rolls in secret, and then tell the players what their characters perceive. They need not know if the vision was real or simply a hallucination brought on by exhaustion. Similarly, a player won't know for sure if his character is blessed, since he won't be certain that that arrow should have hit him in the heart, and not the arm. But the *characters* will probably believe without question that magic works and spirits exist.

Herbalism

Hallucinogens are not the only herbs used by shamans in their arts. Stimulants and plants with medicinal value also constitute a major portion of the shaman's craft. Many shamans will have the Herbary skill. Medicinal herbs are useful in curing, and a shaman will usually try them before resorting to magic. Also, certain herbs are believed to drive off evil spirits – wolfsbane and garlic, for example. Finally, some herbs have spiritual power, making them useful in spellcasting and other shamanistic rituals.

Performance Skills

In performing his magics, the shaman has two potential audiences: the people who seek his aid in one form or another, and the spirits with whom he must communicate.

Spirits: The spirits may require him to "perform" for their amusement before they will aid him. Friendly spirits may be drawn by the beat of the drum or other rhythmic signal, while evil spirits may be frightened away by shrieking and threatening gestures. Every shamanistic spell will have associated gestures, chants and motions designed to intrigue and involve those of the spirit world. Spirits are willful at best, and the heart of the shaman's technique lies in his ability to communicate and deal with them. Often this is much like dealing with recalcitrant children, and should be roleplayed accordingly.

Onlookers: Because of the often capricious and unpredictable nature of shamanistic magics, shamans must become masters of performance. Often he alone can see the spirits he speaks to and combats, so his reputation may depend more upon his ability to make his arts believable than the true strength of his magic. Virtually every successful shaman has some skill in the art of performing. Acting, Sleight of Hand, and Ventriloquism skills are all very useful to a shaman who must practice in the public eye.

Disease: Diagnosis and Treatment

In most shamanistic beliefs, disease can be brought on by a number of factors, from the action of evil spirits to a taboo violation or crime committed by the sick individual. The shaman's job is to discover the true cause and set about finding a cure.

The Aura spell is used for this purpose. Taboo violation might manifest itself as a dimming or staining of the person's aura, and the shaman may be able to sense feelings of guilt. A disease caused by a foreign object might cause a spot or spots indicating points of entry. A person who is possessed will have two distinct auras: his own and that of his possessor. And a person whose soul has been stolen will have no aura at all! The most common treatments are listed, by cause, below:

Physical Injury: The shaman uses the Herbary skill, First Aid, and the Healing spell. The rest is left to fate.

Taboo Violation: The shaman uses Divination to discover the incident which provoked the disease. The situation is then corrected by a cleansing ceremony, sometimes led by the shaman, and often involving the confession of the patient.

Object Intrusion: If an object of evil origin is causing the disease, the Cleanse spell is employed to effect a complete cure.

Soul Loss: The shaman uses the Summon Spirit spell to retrieve the patient's soul from wherever it has gone. The soul resists with its own IQ, or, if it was stolen, the spell is resisted by the stealing spirit.

Possession: The shaman casts Exorcism to oust the possessing spirit from the patient's body. Then, if successful, the shaman must use the Spirit Trap spell to capture the spirit. If this second casting is not performed (or is not successful), the spirit will almost immediately attempt to possess someone else, perhaps even the shaman himself!

Psychopomp

Another important job of the shaman is to serve as escort to the souls of the dead. This assures that they will not return as malevolent spirits to haunt him or his family. This journey is often quite long and dangerous for the shaman, since he must first enter and then leave the realm of the dead.

Each journey requires the shaman to enter a trance state in which he seeks the soul of the dead individual and sends it on its way. To return, he must successfully make a HT roll. External factors such as herbal stimulants and repeated drum beats and chants which call the shaman back may modify this roll at the GM's discretion.

Initiation

A shaman's initiation is the time of his first true trance, heralding his first true journey into the spirit realm. It may be the result of long training, or accidental circumstance uncovering a gift hitherto unknown. The initiation trance is almost always quite long and usually involves a near-death experience in which the would-be shaman explores and returns from the land of the dead. Sleep deprivation and fasting are the most common trance inducers for initiation ceremonies. Various other rituals may also be required, such as the imbibing of hallucinogens or stimulants, and scarification.

Visions seen during the initiation trance are often considered prophetic for the shaman, indicating future aspects of his life. Death visions are not uncommon.

No spells may be cast during the initiation trance.

Magic Items

Magic items in shamanistic magic have inherent spiritual power, affecting anyone who uses or touches them. Such items are very rare, and always natural in origin, though they may have been reshaped by human hands. The GM should be very sparing in introducing such objects. A shaman gets an automatic roll vs. IQ+2 to realize an item is magical when he first sees it, and again when he first touches it.

There are three common effects for shamanistic magic items:

Bless: confers a blessing on the possessor. This effect may be specialized. For example, a magic spear point made from the fang of a sabertooth tiger killed in battle might provide a +1 to skill when attacking herd animals only. The spiritual nature of the tiger defines and limits the item's effect.

Curse: The item is imbued with a spiritual force hostile to humans, and to touch it or have it in one's possession will result in being cursed as with the spell. The power of the curse is left up to the discretion of the GM.

Power: The object is a repository of spiritual power. These are very rare and of no use to anyone but shamans. In order to draw upon this power, the shaman must touch the object while casting the spell. If his spell skill roll succeeds, the item provides 1 or more energy points of the spell's cost – exactly how much is determined by the GM. Should the roll fail, the caster absorbs all

Shamanistic Accoutrements

The dress and accompanying props of a shaman often have as much symbolism and meaning as the ritual he performs. The costume indicates not only a sacred presence, but incorporates symbols which constitute the shaman's view of the cosmos in which he travels.

Clothing is particularly important. Shamanistic ritual is never done in ordinary, everyday clothing, no matter what that might be. Some strip naked for the ritual, using body paint or tattooing to express the necessary symbology, while others don elaborate costumes. It may be as simple as a band worn about the head, a particular combination of jewelry, or a cap sewn with feathers or other important totemistic elements.

Masks are a common element, often frightening in aspect so that they might better warn off malicious spirits. During psychopomp rituals, the shaman may cover his face with animal fat to give himself an aspect of death.

Symbols of flight are also quite common, whether they be feathers, full wings, or artistic recreations of birds, representing the flight of the soul from the body as it travels to other realms.

Mirrors are sometimes incorporated to help the shaman view the world better, or to reflect the needs of mankind in their depths. Mirrors are thought by some to be the repository of the soul, and thus indispensable to the workings of the shaman.

Drums are another common accoutrement whose meaning varies. Some find their methodical beating necessary to enter the trance state. Others use them as a beacon or a summons, to draw the spirit world closer so that they may enter it. Still others use it as a link to the "real" world, providing a path for their return. The making of the drum is often a ritual in and of itself, the materials used having symbolic meaning to the shaman and the tribe, providing a stronger link with the spirit world. Some trances begin with the shaman narrating the history of the drum, even to the component elements – a drum made of deer bone, for instance, may incorporate the spirit of the animal.

energy loss; a critical failure will result in a disastrous backfire in which the object is either destroyed or Cursed (as above).

Spells

Shamanistic spells are a combination of Performance/Ritual and magical ability. Use the rules in the ***Basic Set***, Chapter 19, for spellcasting, with the final skill level being the lower of the shaman's ability with the spell and his Performance/Ritual skill.

Shamanistic spells require the shaman to enter a trance state unless explicitly stated otherwise. Shamanistic spells generally take longer to cast than their "standard" counterparts, though they have fewer (or no) prerequisites and often require less energy. Shamanistic spells may only be learned by those with the World Sight advantage (see p. 94).

Aura — *Information*

Same as the magic spell (see p. M53). Additionally determines whether the subject has the World Sight advantage (or any other divine magic special advantage that the caster is familiar with).

This spell does not require the caster to be in a trance state.

Cost: 3 (for any size subject).

Time to cast: 3 seconds.

Banish — *Regular; Resisted by Spirit's ST+IQ*

Will send any spirit or soul back to the spirit world. To succeed, the caster must win a contest between his IQ + spell skill vs. the ST + IQ of the spirit. Add or subtract any modifiers for the caster's Strong or Weak Will. If the spirit loses, it immediately disappears, and must stay in the spirit world for one year. This spell may only be cast in the "real" world; the caster cannot banish a spirit from the spirit realm, though he may *be* banished from there by an unhappy spirit.

Epilepsy

In most primitive cultures, epilepsy and other disorders which cause seizures are given considerable significance. Often, a person suffering from such a malady is thought to be possessed by demons, in communication with the gods, or to have some special power. Seizures occur when the person is in conflict with a spirit, or when his soul has entered the spirit world. Thus, epileptics may be regarded with a substantial amount of fear or respect – or both.

For game purposes (if the GM wants to incorporate epilepsy into shamanism in his world) an epileptic seizure should be considered an *involuntary* trance. It will come on suddenly, and last from a few minutes to as long as half an hour. The person can also induce the seizure deliberately (for details, see *Epilepsy,* p. B28). He will be completely unaware of his surroundings, and *nothing* will bring him out of the trance early. He will, however, be completely able to see and act in the spirit world. This means that he can use any spell which can be cast in a trance state – if he knows it and has the time – and may see spectacular visions.

Upon coming out of the trance, he will suffer 1 die of fatigue damage, which can be recovered normally. This can be dangerous if the shaman used energy to cast spells during the seizure; if he does not have enough ST left to absorb the fatigue damage, he will lose HT as well!

Should the shaman have a seizure – either deliberately or involuntarily – in the presence of persons who do not know him, the following reaction modifiers apply:

+1 if they already knew he was a shaman and that didn't bother them. Now they know he's for real.

-1 if the viewers have seen seizures before, but didn't know he was a shaman; they don't trust him.

-3 if the viewers have never seen seizures *and* didn't know that he was a shaman. On a poor reaction they will flee, but not attack – it's best not to get involved where demons are concerned!

This spell does not work against undead or any spirit currently inhabiting a corporeal form.

Cost: The spirit's ST + IQ divided by 3. In most cases the caster will not know how much energy the spell will require, and may fall unconscious or even injure himself casting it.

Time to cast: 10 minutes.

Prerequisites: Summon Spirit and IQ 13+.

Bless — *Regular*

As with the magic spell (see p. M62).

Cost: 8.

Time to cast: 1 hour.

Cleanse — *Regular*

This spell cures any disease caused by an object implanted with the Pestilence spell. The caster can remove the object without making any incisions, usually by sucking. If the spell is cast successfully, the disease is completely cured – assuming such an object was the cause.

Cost: 8.

Time to cast: 2 hours.

Prerequisite: Healing.

Control Weather — *Regular*

Allows the shaman to make a slight change in the local weather patterns. He may request one single effect: cloud cover, rain, snow, windstorm, etc. The result is completely up to the GM's discretion, depending upon the oddity of the effect (rain in a desert is a lot harder than snow in the mountains). The change in weather is not instantaneous, but rather a gradual change that will take its course. Once cast, it is virtually impossible to stop. Successive attempts to change the weather within the same month are rolled at -3 for the first, -6 for the second, and so on.

Cost: 10.

Time to cast: 8 hours.

Curse — *Regular*

As with the magic spell (see p. M63).

Cost: 3.

Time to cast: 2 seconds.

Death Vision — *Regular*

As with the magic spell (see p. M72).

Cost: 2.

Time to cast: 15 minutes.

Divination — *Information*

As with the magic spell (see p. M55).

Cost: 8.

Charlatanry and the Shaman

Not everyone who claims to be a shaman has magical powers. In fact, a GM might decide that shamans *cannot* use magic, and that all their "casting" and trances are an act. If this is the case, the performance skills are vital to the shaman. He gives elaborate performances for the sake of his audiences, who *believe* that the spells really work.

Just because shamans don't actually have magical power doesn't mean that they are ineffective. Most anthropologists consider shamans to be primitive psychotherapists. Many of the "diseases" which shamans of modern hunter/gatherer tribes cure do not exist as far as modern medical science is concerned. They are thought to be purely psychosomatic, resulting from the belief on the victim's part that he is possessed, or has sinned, or is under spiritual attack. Since the victim also believes that the shaman has the power to cure him, the cures actually work. Furthermore, all the modern medical techniques in the world would be worse than useless against this sort of problem. The victim must *believe* in the cure.

Shamans may themselves believe that their powers are real, or they may simply consider themselves more intelligent and less ignorant than their fellows. Either way, the cures usually work.

Even if magic really does exist in the game world, there will still be fakes. These individuals must be talented to survive, and their performing secrets will be closely guarded. They will be very careful about choosing cases, accepting only those patients who are likely to recover anyway. Such a person will never be without a ready excuse for failure – "He has violated a taboo and not told me about it," or "The evil thoughts of someone here are preventing the spell from working." If worse comes to worst, a true charlatan can always rely on humility – "I do not know if my meager powers are great enough to drive out such strong evil!"

Time to cast: 1 hour.

Prerequisites: Death Vision, Summon Spirit.

Exorcism — *Regular; Resisted by possessing spirit's IQ*

Drives out any spirits foreign to the subject, ending any possession or control of the subject. Caster must be touching the subject.

Cost: 6.

Time to cast: 3 hours.

Prerequisites: Summon Spirit.

Healing — *Regular*

Restores up to 3 HT to the subject. Does not eliminate disease, but will cure harm already done by disease or wound. This spell is risky if used more than once per day by the same caster on the same subject. Skill is at -3 for first repetition, -6 for second, and so on.

Cost: 1 to 3; same as amount restored to subject.

Time to cast: 10 minutes.

History — *Information*

Cast on any inanimate object (or 1-hex section of a large object), lets the shaman determine the past of the object, its user's personality, events of significance to the object, etc. – but no names! The history can be detailed or general, at the caster's discretion. Detailed history can begin from the present and work back, or begin at some other point in time known to the caster.

Cost: 3 for each month examined in detail; 5 for general sense.

Time to cast: 1 hour for each month examined in detail; 30 minutes for general sense.

Prerequisite: Seeker.

Pestilence — *Regular*

Infects the subject with a loathsome plague (caster's choice, though GM can veto an inappropriate selection) by sending a spirit to attack the subject, steal the subject's soul, or penetrate the subject with a disease-causing object (again, caster's choice). The effects are not immediate, but the disease will take its normal course.

Duration: Permanent until cured.

Cost: 6.

Time to cast: 30 minutes.

Prerequisites: Healing.

Remove Curse — *Regular*

Nullifies any curse. If for any reason the skill level of the subject spell is unknown, the GM's assessment is final.

Cost: 10.

Time to cast: 10 hours.

Prerequisite: Bless.

Shaman Critical Spell Failure

Roll 3 dice. The GM does not have to use this table; he is free to improvise as appropriate to the spell and situation. If a result on this table is inappropriate, or if it is the result that the caster actually *intended,* then roll again.

3 – Spell fails entirely; caster takes 1 die of damage.

4 – Spell is cast on spellcaster.

5 – Spell is cast on one of the caster's companions (roll randomly).

6 – Spell is cast on nearby foe (roll randomly).

7 – Spell annoys spirit; loud moaning is heard.

8 – Spell affects someone or something other than its intended target – friend, foe, or random object – roll randomly, or GM makes interesting choice.

9 – Spell fails entirely; caster takes 1 hit of damage, and his trance is broken.

10 – Spell fails entirely; caster is stunned (IQ roll to recover) and his trance ends.

11 – Spell angers spirits; causes all within sight to have nightmares for a week.

12 – Spell produces a weak and useless shadow of its intended effect.

13 – Spell produces the reverse of the intended effect.

14 – Spell produces the reverse of the intended effect, on the wrong target (roll randomly).

15 – Spell fails entirely; caster temporarily forgets spell – make IQ roll after a week, and again each following week, until he remembers. Caster can study the spell during this time, but it is a waste of time.

16 – Spell angers spirits; a prized possession is broken (GM's choice).

17 – Spell fails entirely; caster's right arm is crippled – 1 week to recover.

18 – Spell fails entirely; an angry spirit appears immediately and attacks the caster.

Seeker — *Information*

As with the magic spell (see p. M54).

Cost: 3. One try per week.

Time to cast: 30 minutes.

Prerequisites: Summon Spirit.

Sense Spirit — *Information; Area*

As with the magic spell (see p. M72). The caster need not be in a trance state.

Cost: 1.

Time to cast: 1 second.

Spirit Trap (VH) — *Regular; Resisted by spirit's IQ*

Lets the caster trap the subject spirit within some object (which must be at hand). The spirit is imprisoned until it can possess the body of someone touching the "trap." It does so by winning a spirit combat (see above), but the spirit rolls at -2. If the trap is destroyed, so is the spirit – permanently. The spirit adds its ST to the object's in determining how easily it can be destroyed.

The wandering soul of a person, living or deceased, may also be imprisoned in this manner.

Cost: 6.

Time to cast: 1 hour.

Prerequisites: Summon Spirit.

Summon Spirit — *Information; Resisted by spirit's IQ*

Lets the caster speak with a disembodied spirit or the spirit of a dead person. If in life the subject was a friend of the caster, it resists at -5. If the spell succeeds, the subject will answer one question, to the best of its knowledge (GM's decision), and one more for every minute it remains.

The spell may also be used to lure a stolen or lost soul back into the body of an ill person. In either case, the shaman must have met the living or conscious (in the case of soul loss) person. If the soul of a dead person is being summoned, the caster must be at the site of that person's death. Otherwise, he must be in the presence of the patient whose soul is to be recovered.

Duration: 1 minute.

Cost: 6 for the first minute; 4 for each successive minute.

Prerequisites: Sense Spirit; Death Vision.

TRADITIONS

Since before the dawn of time, man's search for meaning in the universe has shaped his thought into countless religions. This chapter offers a quick glimpse into a small number of these many faiths.

Animism

The belief that all reality is inhabited by spirits and souls, and that everything is in some sense alive, is called *animism*. Many animists, like the ancient Greek and Hebrew philosophers, believe that spirits and souls are some form of undefined matter. This belief in the "animation of the inanimate" is not limited to ancient or simple cultures. The proud car owner who pampers and polishes "his baby," the angry golfer who curses his club after a failed shot, the gambler who must have his lucky dice – all of these actions illustrate a form of animistic belief.

There are three basic forms of animism. Some believe in and worship the souls or spirits of people and animals, both living and dead. *Necrolatry,* the worship of the souls of the dead, is one form; ancestor worship (see below) is another. Both are widespread forms of animism. Other people believe in freeform spirits that are not associated with any object. This belief, known as *polydaemonism,* refers to the unranked masses of spirits of an animistic world, as opposed to the ranked deities of polytheism (see p. 131). Often both polydaemonistic and polytheistic beliefs are found in one religion.

The Human Soul

Many religions have elements of animism. Hindu and Buddhist beliefs hold that matter is an illusion, and that the soul-spirit is the only reality. Salvation is achieved when individuality is lost by absorption in the *Atman,* or *all-soul*. But most Western traditions emphasis the individuality of the soul-spirit.

The nature of the human soul has long been debated. A common belief is that the soul is an "inner double" which dwells within and pervades the body. Other views hold that the soul is localized, and dwells in specific parts of the body such as the throat, head or heart. Many believe that the soul cannot exist outside the body and that it is created at a specific point in time, such as at conception. Religions which believe the soul can exist separately usually also hold that it is created at conception or birth, or that it has an independent origin separate from the body.

Most religions believe that the soul survives after death. The soul may pass to an afterlife at once, or it may be delayed as punishment for deeds done during the individual's lifetime. Some believe that the soul exists only while living relatives remember the deceased; if they neglect to venerate the soul, it ceases to be. Many believe souls can continue to interact with the living, as guides, ghosts or other lingering spirits.

Reincarnation

A soul may enter a new body after death. Belief in reincarnation is common to many religions, especially Hinduism. Hindus believe that salvation is much too difficult to achieve in a single lifetime. All living things, including humans, exist in a complex hierarchical scale. How well an individual lives determines where upon the scale he will be reincarnated – those who do well are promoted, those who are mediocre remain where they are, those who fail are demoted.

Totemism

Totemism reveres a mystical relationship between an individual or kinship group and a totem. Totemism is common in tribal societies that practice ancestor veneration, from the North American Pacific coast to South America to the Eurasian plains. This totem might be a crafted object that a spirit inhabits, or it might be a living entity such as a plant or animal. If a totem is identified with a primordial ancestor, that animal-spirit will be a guardian or adviser to its living descendants. Harming a totem animal is often forbidden, even if one's life depends upon it. Slaying such an animal for food is unthinkable; some animals are to be slain only in ritual sacrifice, and are eaten only by priests and other holy persons.

Sometimes killing and eating a totem animal is considered to be a holy act of communion, establishing a link with the ancestor or the divine. This is thought to endow the participants with particular virtues, such as strength, courage, bravery or wisdom. In many societies cannibalism serves a similar purpose, granting the diners the chance to participate in the life of the deceased. In cultures that practice ancestor veneration, the dead might be consumed so that the living might share in an unbroken line of continuity that traces back to the first ancestor.

Finding a Totem

There are many different types of totems. Sometimes the link between a family and a totem-spirit is very strong and everyone knows which spirit protects which family. In other cases, each individual in the family must go upon a *vision quest* to find his personal totem. In many of these cultures, no one considers a person to be an adult until he has successfully completed such a quest. Finding this totem is an intensely personal act, usually carried out at puberty. The individual goes on a solitary journey into the wilderness. Usually fasting and other forms of self-discipline are employed. Sometimes hallucinogenic herbs or potions are used to aid the process. The seeker stays in the wilderness until his totem reveals itself. Seekers who fail are never heard of again. They might die, or they might go elsewhere, but if they return without their totem they are considered dead.

In some cultures one's totem is a vital secret; if the person speaks of his special totem at all, then the guardian-spirit will become affronted and leave. In other cultures, people are very open about their totems.

Early Buddhism denied concepts of caste and held that there was no soul, that the concept of self was an impermanent one. One's destiny was determined by karma (see p. 15); those who are not enlightened could be reborn as anything from a god, to a ghost, to a hellish being. Some sects of Buddhism hold that the dead person remains in a transitional state for a specific period of time before being reborn.

Nonhuman Spirits

The most common type of nonhuman spirit is the *nature spirit*. These are associated with some natural object such as a river, lake, mountain, tree, rock or plant. Some nature spirits are connected with forces and processes of nature such as thunder, lightning, fertility and rain. These spirits are related to their objects in the same way that a human soul is related to a human body. Nature spirits have varying degrees of power and definite personalities.

Some spirits are not connected with a natural object or phenomenon, but are rather defined in terms of their intrinsic moral character. Angels, good faeries, demons and devils are prime examples of these *ethical spirits*. "Good" spirits are thought to be benevolent toward humans and their aid is sought though offerings and ritual. "Evil" spirits are considered to be selfish and malevolent – they must be placated with offerings or warded off with protective rituals and charms. Some evil spirits can possess a human being, causing abnormal or dangerous behavior. They may be expelled through rites of healing and exorcism. Other spirits are not necessarily "evil" or "good," but too alien or indifferent to be useful. The realms of spirits often have complex hierarchies governed by sovereign spirits. These sovereigns are either equal in power and opposite in disposition, or totally unequal in power.

Divine spirits are beings of great power, and may even *be* deities. The ancient Greeks made distinctions between their gods and goddesses and the nymphs and satyrs. But often this distinction is unclear and varies greatly. The spirits of Japanese Shinto vary in power from the smallest spirits of rocks and trees to the great spirits who created the world. Generally divine spirits are more "human" in both personality and intention than ethical or nature spirits. Over time, some powerful ethical spirits may evolve into true divine spirits.

Ancestor Veneration

Ancestral spirits are rarely actually worshiped, but rather placated through rituals of honor and homage. They usually require sustenance and attention in order to exist. Those who venerate their ancestors commonly believe that needs and obligations do not end with death. It is the duty of living descendants to care for their ancestors – as their ancestors continue to care for them.

Shamanism

Strictly speaking, shamanism is not a religion but rather a series of techniques. Elements of shamanistic belief are common to many religions and there are many varieties of shamanism. The term is commonly used to refer to the beliefs and practices of those individuals who appear to have magical or spiritual powers.

The word *shaman* is thought to be derived from the Siberian Tungusic *saman* or possibly the Sanskrit *sramana,* meaning ascetic. A shaman is considered to be a healer, diviner, magician, clairvoyant and escort of the dead. Shamans can attain a state of trance or ecstasy which enables them to enter spiritual realms and dimensions. During this tranced state, the shaman's soul is thought to leave his body and either ascend into the sky or descend into the underworld.

Cosmology

A shaman's calling is to break through the cosmic planes in order to communicate with those who dwell in other spiritual worlds. The most common cosmology is three-tiered: the earth, surrounded by a sky-world above, and an underworld below. A unique tree, mountain or pillar often represents the central axis of the world and provides a path of communications between the tiers.

Spirits and deities which dwell within these other worlds can – and do – affect the lives of humans in the middle world. It is the place of the shaman to intervene and communicate with these spirits.

Shamans are common in cultures where the high god is seen as inactive and its role is being filled by nature and ancestor spirits. In other cultures there are divisions between shamans, depending upon whether their actions are benevolent or malevolent. Shamans are highly respected and even revered, but they are usually feared and isolated. While people may rely upon the shaman, they often also blame the shaman when harm or misfortune befalls a community.

Vocation

A shaman either inherits his vocation, or is called to it. Potential shamans are often chosen at a young age from specific lineages and carefully taught and trained until their initiation. Sudden calls of vocation are also associated with illnesses or the arrival of sexual maturity.

Continued on next page . . .

Ancestral spirits are often concerned about the welfare and fortune of their living kin and may intervene in the affairs of the living. If they are pleased and placated by dutiful service, these spirits may offer protection and advice. If angered by neglect, they may torment, haunt or curse the living. Divination is often used to determine how happy these ancestors might be. Sometimes an ancestral spirit might possess a descendant in order to offer oracular advice. Ancestor veneration usually adds stability to the family unit. It can also provide a means of dealing with death – those who fear death may be comforted knowing that they themselves will be remembered and venerated.

Domestic rituals are usually of vital importance. Food, drink and other valued objects are commonly offered at ancestral shrines. Wooden tablets or carved sticks and stools are often considered to be merely representative of ancestral spirits, rather than any sort of permanent home.

Shamanism (Continued)

A shaman's initiation usually involves extensive rituals that result in an ecstatic or visionary experience. Serious illness might duplicate this. Common imagery associated with such experiences includes visions of death and dismemberment, reduction to a skeleton and the cooking and consuming of the body. After this visionary destruction, the shaman's body is restored, more powerful than ever. The shaman also travels, journeying to the sky or underworlds where he meets helpful spirits. Often he also learns special languages, used only for communicating with the spirits.

The shaman becomes able to enter states of ecstasy at will, and break the plane of normal experience. To do this, the shaman is aided by spirits. Only a limited number of these spirits are controlled by a shaman. In shamanistic performances, he will speak in the voice of his familiar spirit. The shaman is not thought to be possessed, but rather touched or transformed, since he remains in control of the ritual.

Duties

Illness is thought to be caused by the loss of the soul or vitality, or by the projection of objects into the body by spirits from these worlds. A shaman travels forth and rescues stolen vitality, or removes the damaging objects. Thus a shaman is also a healer, for only the shaman has the power to deal with malevolent spirits.

Shamans are also psychopomps – escorts of the soul and the dead. This is the most dangerous of the shaman's duties, for it requires that he undergo a symbolic death. He might also escort the spirits of sacrificial animals to their intended destinations.

Other duties of the shaman include finding lost persons and objects, and controlling the weather. Shamans might also engage in spiritual battle with each other, especially in the form of animal spirits.

Shamans often wear highly symbolic costumes and masks. These masks are not used to disguise the shaman, but rather to represent a particular mythical personage or divine spirit. Drums and rattles are other common tools of the shaman.

Dualism

A dualistic worldview believes in two irreducible and ultimate principles which continually oppose each other. They are equally matched, although this may vary from time to time. These principles are both contrasting and complementary – neither can exist without the other. Sometimes each principle is thought to contain a minuscule amount of its opposing quality. The well-known yin-yang symbol is a classic depiction of this. Often these principles are abstract forces involved in an ethical or cosmological struggle. These forces might be personified by opposing deities, or even opposing pantheons.

On a personal level there is the dichotomy of spirit and mind. Mind cannot function without spirit to drive it; spirit cannot express itself without the mind. The relationship between body and soul is also important. Some hold that the soul dwells temporarily within the body – others believe the two cannot exist separately and that the death of the body brings about the dissolution of the soul.

On a grander scale, dualist forces are more abstract, yet balance between them is necessary to ensure a cosmic well-being. Deities are often concerned about maintaining this balance and use both divine and mortal agents. The struggle between order and chaos is a common theme. This is not an ethical or moral conflict – chaos is change, a state in which chance is supreme; order is a stable state of uniformity. Order applied to primordial chaos brings creation, but too much order results in stagnation and the loss of creativity. Balance is needed to ensure prosperity.

Other dualistic forces such as light/dark and good/evil are common religious themes. Light and dark are opposing forces, but their conflict need not be an ethical or moral one. Darkness can be associated with the cold, night, winter, death and mystery; light can represent purity, brightness, fire, summer and warmth. An eternal battle between good and evil often involves absolute archetypes – good is good and evil is evil and never the twain shall meet. This struggle can be supernatural and cosmic in scale, or a conflict between individuals. Such struggles will be dirty, for these boundaries are unclear. Individuals of either side may find themselves compromising their morals to achieve their goals. In this view of duality, everything is in shades of gray. Good cannot exist without evil, and vice versa, for each bears a little of the other within it.

Rituals vary in nature from private offerings to rites involving the entire living lineage. Daily commemorative rituals are common, as are special private requests for advice at times of fortune or crisis. Anniversaries of deaths are important and are often remembered by special rituals. Other rites keep the ancestor up-to-date on family concerns and gossip. Although these obligations may be delegated, it is usually the head of the household who acts as an intermediary between the supplicant and a particular ancestor. In Japan, the daily domestic ritual is often performed by a spouse or close relative.

Public rituals generally address the entire collection of ancestors, both recent and distant, as a group. These rites tend to occur at temples or other sacred locations. Festivals of the Dead and cyclical agricultural rites are examples of this type of public ritual. These rites are usually performed by the senior member of the family on behalf of many relatives, often from multiple households. Non-religious forms can include such traditions as a "roll-call" of friends or classmates who have perished (especially in war).

Earth Religions

Worship of the earth, in its many forms, is the oldest and most widespread form of religion. Earth religions are commonly concerned with the cycles of the world, birth, death and rebirth, the seasons, and the mystical nature of planting, growth and harvest. Often these religions are dualistic and the deity is personified in male-female terms. The earth is often pictured as the nurturing mother-goddess, while the god is often seen as Lord of the Hunt.

Earth religions often have shamanistic and mystic elements – in many cases hidden knowledge and teachings are not revealed until after a formal initiation or some other test of enlightenment. Most earth religions believe that the divine is manifested in everything and everyone who lives. All life is interconnected, and what affects one part of the world affects the rest. Thus all that lives should be respected. Death is not feared, but seen as part of the natural cycle of the world. Life springs from death, allowing for change and new creation. Free will is a basic tenet in many earth religions. Some may emphasize growth, transformation and personal enlightenment, while others are ultra-conservative, wishing to preserve old traditions at all costs.

Rituals celebrating the change of the seasons and the cycle of life, as well as healing and protective ones, are the mainstay of earth religions.

Polytheism

Many religions revere a pantheon of related gods. These gods are usually seen as ruling separate spheres such as astronomy, weather, the elements, life cycles, conflict and culture.

Family Pantheons

This type of pantheon is usually structured in ways that echo cultural values. (The GM must decide if the culture is mimicking the mores of the gods, or if the culture sees their deities in terms of their own society.) If monogamy is the social norm, then the gods will echo this. Marriages and children abound, and much of the politics of the gods revolves around family-type crises and sibling rivalries. Often societal mores (such as those which forbid incest) are ignored by the gods. The very fact of their divinity allows them to break their own rules. If priestly or royal lineages feel that they have been touched or ordained by the gods, they will often ignore such rules themselves.

Court Pantheons

These pantheons are rigidly hierarchal, and have enormous celestial bureaucracies. The supreme being is seen as a ruler, and is often not worshiped directly. Lesser deities serve as lords and officers of the court and report directly to this ruler. Demigods and other divine servants make up the bulk of the bureaucracy.

Opposing Pantheons

Sometimes a pantheon faces opposition from an entirely different pantheon. The relationship between these pantheons might be strictly dualistic, regulated by a neutral force which strives to ensure that the struggle remains balanced. In other cases, differing pantheons might vie for control over a particular world or

Popular and Folk Religion

These religions are characterized by their complexity and their important role in everyday life. Ancestor veneration, fertility rites and sacrificial practices are vital, along with a pantheon of personified deities and beliefs in demons, ghosts, spirits, exorcism and divination. Popular religions are "melting pots," and usually adopt new thoughts and practices with ease.

Most of these religions began in China and Japan, but are now found anywhere in the world to which people of those countries have emigrated.

Household Deities

In popular religions, ancestors and household gods are connected to an enormous celestial bureaucracy. Family members usually turn to their own – more approachable – household gods for protection from misfortune and illness, and appeal to them for fertility, wealth and family harmony and well-being. These deities watch over the family as well as they can, reporting difficulties to their divine superiors.

Small icons or idols are commonly placed upon the altar in each home, along with images of respected ancestors. This altar – the center of family worship – is often located in the main room of the house facing the front door. Other icons of celestial or agricultural deities are also popular. Sacrifices of food, incense and wine are offered at regular intervals. Sometimes every significant aspect of the home or family life is personified in some divine form and given proper and continual ritual attention. An example of an important household god is the Chinese "stove deity," whose image is enshrined above the kitchen hearth. Responsible for the behavior of the family, he reports once a month to the local city gods. Once a year he reports to the head of the pantheon.

Beyond the Household

Outside the household, ancestor worship may be practiced in clan temples and is often associated with educational and economic activities. City neighborhoods and rural areas are usually divided into divine jurisdictions. These local gods, called *t'u-ti kung* in most areas of China, are responsible for the fertility of their particular area. Families in the area usually maintain shrines on a rotating schedule. Shop and trade groups, secret societies and small religious sects all have their own patron deities and saints. Such groups often ignore the normal class strictures of the society and are open to people of varying education and social levels.

Continued on next page . . .

sphere. Younger pantheons might try to overthrow older ones, as Zeus did Cronus and Odin and his brothers did Ymir.

Freeform Pantheons

This type of pantheon is a loose collection of deities. Dozens, hundreds or even thousands of deities might band together, perhaps beneath a charismatic, yet unorganized, leader. This organization is very chaotic, although the deities themselves need not be. New gods and spirits are constantly being born or recruited, older gods fading away or being forgotten. Alliances and rivalries change and shift from moment to moment, or they endure for all eternity. Such deities often have small spheres of influences, or share a large sphere with several others.

Satellite Pantheons

These pantheons are often descendant or splinter groups. If a pantheon grows too large, younger deities might decide to leave and form their own separate alliances. While they are somewhat isolated from the general affairs of the major pantheon, they can be called upon in times of great need.

Geographical Traditions

African

African religions are not usually concerned with dogma or thoughts of personal salvation. Deities and spirits are worshiped because, along with people and animals, they maintain the diversity of an established, natural order. The goal of one's life is to maintain this order. The divine is honored through everyday activity.

Reverence for a supreme being is found in almost all African religions. Triune images are common. These forces flow from the divine to specific clans or locations, such as streams and trees. Humans can call upon each force. In some cultures these forces take on a distinct individuality and are thought of as ministers who serve a greater chief. The divine is invoked through these lesser forces. If the supreme being has entirely withdrawn from the petty affairs of earth-folk, these servants portion out divine favor. This explains disease and ill fortune – the supreme being is good and benevolent, but one must worry about the intermediary spirits. Often the supreme being is thought to be either female or androgynous. Esoteric philosophies often insist that reality and the divine are androgynous, created out of the balance of universal female and male qualities. Matrilineal cultures are common, and the divine is often viewed as a celestial Queen or earth-dwelling Mother.

An unusual theme in African religions is that the divine expresses its active benevolence by remaining in heaven. Everyday life continues without its direct intervention. If the divine comes too close, then sickness, madness or death results. Those struck by lightning are thought to have been chosen by the divine. Shrines are erected to the spirits of these people, for they have become divine intermediaries. Rain and lightning storms are treated with great reverence, worshipers begging the divine to go away.

Popular and Folk Religion (Continued)

Deities

The deities of popular religions often began as human beings and were deified over time as a reward for their works. Deities with a history of triumph over difficulties are particularly popular. These deities usually owe their existence and status to worship by the living. Temple deities are commonly worshiped with great pomp and ceremony. Special offerings, processions and other entertainments may mark their birthdays. Annual festivals are often extremely popular and are strictly observed.

Hostile Influences

Some supernatural forces might work unceasingly to bring disorder, suffering and death to the world. Such hostile forces are usually called "demons." These unlawful forces can be subject to divine command, but they are usually unruly and highly uncooperative. Repeated invocations, prayers and other strenuous rituals are required to restrain these forces. Such exorcisms underline the continual struggle between the gods and demons, illustrating the semi-dualistic nature of popular religions.

Leadership

Hereditary leaders, such as the heads of families, are usually responsible for rituals performed in clan shrines and temples. Leaders of secret societies and sects also tend to inherit their positions. Village temples are served by elders who are often selected by lot and serve for a specific period of time. Spirit-mediums, spirit-writers, healers and magicians are charismatic leaders who have divine or shamanistic ability. They are employed by families who require special aid to heal disease or deal with spirits. Fortune-tellers and geomancers may be consulted when a family needs to build a temple or find a grave site.

Morality and Ethics

Health, long life, harmony, prosperity, continuation of the family and protection from harm are some of the goals important to adherents of popular religions. They may achieve these goals through familial piety, honesty, reciprocal consideration, loyalty to friends, frugality and diligence.

Most adherents of popular religions believe that after death the soul goes to purgatory; once there it will be judged according to concepts of karmic retribution. This passage through purgatory may be aided through purchased prayers and sacrificial rituals. When the soul's guilt has been purged, it passes into the final court, which decides its next existence.

African belief commonly holds that each individual has numerous "souls." Spiritual and physical health must remain in harmony with the environment. Healthy social relationships are vitally important in the maintenance of spiritual balance. Loyalty and generosity to family members – as well as regular sacrifices to ancestral shades – ensure inward peace and external well-being. Ignoring obligations can cause illness, bad luck and even death.

Native American

Native American religions vary greatly, although they do share several common themes. But even religions that hold the same basic concepts and ideas can have different ceremonies, customs and mythologies. The importance of religion also varies from tribe to tribe. Some, like the Zuni, give a special reverence to religious rites, while to others religious practices are an integral part of everyday life.

Codal Systems

These religions have an extensive series of laws and philosophies. They might not involve the divine at all, but rather provide a system of law and ethical thoughts to maintain social behavior. Proper actions, dress and speech are all determined by these long-standing laws. Adherence to these ensures personal prosperity and fulfillment. If the religion acknowledges a deity, that deity is usually considered to be the ultimate judge.

Dispute and Settlement

Many interpersonal disputes do not need to be taken before either a clerical or civil judge. They are commonly dealt with by avoidance behavior, fighting, prayer, verbal insult and feuding. A codal system defines the exact lengths and means to which participants may go to solve the problem.

Legal disputes are typically handled in formal ways, before either religious or civil authorities. There are many ways to settle such arguments. Punishment might be of the "eye-for-an-eye" variety, imprisonment or a standard fine set by the community.

Contests of wit or skill are common. Physical combats may be used to settle charges of assault or murder. The outcome is seen as a divine judgment.

Ordeals may be used to settle conflicts concerning honor, truth, purity, treason and betrayal. They are painful physical tests whose outcome depends upon divine justice. Refusal to submit to such an ordeal is often taken as an admission of guilt. These tests can be relatively harmless, or can involve burning, scalding, bleeding and poison. If innocent, the accused will not be harmed. In the Middle Ages those accused of witchcraft and sorcery were often bound and thrown into ponds or rivers, in the belief that if they floated, they were guilty. If they sank, they died – but they died free of accusation and guilt.

A *moot* is an informal gathering of the community to discuss the conflict. These meetings are organized by the family and neighbors of the disputers. Domestic disputes are commonly settled at a moot.

A court system deals with conflict through formal procedures. Judgments are given out by officials who have both authority and means to enforce their decisions. In a codal religious state these judges – and all other associated officials – will be clerics. Divine or magical means will often be used to ensure truthful testimony and to inflict punishment.

Atheism

There are many forms of atheism, which denies the existence of divine beings and principles. Some hold that any non-believer is an atheist. But some religions actually incorporate atheistic beliefs, such as Theravada Buddhism, which includes the concept of *anatta*. Anatta denies the Brahmanical/Hindu belief in selfhood. Early Buddhism viewed the *atman* as an unchanging, undying, perfect spiritual essence that resided within the body. Anatta insists upon the unreality of the self and denies all cravings and desires, so that the true reality of the divine can be understood.

Atheism is likely to be a common philosophy in a world where gods are absent or inactive. If scientific law and rationalization take the place of mysticism in explaining the way in which the world works, atheism will flourish. An atheist requires irrefutable, rational proof of divine power. An oppressive regime might insist upon a policy of atheism, outlawing all religious worship to secure its own power. If the religion's deity depends upon worship, such political action could influence the deity's power, or even destroy it. In such a situation, a cleric's life would be difficult indeed.

Hunting tribes often have loosely-defined mythologies which describe both a heaven and a world of humanity, sometimes with vague references to an underworld or a cosmic tree. Agrarian tribes often re-enact highly-detailed mythologies in elaborate rituals and ceremonies. A worldview of layers (underworld, human world, otherworld) is common and is often associated with the concept of a world tree. Within the mundane world, tribal areas are strictly defined, usually by geographical terrain. The traditional lands of the Navajo, for example, are defined by four holy mountains. Cross themes (symbolizing the four winds and the four corners of the earth) are very common throughout prairie, plains and southeastern tribes, as are sacred-circle designs. These are incorporated into village layouts, holy lodges and campsites. The Sun Dance lodges of the plains tribes represent the sacred universe.

The Supreme Being

While the concept of a supreme being is common in many tribal traditions, it is not universal. Often seen as a creator, its degree of involvement with people is not standard. While supreme beings may seem to be more powerful than the other gods, they are not always seen to be leaders of those gods. They are usually thought to be intangible or invisible. Often natural phenomena are viewed as manifestations of the supreme being. The supreme being is commonly associated with food (which is provided through the bounty of nature) and the connection with heaven, which symbolizes power and authority. Supreme beings often seem to be distant from humanity (though not unaware of their needs) and are rarely mentioned in mythic tales and stories. A divine representative (such as the hero, the trickster or the twins) is usually the focus of such legends.

The supreme being is often associated with the sun, especially in parts of the American southwest, and is common to both sedentary and nomadic peoples. The Pueblo Indians of New Mexico and Arizona consider the sun a powerful divinity, though only the Hopi regard the sun as creator, and perform special ceremonies at the solstices intended to modify the sun's journey. Gulf and Mississippian traditions are theocratic, with a priest-chief believed to be a divine substitute for the supreme being, the sun. The sun is primarily believed to be a male deity, although some, like the Eskimos, Algonquin, Cherokee and Seminole, depict the sun as female.

Supreme beings are often believed to manifest through atmospheric phenomena such as wind, thunder, lightning and rain. Thunder is often believed to be caused by spirits in bird-form; their flapping wings produce thunder, and lightning flashes from their eyes. Thunderbirds are a common motif in native American art and are often depicted in multiples of four – one for each of the four directions.

The Cosmic Pillar and the World Tree

Another common theme is that of a cosmic pillar holding up the heavens; often this pillar is symbolized in ritual by a sacred pole. Such poles often record the mythic legends and history of the tribe. Such practices are especially common among the coastal and plateau tribes of western Canada. Sometimes the cosmic pillar actually represents the cosmos, or even the supreme being, as in some of the Sun Dance rituals of the prairie and plains tribes.

The concept of a world tree is even more widespread than that of a cosmic pillar. The Iroquois revere the "tree of heaven" from whose roots the mother goddess fell down to earth. While especially common to agrarian tribes, the concept is shared by hunting and fishing tribes as well – the Tlingit of northwest America believe the world tree is represented by the Milky Way. The concept of the world tree implies a belief that the divine is keeping constant watch over a specific people; as such the world tree is often represented in annual festivals and shamanistic rites.

Goddesses

Moon cults are not as common as solar cults, though many divine spirits are believed to have lunar qualities. The creator-goddess of the Shawnee is associated with the moon, and the Zuni revere a goddess called the "moon mother," as do the Apache.

Agrarian tribes commonly revere an earth-goddess, often viewed as an all-powerful deity. As the goddess of birth, she represents the continuance and renewal of life. Vegetation goddesses are very common and often closely linked with the earth-goddess. Some tribes, such as the Pueblo Indians, make a distinction between the Mother Earth and the Corn Goddess. In some cultures numerous goddesses represent a variety of plants; the Iroquois revere the Corn Sister, the Bean Sister and the Squash Sister.

Living with Spirits

Often, certain geographical areas are considered to be the abode of spirits. The Dakota and Cheyenne revere the Black Hills as such a place, while the Pueblo Indians venerate lakes and other openings in the earth as places from which their ancestors emerged long ago. Mountains are also often regarded as holy places; spirits that dwell there are usually greatly feared. The Shoshoni regard the Grand Tetons with trepidation.

While some spirits are feared, others are guardians. A specific spirit – often represented by a specific animal – guards members of a particular clan. Taboos often prevent members of a clan from harming their guardian animal/spirit, or totem. In much of Northwestern America, the totem is a guardian spirit who once helped the clan's ancestral founder. The totem poles common to coastal tribes are heraldic or historical representations, and not necessarily images of gods. Elsewhere – for instance, among the Iroquois or Zuni – members of a particular clan are believed to be actual descendants of their totem. Protective talismans and medicine bundles are often thought to be given or blessed by totem spirits. Guardian spirits may also be found by performing a vision quest. Such quests are often part of puberty initiation rites. In some tribes, such as the coastal Kwakiutl, people with the same guardian spirit join together in secret societies. Such societies have their own traditions, mythologies and rituals which only members share. (See also *Totemism*, p. 127.)

Medicine Men and Shamans

Shamans and medicine men are important members of many tribal societies. The word "medicine" was used by translators to describe various manifestations of supernatural power. Often these supernatural gifts have been received through visionary quests. Ordinary people believe a shaman or medicine man is more mystically gifted than they. Medicine men or shamans also heal, and most importantly, use their powers for the benefit of their societies. This service to the community often gains the shaman both prestige and political power. Not all native American "medicine men" are shamans; only those

Agnosticism

Agnostics believe that, given the limits of the mind and human perception, it is impossible to truly *know* if the divine exists. Agnosticism does not actually deny the divine, just one's perception of it. Agnostics do not *believe* in the divine, but they can, perhaps, be convinced otherwise. Agnostics could be found in any game world where divine activity was unknown or exceedingly rare.

who can establish contact with the spirit world are called shamans. Medicine men are often religious authorities without this special talent. Many tribes have female medicine "men" and shamans, especially native American tribes in northern California and Oregon. Transvestitism is very common in some North American tribes, such as the Netsilik, Sioux and northern Californian tribes. Such an individual (often called a "berdache") represents both male and female aspects, thus holding a particularly potent supernatural power.

South Asian

South Asian traditions have a common belief in the interaction between people and spirits. Often there is an underworld inhabited by the dead, deities and spirits – but some cultures do not believe in an afterlife at all. Divine forces are usually believed to be invisible and limited in power. Many deities are utterly dependent upon regular sacrifices, and get angry if they are ignored.

Benevolent deities are rarely supplied with material offerings – worship and attention pleases them more. Possession by a deity or clan spirit may occur when the worshipers need to be reminded of some failed duty. The supreme deity – usually associated with the sky or sun – is rarely given more attention than the lesser, earth-bound deities. There is no concept that such a deity stands in opposition to any "evil" force, or that there even *is* such a malevolent, hostile force.

Divine forces are totally indifferent to the moral conduct of their worshipers. So long as the proper offerings and rituals are carried out, the divine will grant protection and blessings. Breaking a *taboo* will bring misfortune, but not divine retribution. Few tribal languages have a word for "sin." A priest's duty is to maintain good relations between the people and the gods. He is not responsible for influencing the behavior of his fellows. Priests discover the causes behind ill luck and illness, and if a god or spirit is responsible, then they act to appease divine wrath.

Southeast Asian

Almost all of the religions in this area are dualistic, with strong oral traditions, shamanism and ancestor worship. Many

Metaphysics

Metaphysics is the philosophical study of the nature of the intangible. It uses scientific methodology to study the nature of reality and challenges all belief, even the assumption that the divine exists. Metaphysicians describe their work as a study of ultimate, irrefutable proofs.

What Exists?

Plato conceptualized what he called the *form*: an archetypical structure which denotes some primal aspect or substance. A *particular* – a concrete object which took on an aspect of a form – only received some appearance or element of the form's reality and was unable to attain the purity of the true substance. Aristotle argued that *forms* were actually abstractions of *categories* of reality apparent in a particular. These are abstractions of universal substances, while Plato claimed that his forms truly existed and could be discerned, not by the eyes of the body, but by the eyes of the soul. This conflict between the reality and the abstraction of primal substance was later dubbed the problem of the existence of *Universals*. Other philosophers took the argument even further, denying even Aristotle's abstract categories of substance. Some held that any sort of classification was artificial.

Most modern metaphysicians discuss reality in terms of processes and events. The terms "soul" and "mind" are used interchangeably. Material substance occupies space, but mental substance – with God as the supreme example – exists in the mind. Life consists of the intertwining of these two disparate substances. Space and time are often seen as being ultimately unreal. Reality does not endure throughout time, nor is it subject to the dimensions of space. Time and space are by definition limited – one space excludes another and no two times can be simultaneous. God is infinite and omnipresent and so must exist outside of time and space.

see the afterworld as a mirror image of the living world. Illness and death are believed to be caused not only by malevolent spirits, but also by sorcerers. Shamans not only perform cures, but also determine who or what is to blame for the problem.

Sacrifice of domesticated animals, and even people, is a common tradition. Large animals are offered (usually burned) to gain large favors. Hunter-gatherer tribes practice a form of self-sacrifice by offering their own blood. The ultimate sacrifice is a human head. Raids to obtain these are often an important part of mourning and funeral rites, and heads are often mounted upon gates or walls. The ghosts of such heads become guardians of the community, and protect the village from spirits which might cause illness or crop failures.

Melanesian

These societies revolve around commercial transactions and reciprocal giving. Conscience and morality are achieved through reciprocal relationships. Transactions determine both kinship and friendship. It is necessary to understand the powers of nature to gain success in farming and hunting. Secret rituals and spells, usually chanted jingles, grant some control over rain, blight and other natural disasters.

Ancestors and clan guardians are seen as benign, yet sometimes troublesome spirits. People must appease these spirits by offerings of produce and pigs. These are made with great ceremony; such feasts are used to extend one's range of transactions. It is impossible to equally reciprocate the powers of a storm or earthquake. When a person (such as a sorcerer) shows such nonreciprocal power, he should be struck down to restore the balance of power. (Sorcerers are thought to be responsible for illness and misfortune, caused by their attempts to express power over other people, even spirits.) The individual is first forced to admit to his mortality, and then is often killed for denying the harmony and necessity of the equivalent transaction.

Polynesian

Ceremonies abound in these societies. Rituals involving pig and human sacrifice and even cannibalism are performed in elaborate temples of stone and wood. In such cultures, personal integrity lies in the legitimate use of coercive power. The identity, power and worth of an individual depends on maintaining the favor of a multitude of gods.

The supreme being is seen as an obscure force, vaguely associated with the East and the rising sun. The creative forces are a duality. The primary creator is male, associated with the sky, birth and harvest. The female is both a destructive and creative force, associated with the earth, underworld, earthquakes and volcanoes. From this mating of earth and sky was born a host of lesser deities. Many other spirits arose independently. Every bush, grove, stream and even sea current was the province of some spirit or another. These spirits are appeased by feasts, rituals and sacrifices. All crafts and abilities have divine patrons or spirits, as well as enemies who strive to thwart such activities.

Mana in such a culture is the "demonstrated power of effectiveness," and is evidence of divine favor. A high chief has the most mana. Lesser chiefs are subject to him and so have less mana. In some tribes, only men have mana; women have none, but they can drain male mana. In other tribes, only women have mana or other divine power. A hierarchy of priests offers advice and organizes all the various feasts and rituals. *Seers* have animal familiars and are consulted

Maltheism

Maltheistic religions are those which encourage or support "evil" activities, particularly those against people. Their deities are dark and twisted beings, with no redeeming qualities. They encourage their followers to perform violent, sadistic acts of worship. A clear understanding of the nature of evil is central to these types of religions. There is an evil, and they are it.

Worshipers are drawn from the malcontents of society, the sadistic, the insane, or those who seek their own survival. If a maltheistic deity is intent upon devouring the world, people may flock to its worship in the hope that if they must die, they might at least be eaten last. Maltheistic religions are usually underground, hidden things which rebel against the societies of which they are a part.

Examples of maltheistic religions can be found in literature, such as Lovecraft's cthonic deities. There are no documented examples of true maltheism in the real world. Many religions which the popular press, and others outside the religion, consider "maltheistic" – such as the worship of the Hindu god and goddess of destruction, Shiva and Kali, and Satanism – are in reality fairly ordinary religions meeting the spiritual needs of humans. (A Hindu, for example, believes that Shiva and Kali destroy such things as worldly desires, making it easier for an individual to avoid accumulating karma. Satanism is a religion of rebellion – followers do everything backward to obtain prosperity.) Unfortunately, a religion can get a reputation as maltheistic, from something observed and misunderstood (as has happened with voodoo), or because the religion is so secret that rumors about it are not contradicted. At that point, the twisted, the violent, the sadistic – those at the margins of society – begin to claim membership as an excuse for their transgressions. Their beliefs may have little or nothing to do with the religion or its actual practice.

Maltheistic religions can, however, play a part in a game world, especially if a GM wants a clear-cut "bad guy." These types of religions may also be useful in horror campaigns or classic quest adventures, where the characters are the only hope remaining between the evil gods and the destruction of the world. (See, for example, "The Lord Beneath the Ice," ***GURPS Horror***.)

for divinatory advice. They are susceptible to trances and spirit possession, but they do not share the healing abilities of the true shaman. In some tribes only women can be true shamans.

Tapu is the concept from which the term *taboo* is derived. In meaning, *tapu* is a combination of "sacred," "holy," "forbidden" and "not done." There is a definite connection between *mana* and *tapu*: at one end of the scale is coercive power and freedom, at the other many restrictions. As the gods have power over people, so people desire power over others.

Australian Aboriginal

Oral traditions flourish in Australian societies. Guardian spirits and tutelary deities – usually associated with specific places or kin groups – are very important. Religion is vital to both economic and political activity. These cultures have a strongly developed sense of moral integrity and identity.

Australian aboriginal belief starts with the *Dreamtime,* during which creatures with human, animal and divine attributes wandered about. They flew through the air, traveled underground, transformed themselves, hunted, made laws and generally created the order of things. This order has continued down through time to the present, and is remembered in myth and story. People, animals, plants, stars, rocks, streams and winds are all seen as part of the Dreamtime. Some myths are the property of specific totemic groups, others are known to all. All the myths, activities, rituals and stories that came from the Dreamtime are considered to be a part of a sacred heritage: they make the *Law.*

Status and prestige within the group is dependent on one's understanding and interpretation of the Law. Elders govern aboriginal life according to their wisdom and this law. Birth is seen as a reincarnation of a Dreamtime being. The place where the child is born (or where the mother first felt it kicking) determines the totemic attributes of the child. People who challenge the harmonies of the Law, such as sorcerers, misuse the Law for their own selfish means. Thieves and adulterers are considered sorcerers, as are those who cause illness and death.

Whose Chaos Is This, Anyway?

Part of the problem in discussing chaos is the definition of the term (which, like the term "chthonic," has meanings that predate Lovecraft). "Chaos" has very strong connotations to gamers – connotations that don't apply in a religious perspective. These particular *gaming* connotations mostly stem from Moorcockian fantasy.

Chaos in a religious sense deals not only with randomness but with change, and with life and death. Some hold that life-force by its very nature is chaotic, since life *is* change. Chaotic deities often deal with creative/destructive forces, cycling through them from one divine aspect to another – chaos to substance, substance to chaos – or even both forms existing together. The worship of Kali is a prime example. Much of India still worships her as a divine mother, but until the 19th century (and British interference), the Thugee sects also flourished in northern and central India. These groups worshiped the chaotic and destructive form of Kali, Bhavani, and chose their sacrificial victims to honor her. Not only was the sacrifice an act of worship, but the manner of death – strangulation or decapitation – was as well. These acts echoed the goddess' own actions. Devotees decorated her statues with the severed hands and heads of her offerings, and heaped the bodies at her feet. Sometimes a valued worshiper was sacrificed as well.

In some religions, chaos is seen as the absence of all restraint, a state of anarchy and disorder, a whole-hearted denial of all societal mores. Society often views such worship as divinely-inspired madness. The most devoted worshipers of Dionysus, or Bacchus, sometimes came together in drunken bands that roamed the countryside, attacking and even dismembering any who would not join in their revels. Some thought that Dionysus himself led such bands, while others believed that his followers merely copied the god's debaucheries.

SAMPLE RELIGIONS

8

The preceding chapters give you all the tools you need to create imaginary religions – like these six samples. There are religions here for aliens, for spacefarers and netrunners, for medieval or near-future times, for strange cultures. Now create your own . . .

T'Si'Kami

From before time Herself began, there was the iShaka, the Breath. And in the darkness the iShaka whispered, and from these whispers were born the Winds of Time. Fierce and free, the Winds blew through the Celestial Heavens, scattering Light from Dark, and Water from Land. And as Light fled from Dark, the Celestial One stepped from the Shadows and called the Winds to order, sending one to each of the four corners of the World. But the Fifth Wind remained and clung to Her Fingers. Then She spoke, and Her Voice was the iShaka and it breathed upon the Fifth Wind, scattering it from Her fingers. Through the Heavens the scattered fragments fell, until they came at last to rest upon the rocks at Her feet, bringing Life where there once was none. And so the kami, the children of the Fifth Wind, gave birth to ShiShaka.

The ShiShaka rarely leave their island homes. Family ties are of utmost importance to them – someone without a family is not truly alive. Their society is extremely stratified, each family having rank according to the occupation of its members. Each island has its ruling family, with several noble families beneath that. Fishers and sailors rank next – they are given high respect, for it is they who dare the treacherous currents of the Da'kasha sea. Beneath that are craftsmen, merchants and farmers. Families make alliances within their own ranking. Only the noble and ruling families ally with those of other islands.

All ShiShaka follow the ancient tenets of T'Si'Kami. This is "the Way of the Spirits." All aspects of the world and nature, the wind and rain, fire and water, lightning and thunders, forests, rocks, mountains and trees have their own guardian-watchers, the holy *kami*. The human spirit is different, for only humans do not have a kami. Their souls are called *tala* and are received at birth from the ancestor-kami of the family. A tala departs the body at death and floats upon the winds of time until 49 years have passed. The living must remember the deceased during this time; if they do so well, then the tala joins the ancestor-kami. If they do not, the tala may become *ni'kami* – a spirit which will torment them until they change their ways. If a person has no family to perform the rites and the tala is forgotten by the living, it is lost forever upon the winds of time, never to become a kami.

The living have specific duties, according to the T'Si'Kami. First, they must be grateful to the kami, and diligently observe all the festivals and ceremonies, performing their duties with all sincerity, cheerfulness and purity of heart. They must give help where help is needed, without thought of reward. It is important that they think long and ponder upon the will of the Kami. And finally, they must live their life in harmony according to the will of the Celestial Empress, praying that the country will flourish, according to her need and will.

Organization

The Celestial Empress is the head of the Divine Court. There are many *Hai'ka'i* – minor courts with their own *Hai'do,* or Minister. These courts

The Divine Court

Once upon a time on the far islands, a young man knelt within his family shrine and prayed for help in his courtship. One of the ancestor-kami had a very soft heart and decided to take matters higher up. So he cleansed himself in the fumes of incense that filled the shrine, dressed himself in his best intangible robe, and flew upward, toward the mountain of minor courts, toward Hai'si'ka, the Court of Domestic Relations.

Hidden in the clouds upon the mountain's highest peak was the finest castle that the ancestor-kami had ever seen. He swept in through the door and was confronted by the seventh minor undersecretary to the fourth subminister. The ancestor-kami bowed deeply, kneeling, touching his head to the floor the required five times. With great respect he explained his task.

Fortunately for the ancestor-kami, this was a very slow day for the seventh minor undersecretary to the fourth subminister, who went to speak to the sixth minor undersecretary to the fourth subminister. After some consideration the sixth minor undersecretary agreed to carry the plea further.

As so the petition continued on, from minor undersecretary to subminister and then on again, until finally the plea came before the second subminister himself.

The second subminister was a grand old kami, dressed in five fine intangible robes, his offices decorated with wispy clouds in the Edo style. He shook his head sadly and looked down at his first undersecretary.

"This appeal really should have gone through proper channels, to the Ministry of Record. They are the ones who handle family alliances."

The first minor undersecretary to the second subminister cleared his throat tentatively and offered, "The subminister is of course correct. But the ancestor-kami points out that since the petitioner and his intended are ninth cousins four times removed . . ."

The second subminister frowned slightly, then nodded. "Well, that is all right, then. Make out the papers."

And so the first minor undersecretary to the second subminister did just that. He handed the papers to the second minor undersecretary, who took them to the third minor undersecretary and so on until finally the seventh minor undersecretary to the fourth subminister stood once more before the ancestor-kami, papers in hand.

Continued on next page . . .

handle the affairs and appeals brought to them by each island's *Hai'no'sai,* or divine lobbyist. The most important of the minor courts is the *Hai'si'ka,* Court of Domestic Relations, which handles all matters concerning internal family problems and obligations. The *Hai'ki'lan,* the Court of Honor, deals with matters of personal duty, or *jiri*. The Court of Record, the *Hai'i'hai,* deals with the histories and alliances of each family. Pleas to avert divine wrath are handled by the *Hai'so'ki'da,* the Court of Appeals, and even the lowest ranking ShiShaka can pray for attention from the *Hai'da'ki,* the Court of Common Pleas.

Major appeals to the kami of the Divine Court are generally made by the family head. Direct personal appeals are allowed but considered somewhat disrespectful. It is better manners to appeal to the family kami, or ask a wandering priest to intercede. Once the problem has been brought to the attention of the court, the relevant *Hai'do* may either question the family kami further on the matter, or pronounce a judgment.

Each of the Hai'ka'i has specific colors associated with it, as do their festivals. Five is a holy number, for there are five holy winds, five elements of the world and five stages of life.

In contrast to the divine bureaucracy, there is little hierarchy among the mortals of ShiShaka. The head of each family or clan serves as its priest and is responsible for the household rituals. An alternate may be appointed for the minor rituals, but it is considered disrespectful if the family head is absent from the greater rituals. In addition, enlightened individuals can serve as wandering priests. A visit by such a person is a great honor.

Shrines

The *Shi'da'kami* is the center of each dwelling, no matter how great or humble. It is here that the kami are worshiped. While each family strives to create the best shrine it might afford, simple elegance is preferred. The altar is stone or dark wood and upon it is a veiled mirror. Hidden from sight within the altar is the *Sh'kein,* a sealed vase that holds the ashes of ancestors. Bone chimes hang about the room, and a gong calls the family to worship. Incense and fragrant *shokha* wood are burned upon a brazier. A bone flute lies upon the altar – carved from the thighbone of an illustrious ancestor, it is played during the greater rituals. Swords and silk paintings are also revered as holy objects and often found with the Shi'da'kami.

Rituals

Minor Rituals

The ShiShaka are very concerned with purity; minor purification rituals are performed before all important actions. Each family has several *Hara'jashi,* purification wands made from the bone of an ancestor.

The *Ke'sai* are personal rituals and usually take place in the home. The Ke'sai rituals ensure external (or physical) purity and are performed before joining a festival celebration or before visiting a shrine or other holy place.

Upon entering a shrine or other holy place, a second purification ritual must take place. The *Ha'Sai* purifies the adherent spiritually. This rite is performed by a priest who passes one of the family's Hara'jashi over the supplicants.

Other minor rituals include daily offerings of highly stylized prayers and poetry. These may take place either in the family home, or in an outdoor location of particular beauty or sanctity.

The Divine Court (Continued)

The ancestor-kami bowed many, many times, and, tucking the scroll into the depths of his intangible robe, he flew back to the shrine where the young man still prayed. He laid the papers upon the brazier and the fire leapt up. The young man exclaimed in joy, for he knew then that his boon had been allowed, and after much thankful prayer he left the shrine to seek out his bride.

GMing the Divine Court

Each spirit, once adequately sent on by its descendants, enters the Divine Court, working its way through the many levels of the spiritual bureaucracy. Ancestor-kami are expected to hear appeals from their descendants, which they may or may not choose to answer.

How can this be handled in game terms? Using the *Miraculous Magic* system (see pp. 113-115), give each family priest the Divine Favor advantage, with the family's ancestral kami as the patron deity. The base cost is 15 points, and the kami will respond to requests on a roll of 15 or less. Reaction modifiers indicate the ancestral kami's status in the Divine Court.

Any appeal for aid must first capture the attention of the ancestral kami. The family priest performs the appropriate ritual, rolling against his Performance/Ritual skill. If he succeeds, roll to see if the kami is listening. Kami will never appear for an improperly performed ritual.

By responding, the family kami has indicated a willingness to present the problem to the Hai'ka'i. The GM then checks results against the NPC Reaction Table (pp. B204-205), to determine the ancestral kami's luck with the courts. The kami's reaction modifiers (as determined in the Divine Favor advantage) are considered, as well as the worthiness of the request:

+1 if the request is very simple.

-1 to -3 if the request is complex or unreasonable.

+2 if the request is just; -2 if unjust.

Wandering priests are different, in that they appeal directly to the Hai'ka'i. Thus they take the Hai'ka'i, rather than an ancestral kami, as a patron. The Hai'ka'i has a base cost of 20 points, and the reaction modifiers determine the priest's influence with the Hai'ka'i spirit.

Appeals often take days or even weeks to clear the levels of divine bureaucracy, but there is always some response.

Funeral Rite of the ShiShaka

In the predawn darkness the small braziers burned fiercely as Shana-ka sprinkled powered incense over the flames. At the doorway his small sons stood in silent vigil, the mirrors in their hands dark and veiled.

Shana-ka stepped closer to the bier of his father, bowing deeply before lighting the thin candles that lined the edge of the bier.

Soon it would be time to leave. He could hear the muffled sounds of the household procession forming outside. Bowing again, Shana-ka turned to a small gong that hung beside the bier.

With his balled fist, he struck the gong, once for each year in his father's life. He paused between each strike, letting the mournful reverberations fade slowly away.

When the last sound was gone from the incense-heavy air, Shana-ka turned, bowing to his brothers, who now stood behind him. Silent, he stepped aside, letting them take up the honor of their father's burden.

Slowly the bier was carried from the family shrine, the youngest sons of the clan walking so seriously before. After the bier, Shana-ka walked, darkly resplendent in his crimson robes, the long golden tassels knotted and tangled in mourning. In his hands, Shana-ka carried the Sh'kein of the house, a fine tall vase of greatest antiquity.

Continued on next page . . .

Major Rituals

The most important rituals of the ShiShaka are those concerning the five stages of life.

Sai'wak'i – Rite of Birth

It is the duty of the mother's sister to take the newborn into the Shi'da'kami, where the father presents the child to the ancestors. If the mother has no sister, the duty falls to a favored female cousin. Five days after the birth both mother and child are purified. The child is named by the father's mother; if she is dead, the father gives the child a variation of her name. If the father is dead, his brother or a favored male cousin stands in his place. If the mother did not survive the birth, the child is given a variation of her name.

Sai'ko'do–Rites of Childhood

There are three rites of childhood, all involving purification and presentation. When the child is weaned a silken cloth is touched with the child's blood and then burned. When he first walks, a lock of hair is cut and burned upon the altar. When the child first speaks clearly, he is anointed before the altar and given his second name by his mother's mother. If she is dead, the mother gives the child a variation of her name. If the mother is dead, this duty falls to the mother's sister, or a favored female cousin.

Sai'ot'suri – Rite of Adulthood

At puberty the child is tested and questioned about tradition and duty by the eldest of the clan. If successful, the child is pronounced an adult and given his adult name. If not, the child is sent to study with the priests and the rite is repeated after 49 days. If there is another failure, the child remains a child forever, becoming a ward of the priests, never to marry or assume adult responsibilities.

Sai'kan'ai – Rite of Marriage

Five days before the marriage (which usually takes place during the Tsu'ki'shi Festival), both the bride and groom are secluded in the shrine, tended to by their same-sex siblings. It is a time for private prayer and devotion. On the day of the marriage, the elders of both families gather in the shrine with the couple. A lock of hair from both is knotted together, then burned. A common cup of rice wine and sticky-rice/almond balls are shared. The elders call upon the kami for their blessings, and then they leave the shrine for the clan hall to celebrate.

Sai'shi'nu – Death

Death is a time of solemn and elaborate ceremony. The body is taken to the *Da'kein,* the clan shrine. It is here that the funeral and cremation take place. The ashes of ancestors are burned with the body and then placed within the Sh'kein for return to the family shrine (see sidebar, pp. 142-143).

Festivals

Shi'ga'shi – Festival of the Turning of the Year. Houses are rigorously cleaned in preparation for this festival, which lasts the first week of the year. Doorways are decorated with finely braided ropes. Special foods are enjoyed and ritualized visits made. Students visit their teachers, children visit their parents.

Da'ga'shi – Festival of the Lesser Year. This festival occurs a little after the *Shi'ga'shi*. Rites of purity are strictly adhered to during this week-long festival. At the end of the festival the shrine fires are lit, and special rice offerings are made.

Ka'an'shi – Festival of Beans. This festival is a lighthearted family ritual. Children throw toasted beans from the house, along with chants and much laughter, chasing out ill luck and calling the little kami to visit them.

Hin'a'shi – Festival of Dolls. Elaborate displays of dolls are set up within the main room of the house. These dolls represent the nobles of the Courts. Toasts are made and drunk. Marriage arrangements for children are often made at this time.

Ha'Kami'an'shi – Festival of the Spring Kami. This is the day set aside to especially honor the kami that watch over the town or village that the family lives in.

Hi'gan'shi – Festival of Family. This is a time to visit family and far-distant relatives, bearing gifts of wine, rice and incense. Grave shrines are also visited at this time.

Ma'sa'shi – Festival of Flowers. This is a day for family celebrations. The family climbs to the top of a nearby hill and gathers wild flowers. Special toasts and offerings to the wild kami are made. Rice-field ceremonies are also very elaborate at this time.

Seku'an'shi – Festival of Wind. As with *Hin'a'shi,* an elaborate display of dolls is set up within the main room of the house. Streamers of bright silk are hung from the rooftops, and armed dolls are set up at the doorways. Arrangements for children's training and apprenticeships are made at this time.

Su'jin'shi – Festival of the Water Kami. This festival is of utmost importance. During this long festival, many rites of purification are performed. On the last day of the festival, special rites are performed in the shrines of the village and town deities. The Celestial Empress herself performs secret rites on behalf of the people.

Tan'a'shi – Festival of Stars. This is an ancient festival, honoring the distant kami of the Celestial Heavens. Poems are written upon bright scraps of paper or silk, and tied to bamboo leaves. At nightfall, the leaves are placed upon the water and allowed to drift away.

Bon'shi – Festival of the Dead. This is a serious, yet joyous, festival, for this is the time when the ancestral kami are welcomed back into their homes with gifts of food and incense. Graves are tended and decorated.

Tsu'ki'shi – Festival of the Moon and Winds. This is a time of joyous celebration, in which many parties are held. This time is considered to be particularly fortuitous for marriages and betrothals.

Funeral Rite of the ShiShaka (Continued)

Behind Shana-ka the rest of the household followed, the men silently carrying faggots of dark shokha wood, the women carrying wrapped bundles in their hands. Their white garments were torn and streaked with ash, their unbound hair wild and tangled.

The procession made its formal way up the curving mountain path, toward the Da'kein, the most holy shrine of the Clan. The younger brothers waited silently while the other men carefully built the Ka'pan'an from the shokha wood they carried. Then the body of the Eldest of the Clan was laid to its rest upon the Ka'pan'an.

Silently the clan stood, and waited.

Then, when the first pale glow of the dawning sun touched the high mountains, Shana-ka raised up the Sh'kein. Behind him, the women of the clan dropped the scarves from the chi-dai chimes they carried.

Shana-ka stepped forward, and slowly tipped the Sh'kein toward the bier, his voice strong yet sorrowful as he poured the ancestral ashes upon the body of his father.

"Most honorable Kana-ka
We speak your praise
We remember your wisdom
We honor your spirit
We mark your passing
We rejoice in your reward
Rejoin us now
O father
Rejoin us now
O honorable clan
Rejoin us now
O light of the heavens
Rejoin us
Remember us
Rejoin us . . ."

The chant continued, Shana-ka's voice accompanied by the eerie chimes shaken by the women. The Sh'kein empty of its ashes, he stepped back, the ancient vase nestled in his arms.

As the sun crested the mountain peaks, he nodded to his young sons. Each stood at one end of the bier and they unveiled the mirrors they carried, holding them to catch the rays of the rising sun and so set the bier alight.

The eerie chiming of the chi-dai was soon joined by the crackling of the flames.

And when naught but ash was left, Shana-ka knelt and reverently gathered up the ashes of his father and ancestors, and refilled the Sh'kein.

Their duty done, the clan returned to their home, the Sh'kein replaced once more within the family shrine, that Kana-ka's wisdom should not be lost.

Flatliners

He was a punk like any other punk, but he had a talent along with his attitude. A talent for the box. The first time he wired into the Net, he thought he'd found God. People laughed. But he wasn't lying . . .

The Net started simple, just wires connecting machines. But it's more than that now. A whole new world, some say – a place inside the mind if you're a 'runner, a place that leads to every other place, even some nobody really expected. It was the punks that realized it first. The bad boys, high on life and too many drugs, ready to burn their mark into the world. They found the first one cold at the keyboard. Flatlined. The powerboost took down a whole block of the city. But not the Net. Nothing could take down the Net at that point. It happened again, here and there, discounted by the corps and the feds . . . who cares about a stupid punk? But the street learned. The street knew.

They'd found God.

Well, maybe not God. But something. All these years of mystic mumbo-jumbo, who'd have thought that computers would show the Way? Not the corpzecs. They still didn't believe it. But the street knew. The machine. That was it – the missing link. The one perfect accomplishment of man that made him worthy in God's eye. Linked to the Net, those with the touch could find it. Even, with practice, use it. Man to machine to God – that's what the street knew. Cyber became more popular than ever. Metal, wires, electronics – the cold, pure logic – that was the path. The Way. The corps laughed, but they're not laughing any more. Shamans, they call them – Net Wizards. They touch God and bring him back.

Now the corps are getting scared.

GMing Net Shamans

Trancing

Trancing is particularly important for Net shamans. Without the trance, they are simply talented netrunners. With it, they become much, much more. First the shaman must connect into the Net with a neural interface. Then he uses one or more of the techniques listed in the main text (see *Shamanism,* pp. 118-119) to transcend the usual Net experience and attain a trance. The Autotrance advantage is particularly useful for Net shamans.

Breaking a trance suddenly is quite traumatic for the shaman. The only real way to do this is to unplug him from the deck – even physical damage will not affect him otherwise. Should this occur, the shaman must roll against HT. On a failure, he goes into systemic shock, taking 2 dice of damage.

Performance

Unlike their more primitive counterparts, a Net shaman has no need to put on a grand display or performance. If he wishes to convince others of his abilities, he can plug them in and let them piggyback along. This tends to disrupt his concentration, however, and all rolls to establish the trance state are at -1 for each additional person.

Piggybacked viewers will get the shaman's view of the Net. Any interaction with the ghosts or spirits he encounters will appear to them as unusual entities within the Net. However, only the shaman may interact with them. The others may only watch.

Talents

Physical healing, psychopomp duties, and magic items have little meaning in the cyberpunk world. The Net shaman's talents are turned more toward vision and observation than the other shaman duties, though there have been instances of curses, blessings, and spiritual healing. Some claim to have been haunted by malign spirits or *gremlins* at the behest of Net shamans. For the most part, the shamans are still defining the scope of their abilities. The GM should allow anything that has a proper feel and does not unbalance the game too much.

Continued on next page . . .

Shamans

Shamans are netrunners with a special talent. Punks, mostly, they combine the simple skills of any 'runner with an inborn talent, an ability to use the cold, featureless landscape of the Net to reach something beyond. Nobody really understands it, least of all the Net designers. The Net traveled beyond the sight of any one person long ago, beyond everyone but its true master – the shaman.

Plugged in, wired, often cybered, shamans turn electron dances into dreams of reality. The Net creates its own world for them, filled with graphic images, the river-like streams of data flowing, the buzz of minds and realities that sculpt the texture of the Net, and the flickering afterimages of phosphor-dot ghosts. No two shamans view the Net the same way. Each plays a slightly different tune, a different construct of reality. But they all see the ghosts – the flimsy coils of energy that extend in and out of the Net, the machine, themselves, wrapping misty fingers about all who live and breathe, connecting them to all of that which does not. The first shaman fried his brains out in the contemplation of his new world, body cold at the keyboard, eyes turned upward in an expression of ecstasy. The word on the street was that he'd finally found God. Flatline – that was their nirvana, their paradise. To encompass the whole of the universe in a single instant.

It is a terrifying fate to some. But for those willing to search, there is almost unlimited power. Power to reach these ghostly filaments, and bind them to a purpose, to see beyond the normal vision, to call them forth or send them hence, to tap the raw, wild power beyond and find uses for it here. It is dangerous work, magicking the Net, focusing the power of the machine to drive the world beyond the world, but its benefits are many, and quite real. Its potential stretches far beyond the grimy world of the street. Many shamans die young – they all die eventually, in the contemplation of their art. Most say they are the lucky ones. The ones who found something real. While they live, they are worshiped on the street – cared for, protected, coveted, and feared.

Abilities

So what can the shamans do? Much like their primitive namesakes, they transcend this world to enter a realm of ghost and spirits. Using the cold logical progressions of the Net, they gain a true view of this and other worlds.

What this means to the individual shaman can vary greatly, especially since most are still self-taught. Some things are common, however. To attain this new "sight" the shaman must first plug into the Net, and then enter a trance state. Some find this an almost natural occurrence; others need hallucinogenic drugs, meditative exercises, or periods of fasting and physical deprivation to reach it. While tranced, the shaman is completely unaware of anything that occurs about him in the physical world.

His awareness of the Net, however, is incredibly heightened. He gains an almost instinctive understanding of the geography of the Net – not of any particular subsystem, but of the thing as a whole. It is, to him, a huge living landscape that stretches out before him. He can ignore normal movement rules, simply willing himself to a particular area. He can even "hop" systems, moving from one local network to another, as long as any sort of physical connection exists, completely bypassing usual security rules. His "vision" is far more than the usual direct line-of-sight. If he concentrates on a particular locale in the Net, he can gain an immediate understanding of its architecture and current operating status, though not anything detailed or lengthy – he will know that a

GMing Net Shamans (Continued)

Spells

There are two different categories of spells for the Net shaman. The first relate particularly to the Net itself, while the second are the more traditional effects relating to the spirit world.

Net shamans may learn to duplicate program effects with their own powers. To do this, the shaman takes any single program and learns it as if it were a Mental/Hard spell. Casting time is equal to the program's usual execution time, and the shaman's Speed Index is his DX attribute divided by 2. Energy cost is measured in fatigue, and is equal to the equivalent program's complexity. His skill in casting any "spell" can never exceed his Cyberdeck skill. Since the shaman is, himself, performing the effect rather than having a program do it, any successful attacks against the spell affect *him* personally. For example, a crash would force the shaman off the Net and out of trance (with the associated HT roll).

Continued on next page . . .

GMing Net Shamans (Continued)

Net shamans may also learn to cast a limited number of the usual shaman spells. The Banish, Bless, Curse, Death Vision, Divination, Exorcism, History, Remove Curse, Seeker, Sense Spirit, Spirit Trap, and Summon Spirit spells are all applicable. The effects of each should be translated to the cyberpunk milieu by the GM. Additional spells may be created by players, subject to the GM's approval. Spiritual spell effects are particularly draining for a Net shaman, and will most likely be accompanied by power surges and local system crashes of the Net. A successful roll against his Cyberdeck Operation skill must be made, or his deck will be ruined.

Spell failures are particularly nasty for the Net shaman. Net-affecting spells which fail are treated exactly as programs which failed to execute. Critical failures will either dump the shaman out of trance and off the Net (with the associated HT roll), or "freeze" him in his current locale, unable to escape – usually, whichever is worse. Spiritual spells which fail will always result in the destruction of the cyberdeck, and force the shaman to make a HT roll at -2. On a successful roll the shaman takes 1 die of damage; if he fails, he takes 3 dice. If it is a critical failure, the shaman flatlines.

program is being executed and a general sense of its purpose, but not exactly what data is being accessed. Most shamans still rely upon the standard programs for attack and defense, but some have found that they can duplicate program effects by using their enhanced interaction with the Net. In this case, shamans will learn "spells" that are roughly equivalent to program abilities.

These abilities are enough to unnerve the few corp execs that are aware of them, but shamans are more than super netrunners. In addition to their heightened awareness of the Net, they can push beyond, into the true realm of spirits and ghosts. From there they can duplicate many of the traditional shaman's abilities – gaining visions of the present, past, and future, summoning spirits or "ghosts" to their aid, altering events in the form of blessings and curses, and cleansing or curing those affected by maladies of the spirit. Some even claim to speak with the ghosts of past shamans, gaining valuable insight. This is the least understood part of any shaman's powers, and is always associated with dangerous electrical surges on the Net. Shamans go through a lot of cyberdecks. And their fate is always the same. Eventually they are either overwhelmed by the forces they are attempting to control, or they reach some new level of fundamental truth beyond which life has no meaning – Flatline. There is no halfway, no catatonia, no near misses. When a shaman goes, it's always spectacular. The survivors dream of attaining this final moment, the ultimate ecstasy where they become one with God.

Training and Initiation

The discovery and training of those with shaman talent is still quite haphazard. Most still realize their ability on their own, and (if they survive the initial experience) train themselves by trial and error. As the gangs grow, however, and the Net shamans learn more techniques, they are more likely to be sensitive to those with the talent around them. Many of the larger gangs have apprentices or assistants aiding the primary shaman.

It is even possible for multiple shamans to join together on the Net, and add their individual energies together to achieve a much greater effect. This takes a great deal of cooperation on all sides, however, and has not often been attempted.

The Tribe

Like the shamans, those who follow them are mostly punks – street trash. They have found their new savior, the power that can lift them even higher than the almighty corps. Shamans are revered, or at least respected. And the machine becomes their ally. The tribe members cyber themselves as much as they possibly can, for only in the cold purity of logic can they hope to find their future, their enlightenment. The flatline – the symbol of ultimate rebellion, the crimson line and heartbeat symbol on the black background – is their icon, their hope – life recorded, seen, enhanced and then erased by the machine. They are often fanatics.

Organization

Each shaman builds a gang of followers. These are his people, his tribe, who protect him as much as he protects them. Different gangs are often quite introverted, keeping secrets from one another, even to the point of gang warfare. Only one thing binds them together – hatred of the corps and feds that rule their world, and desire to realize power through that of their shaman.

When a shaman dies, the tribe either searches for a new shaman to lead them, or disperses, its members often joining other tribes.

Corps

The one true enemy of the Flatliners is the conglomeration of corporate and government entities that provide the backbone of the Net they rely upon. To the corps, the Flatliners and their shamans are parasites, drawing resources out of the system and returning nothing. Many of the shaman's more impressive magicking results in severe power demands on the system, all too often leading to local outages and system crashes.

Most corps completely disregard the mystical claims, chalking them up to fanatical ranting and hacker's tricks. Some few, however, have begun to realize the grains of truth behind the wild claims. They have one of two reactions: fear, followed by intense search-and-destroy efforts, or curiosity. No few shamans have been "collected" for experimentation.

What has happened to them is not exactly clear.

Truth

So, what's really out there? The folk on the street don't really know, and those shamans who reach an understanding always die in the process. There is speculation, of course, leading to two schools of thought.

The first holds that the true power is the Machine. In its design, man has finally overreached his own potential, and created God. These believers glorify anything related to computers – cyber, robotics, electronics, and so on. They believe that the machine is the perfect form, and they wish to attain it as quickly as possible.

The other school of belief is a more philosophical one. They hold that it is the interaction between the neural interface of the netrunner and his own subconscious mind that brings about the state in which penetration into the next world is possible. The machine merely provides a convenient pattern of consciousness that touches the soul of the shaman 'runner, and allows him to reach beyond.

The truth of the matter is left for the GM to determine. It may be one of these two, or something completely different. Whatever the case, there is *something,* and its true nature should not be easy to discover.

THE KALM OF SEQUAN

In the beginning was the seed, planted deep within the void. And as Time grew, so did Sequan, the Great World-tree. Glorious are the branches of Sequan, for they reach to the upper world, the heavens, the realm of C'lanan. Strong and deep are the roots of the Sequan, for they delve far into the underworld, the realm of Kas. Upon the center of the world, the Sequan stands, the way to all that is.

The Kalm are a reclusive cat-like race inhabiting the lush jungle world of Sequan. They are mistrustful of the off-worlders who trade for the rare pharmaceuticals found on Sequan. Their society seems primitive to many, but their history stretches back nearly three millennia. In ancient times they were a warring tribal people, but now they are a strictly hierarchical society. Personal and family honor is of vital importance to them and blood feuding is common. Yet they consider themselves to be peaceful folk – so long as honor is held holy.

Castes

There are three castes of Kalmis – the Claw, the Pride and the Ka.

The Claw is the warrior/hunter caste. Consisting of both males and females, they are responsible for provisioning and defending their lineage. They mate within their caste, or with those of the Pride.

The Pride makes up the bulk of Kalm society, consisting of non-warrior adults and children. A child may be adopted into the higher caste if one of their parents is of the Claw.

The Ka are the spiritual and temporal leaders of the Kalm. There are three sub-castes within the Ka – the *Shika,* or shamans, the *Shani,* or scholars, and the *Seda,* or leaders. The Shani are responsible for the extensive oral histories and lineage records of the Kalm. The leaders rely both upon their wisdom and upon the knowledge of other realms gathered by the Shika.

Belief and Practice

Religion is an integral part of Kalm life. Their world consists of three realms – the upper world of the heavens, the middle world in which the mortal Kalmis dwell, and the underworld of Kas. Off-worlders are thought to come from distant realms beyond the heavens, and so dealing with them is left to the Shika.

The Tale of Kis and Kas

Long ages passed and the world was empty and quiet, and the realm of Kas lay empty, and began to rumble. These rumblings grew so fierce that they shook the very trunk of the Great World-tree, and rattled the branches that reached into the higher realm. So hard did they shake the tree that a spirit fell from the Realm of C'lanan and fell into the middle world.

And this was Kal, the first shaman of the Kalmis. But Kal was lonely, and so after a while she gave birth to twin sons, who were very unlike each other. Kis was born in the normal way; but Kas refused to follow and be second born. So he clawed his way out of the side of Kal and she died. She was buried in the earth and from her body grew all the holy plants and herbs. And from her blood the Kalmis were born.

Kis and Kas went their own separate ways. Kas created fierce and monstrous animals, ferka and brahgs and ools, and huge biting ickles. Kis made all the useful and harmless animals, like threnkies and klare and rits. Kis and Kas followed the rits as they flew, and they led them back to the little Kalmis, as young and helpless as plets they were. Kas growled and immediately began to gobble up the Kalmis, but Kis hit him, and Kas died, and went away into the lower realm. It was then that Kis taught the Kalmis to fight, to kill and eat. And it was Kis who first traveled to the Realms of Kas, to speak to the spirit of the first shaman, Kal. And when he returned he brought back with him the first kahan.

And so it is that the Kalmis came to be.

Once a Shika has undergone his initiation, he can enter a state of trance at will to travel in the spirit. The upper world is the world of spirits and knowledge. It is to this world that the Shika travel to confer with their spiritual helpers. These spirits help the Shika gather and prepare the pharmaceuticals that Kalmis and off-worlders both value. Each Shika has several spirits which will aid him, both here and in the middle world.

The lower realm is the underworld of Kas, Lord of the Dead. It is Kas who guards the spirits of the dead and judges the honor of the living. At death each Kalm is guided here by a Shika to be judged. If honor is pure then the soul may remain. If at fault, the soul is devoured by Kas, forever lost to its lineage. Souls that remain may be contacted by a Shika at the request of their family if needed.

The Kalm belief in the mystical relationship between the three realms can be seen in the practices of everyday life. Honor is of utmost importance. The Kalmis have no written language and a spoken oath is unbreakable. To call a Kalm a liar is to touch off a blood feud.

Each named adult has a *kahan*, or ritual knife, that is not only the seat of his soul and honor, but is considered to *be* his soul. The handle of this knife is carved from the bone of an ancestor. If the kahan is lost, a Kalm will do anything within the bounds of honor to regain it. A Kalm without a kahan is considered to be cursed, caught between the worlds of the living and the dead. A Shika would certainly be sought to help find the kahan in such a case. If the kahan is destroyed, then the Kalm is considered to be worse than dead – with the soul dead, the body must follow. Suicide, in some public and spectacular manner, is the only recourse. A kahan-less person – such as an off-worlder – is considered, at best, to be a child. At worst, they are mere animals. Only members of the Ka (and those of the Claw specifically bound to protect them) deal with off-worlders.

Rituals

Kalkah – Rite of Naming. It is vitally important that a Shika (preferably female) be present at a birth, especially a birth among the Claw. The Shika protects the newborn soul during the trauma of birth, and travels to the underworld to find a soul-patron for the child among its ancestors. Such a soul-patron acts as a spiritual guardian for the child until its Rite of Souling. (Until the Rite of Honor, the child is known by the name of the ancestor, with the prefix *da-* attached. Thus, the ward of the soul-patron Glyss would be called da-Glyss. Bone once belonging to the ancestor Glyss would be blessed and prepared to become the hilt of the child's kahan, should it survive to adulthood.)

Kalkahan – Rite of Souling. This rite marks the transition from child to adult. The adult-to-be is presented with the kahan before a gathering of ranking adults. A ritual battle takes place between the supplicant and a Claw warrior of the same lineage. The warrior slashes the supplicant three times (one for each realm) while the supplicant attempts to kill the warrior. The battle complete, the newly-made adult bloods his kahan in his own blood and claims an adult name. (If by some fluke the warrior is killed, the supplicant claims that name. This is the only instance in which blood feud is *forbidden* over a killing. Rather, it creates a deep bond between the new adult and the offspring of the dead warrior.)

Kalkiska – Rite of Honor. This is a ceremony of vassalage or allegiance. Obligations are announced before a gathering of those concerned. The kahan of the lesser-ranking Kalm is offered into the hands of the higher, signifying that the one trusts the other with the guardianship of his honor and soul, a state called *kadiss*. A Kalm under kadiss is not responsible for the honor of any act the other requires him to commit – all obligation falls upon the other.

The state of marriage is considered to be a state of mutual allegiance among the Kalmis. It is a simple ceremony before witnesses in which kahan are exchanged for a brief moment and then returned. A marriage can be ended only by the Rite of Duel.

Kaldesha – Rite of Duel. This is a ritual of determination through combat. Conflicts of honor between individuals are settled upon the *Sakiska,* the field of honor. A challenge of Kaldesha cannot be refused.

There are two forms of this rite. The first is *Redesha,* the naked duel. Combatants fight naked, using only claws and teeth. Redesha ends when one combatant submits his throat to the other. The second rite of Kaldesha is *Rekah,* a duel in which kahan are used. This duel ends in the death of one (or both) of the participants.

Kalkors – Rite of Blood. This is the rite of feuding. There are two forms of the Kalkors. The first is *Korskal,* a personal vendetta. If a Kalm feels that his honor has been insulted beyond repair, he calls Kalkors upon an individual *and* all his lineage within a certain degree of kinship. Kalkors is declared by slaying a close member of the lineage in a ritualistic fashion and presenting the body to the challenged party (see *Kalkessa,* below). Such feuds end quickly, though they garner much honor for the outnumbered challenger. Death through Korskal is an excellent reason to call the second form of Kalkors, *Korska*. This involves entire families, and continues until either honor is satisfied, or there is no one left to fight.

Kalka – Rite of Spirit. This is the initiation rite of a Kalm shaman. About the time of puberty the would-be Shika disappears into the forest for several days upon *Shalel,* or vision-quest. The supplicant wanders and fasts, drinking only his own blood until he falls into a trace state and travels for the first time to the upper realm. It is there that the C'lanan, the great spirit, touches him and grants him his spirit helpers. When the new Shika returns he joins the ranks of the Ka. Shika can be drawn from any of the three castes, although Shika rarely come from the Claw. Those born to the Ka caste who do not become Shika train as Seda or Shani instead.

Kalkessa – Rite of Feast. This is one of the most important observances of the Kalm, in which the bodies of the dead are consumed. It is considered the utmost insult to refuse to eat a vanquished foe (hence the horrible consequences of returning the body in the Rite of Blood, above). The kahan of the slain are given to the Shika, who travel to the realm of Kas with the soul.

Kaltas – Rite of Clan. This is an extremely rare rite involving adoption. If honor demands an obligation of such import that even ritualistic suicide cannot repay the debt, the honored person may be adopted, creating bonds of blood and honor that nothing can erase. Before a gathering of the entire lineage, the adoptee is blooded by the kahan of every adult member. In turn, the adoptee drinks from a cup in which blood from the entire lineage – including children – has been mixed. (If it happens that the adoptee is not strong enough to survive the rite, he is consumed in a Rite of Feast with great ceremony.)

Rite of Naming

Suzsha crouched in the center of the birthing circle, sweat matting her once-glossy fur. She snarled as another contraction hit, claws raking deep into the hard-packed soil. Nearby her sisters and mother, fellow warriors of the Claw, waited, patiently watching. They guarded the clearing, making sure no one dared to come too close. Above, the hot noon sun broke through the canopy of leaves. Beside her, the Shika Tshosa continued chanting, her gnarled fingers striking a slow beat on the ground with an ancient thigh bone. Her apprentice crouched nearby, slowly adding holy *sezza* leaves to the small fire. The pungent smoke rose up in lazy waves, making Suzsha's senses waver. Tshosa's voice was a sibilant stream of prayer.

"Come oh honored one
Heed the call of bone
Heed the call of blood
Heed the mew of a new soul
Come oh warrior
Heed the cry
Come oh guardian
Heed the blood
Come oh ancient one
Return to your blood
Return to your kin
Come oh honored one . . ."

Suzsha's panting snarls became a sharp series of pained yowls as the child forced its way from her body in a gush of blood and fluid. Her cub lay upon the ground between her haunches and Suzsha howled in triumph. The Shika Tshosa moved closer, dipping the thigh bone in the blood. Her chant continued as she reached out, one sharp claw gently scribing a holy rune onto the shrieking child's belly. Blood swelled up from the cut; the Shika wiped it off with her fingers, anointing the bone she held. Suzsha's howls faded away as she waited the Shika's announcement.

"Isshan has returned to us."

Around them, the other women broke into howls and screams of joy. Suzsha's lips pulled back from her sharp teeth as she smiled in victory and bent to pick up her daughter, the cub da-Isshan.

Disciplines of Change

It was the year 2042 of the old calendar when Dr. Mary Kelly first demonstrated her incredible power to the world by healing an entire ward of terminally-ill patients. She became a public icon overnight, an object of adulation, fear and worship, hailed as a new messiah, and was eventually driven into seclusion by those who sought her healing touch. She lived in near-solitary confinement for the next 10 years with a handpicked group of students, until her death in the year 2052 at the hands of a rabid mob who feared her power. But her work survived her. Entitled the Doctrine of Change, it spoke of a new way, foregoing faith and religion for rational thought and scientific discovery, emphasizing her own exploration of the mind. From this work, preached and publicized by her chosen students, sprang forth what later came to be known as the Disciplines of Change.

Excerpted from *The Facts Behind The Myth – The Life of Dr. Mary Kelly*

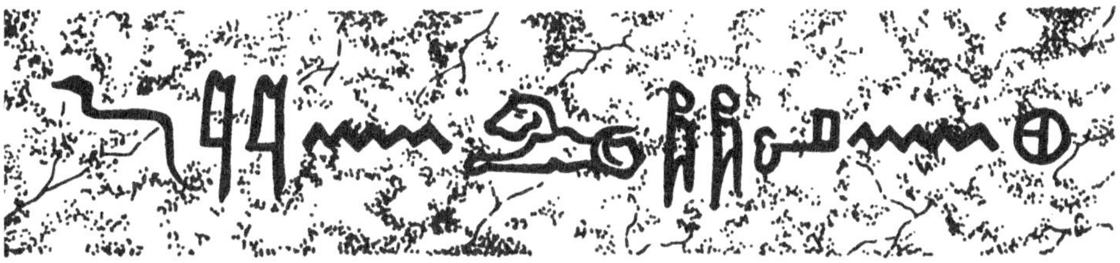

Beliefs

From the words and writings of the prophet Mary came the Disciplines of Change. The Disciplines center about the following tenets:

Knowledge over faith. Perception over belief. Faith, wrote Mary, is the root of all prejudice in the world – faith in religion, faith in country, faith in truths that bear no relation to reality. Those who had opened their minds to knowledge knew the power of questions, and the sadness of ignorance. "Believe only that which you can demonstrate. That which cannot be known does not exist."

Power lies within ourselves. "Those who seek the divine need look no farther than themselves. Accept the power and the responsibility for yourselves, your actions, and their consequences. Seek the keys to unlocking the mind, for within lie the purest truths of all."

Change is the only constant. Change is, of course, the central doctrine of the Disciplines of Change. Mary viewed change as the major power of life. "Through change we grow, leaving behind the old and embracing the new. Change through knowledge is a path leading ever closer to enlightenment."

Learning is the primary motivator for change. "Learning disciplines the mind, leaving it open to change. Without learning we become stale, wasted, static."

Only through scientific exploration can we learn. "True learning must be experienced, explored, quantified and categorized. Rote memorization is worse than useless; it teaches faith rather than knowledge. Random questing can lead one astray. Hypothesize, experiment, and draw conclusions from your own experimentations. Believe nothing but that which you can constantly reproduce."

Without trial, complacency results. "Suffering is one of the prime motivators for change. Fear, starvation, disease, all cause us to seek answers and grow Contentment breeds complacency. Decay is the result. Suffer, and be changed."

Mind Powers

As Mary Kelly proved, the mental powers sought by adherents of the Disciplines of Change are real. It was her belief that all people had one or more latent powers which could be discovered and trained. This may be true, or it may be that only special individuals with true latent talents will be able to reach this "enlightenment." In any case, it won't really matter to those who believe. Despite considerable attempts to quantify and rationalize the process, the sequence of steps each person goes through to discover his own talents is slightly different. Those who do not achieve such powers have obviously not found the proper path, or are not concentrating upon it adequately.

In game terms, the mental powers begin as latent Psionic abilities and are developed through study and discipline. Techniques include hypnosis, sensory deprivation, meditation, biofeedback and careful consumption of hallucinogenic drugs. There are two aspects to developing a power – achieving or increasing the power of a particular psi ability, and then developing the skill to use it in certain ways. The GM decides whether powers have upper limits, and whether the power for a particular ability is innate (and therefore immutable) or can be increased with further study.

Crystals

Crystals may be used to focus psi power through meditation. The individual clears his mind and concentrates on the chosen crystal. On a successful Meditation roll, the crystal will effectively increase his psi power in whatever ability he attempts to use thereafter. Each 10 carats of crystal (round down) will increase the psi power by 1. The crystal should be pure – without flaws or fractures. Each flaw reduces its effective size by 10 carats. Large, pure crystals are exceedingly rare.

For example, Adrienne, with a Telepathy power of 2, concentrates upon a pure crystal of 25 carats. Assuming a successful Meditation roll, the crystal will increase the effective power to 4, allowing her to Telesend up to 2 yards away from her current location. She must still make a successful Telesend roll against her usual skill level.

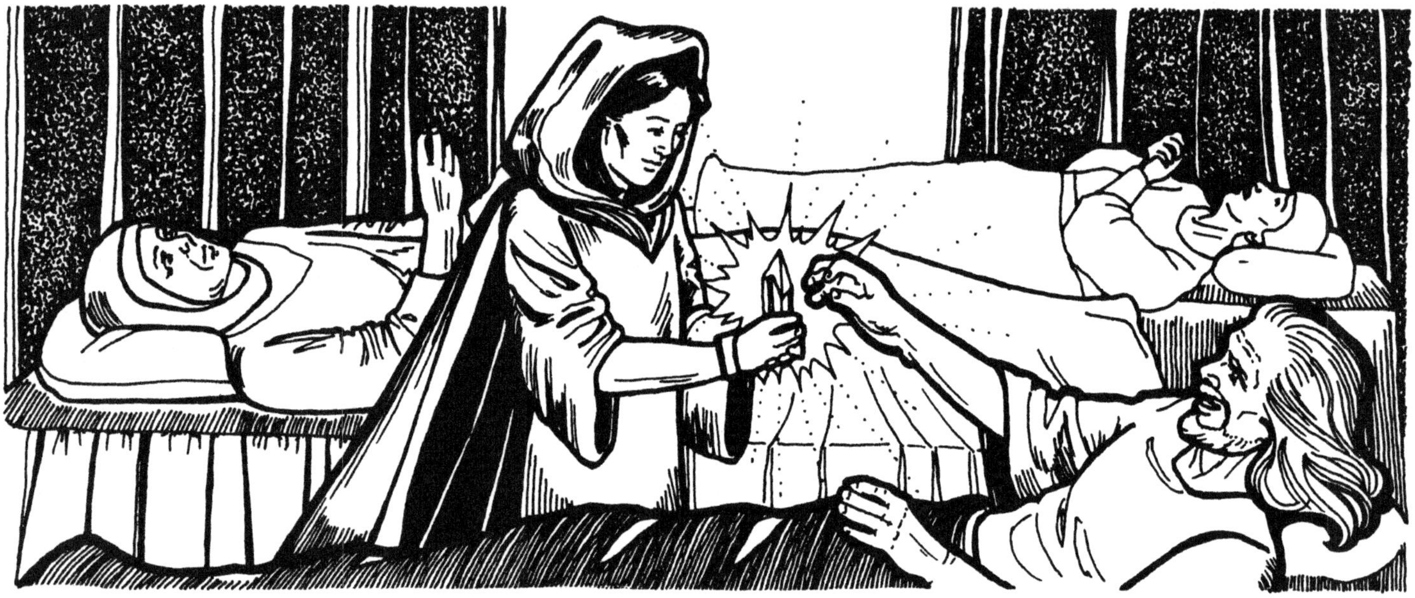

All perception is flawed. Truth is relative. Perhaps the most difficult of the tenets, Mary also realized the relative nature of perception, and the truth that results from it. "Your truth is not always my truth. Thus you must always seek the answers that are your own. By examining the works of others you can gain insights and ideas, but only through rigorous testing and cross-examination can real truths be found."

Exploration of the Mind

Mary's own field of expertise was the study of the brain and the thought processes of the mind. She wrote many papers on the nature of hallucinations, dreams, and the keys to unlocking the inherent power of the mind. She believed that all people had latent talents which could be trained and developed by scientific methods.

Her research revolved around her own "evolution," as she called it. Beginning with biofeedback techniques, sensory deprivation, and the closely-monitored administration of certain drugs, along with Eastern mantras for centering and focusing the flow of thought, she tapped into her own latent powers and awoke her healing gift. The notes she left were copious and detailed. Her experiments were unorthodox on several levels, but her basic techniques were sound. Her results were unquestionable. Mary had achieved something – something people flocked in record numbers to seek for themselves.

Purpose

The purpose behind the Disciplines of Change is to learn the true nature of the universe and the self. Its disciples hold truth and knowledge, especially self-knowledge, above all else.

Though they stress the internal development of the mind, the leaders of the Disciplines also encourage students to interact with others and share what has been learned. They regularly hold seminars and meetings on all that they have discovered in their personal research. Through the professional quality of their work, proponents of the Disciplines have gradually received approval and acceptance among the scientific community.

The Martyrdom of Mary

Considered a holy figure by many, Mary's death caused considerable outrage and furor. Not a few venerate her as a martyr of the common age, and have adopted her as an icon for peace against an increasingly violent society. Many without access to the training to appreciate her works see her as a figure worthy of devotion and worship. Some find their way into one of the many sects of the Disciplines, but others ignore her teachings, preferring to view her as a reincarnation of the Virgin Mary. Within the Catholic church, there has been a resurgence of the Cult of Mary, with Mary Kelly as its new focal point.

Needless to say, adherents of the Disciplines decry any attempts to deify their prophet, pointing to Mary's own words. However, their actions have had little or no effect on the growing movement.

Organization

There is no true organization to the Disciplines, no established central body. Mary specifically denounced "archaic and static hierarchies."

Despite her desires, however, certain distinctions are commonly made among followers of the Disciplines. Those new to the Disciplines are known as *Students*. Once they have mastered the basic principles, they are accepted by the community at large as *Associates*. Associates form the majority of the membership. Those Associates with particular initiative and insight will eventually develop a reputation among their peers, and may, with the approval of the majority, be accepted as *Principals*. Principals gather into informal collectives which judge new proofs and theories based on scientific merit, and write papers on their own experiments for others to study. They provide a focal point for the energies and ideas of the whole, and serve as a repository for the information collected by the members. Archives exist in many places, often supported by research grants and various scientific bodies.

Those members who achieve demonstrable mental powers are venerated by their peers, but hold no special rank.

Sects

As time goes on, the loose structure of the Disciplines has led to different sects, each focusing on some particular theorem derived by one of their Principles. Some of the sects merely provide a focus for learning, while remaining open to diverging points of view. Others have become almost hostile to this lax approach, declaring that certain fundamental truths must be accepted in order to ascend to the next state of knowledge. Two of these, on completely opposite sides of the spectrum, conflict openly.

The Relativists believe that since all knowing is relative (especially self-knowledge), the scientific slant of Mary's writings is but one expression of the real truth. They accept all member testament as fact, no matter how poorly documented, and build their theories in whatever manner suits them best. Much of their focus centers around the study of parapsychology and the awakening of mental gifts. Their claims far outstrip any other sect, and thus they tend to draw the more idealistic and enthusiastic adherents.

The Logicians, on the other hand, discount anything that cannot be empirically proven. They distrust many of the Relativists' claims, accusing them of being little better than a charlatan's parlor tricks. They deal only with that which can be easily quantified, and prefer to remain in the more familiar realm of metaphysics and philosophical proof. It is the work of the Logicians which has received the most scientific scrutiny and approval, and as time progresses, they feel more and more weighed down by their less-rigorous Associates.

The Future

As time progresses, the differing sects grow farther and farther apart. Some of the collectives gather in monastic communes, citing the difficulties of focusing mental powers like telepathy and empathy in overcrowded cities. One particularly radical sect seeks to build its own space station, claiming that the magnetic fields, background radiation and overwhelming population of the earth have negative effects on its studies. Someday splinter groups may seek their isolation in separatist colonies, whose membership is limited to those who have achieved demonstrable and repeatable mental powers.

Crystals

Quartz, or rock crystal, has become a common token or talisman worn by followers of the Disciplines. Though crystals were not mentioned by Mary in her writings, her student Maratsu discovered that they seemed to be useful in focusing the mind. Further studies have proved that many of the claims of crystal enthusiasts through the years are true ~ crystals form a naturally balanced energy field which can be used to manipulate flows of psychic energy.

Jealousy and Fear

As techniques for waking mental powers become more advanced, those who practice them have been forced to be more and more careful about how they approach the public. The outrage at Mary's death halted much of the initial fear-mongering, but it is not completely gone. As the Disciplines grow and expand an ever-growing portion of the world population fears their use and potential abuse. Some of the group's more notorious members have been forced into isolation to escape threats of violence, while others have been approached by everyone from government agents to business interests interested in exploiting their talents.

Dhala, Destroyer of Worlds

"The ages of creation are past, the days of our glory have sped into darkness. The supreme night is upon us – Dhala, who swallows all things. Upon the corpse of the universe she stands and we are the sword in her hand. Dissolution of all is her triumph, all that is colored shall fade into darkness, all that is shaped shall be dispersed. O enfolding darkness, o divinity of night, thy power is boundless, thy visage most terrible."

The Dhala are an ancient people, their origins lost in past millennia. They take their name from their goddess. At the height of their glory they ruled the galaxy, their technology so perfected that little was beyond their capabilities. Now they are a shadow of their former selves, their empires collapsed and forgotten, their worlds abandoned cinders. The few remaining Dhala travel the universe in their great world-ships, destroying all they encounter with single-minded fanaticism.

The Dhala are multi-armed, vaguely humanoid beings, genetically manipulated countless generations ago to resemble the image of their goddess. They reproduce by cloning – when one of their number is killed or undergoes the rite of Ysa, a replacement is made. The race must continue until the final immolation of the universe, at which time Dhala will consume them all. They possess psionic abilities and are especially adept at telekinesis, pyrokinesis and other destructive mental skills.

Belief and Practice

The Dhala believe in *Riksa,* the eternal cycle of creation and destruction. The universe has entered the second half of the cycle, the journey to entropy and final destruction. And it is their divinely appointed task to ensure that the cycle continues.

While the Dhala are monotheists, they believe that Dhala has many aspects, all involved with dissolution and destruction. (The creative aspects once ascribed to her have been downplayed and are all but forgotten.) Fire is the primary aspect of Dhala. There are ten forms of fire – five natural and five ritual.

The Duality of Dhala

Dhala is the deity revered by the Children of Dhala. Though her people forgot her dual aspects long ago, they still remain part of the goddess. At present, Dhala the Destroyer is foremost, but once the universe is truly unraveled, the creative side will flourish and life will begin again under Dhala the Creator. Such is the nature of duality – opposite sides of the same coin (see *Duality,* p. 130).

Dhala was born in the act that first created the universe. As it cycles, so does she, her aspects shifting from creator, to a balance in harmony, to the destroyer, in order that the whole shall begin again.

She is archetypal, in that she represents the primal forces of creation and destruction. As creator, she also symbolizes birth, mercy, and light. As destroyer, her primary aspect is the flame that shall consume all being.

Dhala is omnipresent, existing in all things simultaneously, as well as being omnipotent, though her cares are for the flux and flow of the universe rather than any particular individual fate.

The dualistic image Dhala presents to her believers is that of a multi-armed humanoid female. In her right hand she holds a newborn babe, while in the other she cups the flame that is her destructive potential. In reality she has no true physical form, but rather exists as an abstract force that is actualized through her chosen people.

Continued on next page . . .

The Natural Forms of Fire

Aga – The common fire of fuel. It is the spirit of Aga that speeds the Dhala on their path of destruction through the universe.

Vaga – The fire of space. It is the spirit of Vaga that powers their weaponry, that brings conflagration and destruction upon the universe.

Saya – The celestial fire. This is the fire of a nova sun which illuminates a world in the last days before its annihilation.

Nara – Life-fire. This is the all-pervader, the power of consumption found within all living things. It supports life, yet it is holy to Dhala for it consumes and destroys to do so. Pyrokinetic abilities are evidence of the existence of Nara.

Ignis – This is Dhala's most fearful form, the ultimate fire of destruction. The power lies deep within each world, and it is the awakening of this fire that destroys worlds.

The Ritual Forms of Fire

Ima – Essence-fire. This is the burst of divine fire that appears at the time of a sacrifice and consumes it utterly.

Iga – Priest-fire. This is the eternal fire found at the core of a Dhala world-ship. It is preserved though worship and sacrifice.

Hisa – Blood-fire. This is the fire that burns at a private shrine. It is the center of personal worship and is fed by the supplicant's blood.

Haga – Ancestor-fire. This is the fire of purity and preparation. It is the fire of memory that recalls the deeds of ancestors so that the living might be strengthened and inspired.

Ysa – Immolation-fire. This is the fire of personal destruction, never approached by the living. A Dhala called by the goddess will set himself alight and throw himself into the Iga at the core of the world-ship.

The Image of Dhala

Dhala is most commonly depicted as a four-armed being perched upon a broken corpse, flames issuing from her mouth. She laughs in triumph for she holds utter dominion over all that exists. She mocks those who hope to escape her fury. The body on which she stands is the corpse of the universe. At the end of time, only the power of destruction – Dhala – remains. The sword she holds represents her people – the power of her wrath. She is naked, for she is clad only in the vast emptiness of space. And she is black – as are the ships and colors of her people – for she is the ultimate energy in which all things and all colors disappear, all shapes returning to the entropy of the everlasting night.

The Duality of Dhala (Continued)

Being essentially abstract, as well as omnipresent, Dhala exists everywhere simultaneously, having no particular realm or dwelling place. Though her universe may be consumed in flame, she is never destroyed.

Dhala the Creator is a benevolent deity. Dhala the Destroyer is malevolent, destroying all that comes before her with equal abandon. Generally speaking, she is an indifferent deity, not concerning herself with the piddling affairs of mortals. She will almost never interfere directly, though her devoted followers may call upon one of her two aspects – the light of healing, or the flame of destruction. She is almost always oblivious to the actions of her creations or the suffering of her destruction. She simply is, as she will always be.

Dhala's worship is one of mystery and discovery. She recognizes no other form of divinity besides her own, and thus has no divine ties.

Dhala is subject to no divine law except her own. She depends upon her followers for little – they but speed the process of her work. It would occur, and she would exist, with or without them.

Dhala has no associated demigods or divine servants.

Organization

The *Ris'da*, or priests, lead the Dhala. They are considered to be beyond rank. Occupation determines the rank of the remaining Dhala. Those who deal with weapons systems are ranked highest, those who deal with ship maintenance are lowest, with all others scaled somewhere in between. All Dhala, regardless of rank, consider themselves to be warriors in a holy cause and spend much of their off-duty time honing their martial skills.

Each world-ship, or *Dhak*, is totally independent of the others. The Ris'da maintain only enough contact between ships to ensure a certain level of planning in their destructive courses. The Dhala delight most in destroying entire planetary systems by awakening the Saya, causing the sun to go nova by use of their ancient technology. Spacefaring races that oppose them they destroy in great battles, reserving the most honorable fate for their defeated foes – those planets they destroy individually, by piercing the world's core with their weaponry and awakening the holy Ignis.

The Gods of Bethany

Long ago, before the age of Man began, before even the Elves awoke and the stars began to shine, there were Daisha, the Queen of Earth and Lystran, the Lord of Light. Many were their children, and the world was peaceful and golden, without flaw and unchanging in the perfection of endless time.

– *The Lay of Light*

Long ago, when the very thought of man was but a whisper in the wind and the elder folk had not yet ventured forth into light of day, the world was wracked and broken by the arguments and wars of the gods. Now, we call this the Sundering, for it surely changed the world.

In those days, there was no Sleeping God, for Wylan was awake and wandered the world as he willed. All the magic and the mysteries of the world were known to him, no secret was held safe from his sight, and his will pierced the Darkness and gleaned all from it.

– *The Tale of Wylan*

Those who live in the lands of Bethany worship the Holy Children of Daisha, the Queen of Earth. Daisha had two consorts, the Lord of Light and the Dark Hunter. Most follow the children of the Lord of Light – Keldan, Dorn and Asta. Worship of the Dark Hunter's children is discouraged (and in some cases outlawed) by the church of Keldan. (See sidebars, pp. 163-166.)

Keldan Lawgiver

The firstborn of Daisha by the Lord of Light, Keldan is the Giver of Laws, the Defender, the Protector of Oaths. His spheres of influence are truth, honor, justice, resolve, loyalty and strength. Keldan dislikes magic and sanctions its use rarely, and then only in Dornite hands. He is a militant and chivalric god. His symbols are the light and the sword; his colors are the gold of light and the white of purity.

Creation Myths of Bethany

The Lay of Light

Each of the Holy Children had duties in the world, as the Lord of Light in His wisdom decreed. High among these were Keldan, Lightbringer and Lord of Truth and Honor, and Dorn, the Lord of Wisdom who spent long ages at Lystran's knee, drinking of His knowledge. And most beloved was Asta, whose beauty and fair spirit caused all to grow in glorious abundance. Birds broke into song at the sight of her, and flowers sprang up where she stepped.

But sadness came into the world, for where the light of Lystran did not fall, there grew darkness and shadow, giving birth to He-who-is-not-seen, the great Deceiver, the Dark One, the Hunter of Life, Souldrinker. Many are His names, and great His evil.

As darkness grew, the Lord of Light weakened and grew wan. So the Queen of Earth sought out the Dark One. First She demanded, and struck at the foul darkness, but such ill suited her, and even a goddess may not kill what does not live. Then She tried the guiles and crafts of women, and pleaded for mercy. Her pleas moved the Dark One not, though Her beauty inflamed him. And so in dishonor and darkness did Volt come into the world, born of Daisha's strength and fire. Then came Wylan the trickster, born of Her witchery. And last, born of Her guile and beauty, came Cara Gildenheart, the temptress.

And while Darkness reveled in the birth of His children, Daisha crept away in Her shame, and was lost to the world.

So Keldan Firstborn, guided by Dorn's wisdom and craft, forged a sword of Light and Law, and tempered the blade within the fire of Lystran's fading glory, so that forever more might Lystran's light be with the world. And Asta wept, to see her beloved step out to war, Dorn at his side and a great host behind them. With her tears, the stars were kindled, to shine brightly and illuminate their way.

And so began the Sundering Wars.

Long ages they fought, brother god against brother god, until the very face of the world was changed. In those times even Volt fought against the darkest one, for he was shamed by Daisha's fate, and sought vengeance against his father. Wylan hid in the shadows and worked his witchery and dreamcraft. But such could not withstand the light of the Sword of Keldan and the righteous flames of Dorn's wisdom. And so Wylan hid behind the skirts of Cara, who by her guile kept all others from him.

Continued on next page . . .

Keldan's physical form is that of a tall, blond, golden-eyed knight wearing robes of white with a cross emblazoned in gold. He wields the Sword of Light, which represents both his strength and his purpose – to cut through the darkness with light, and to protect the defenseless.

Keldan is a benevolent but harsh deity. He requires much of those who follow him, and accepts little deviation from his laws. He keeps a close eye on his worshipers, and will even appear directly to his special chosen ones (known as Trueswords). He has a forthright and lawful nature, and demands the same of all who worship him. His weaknesses are an unforgiving character, and a tendency to view the world in terms that suit him best. Keldan opposes all things of chaos, darkness and deceit.

Those sworn to Keldan never lie or break an oath or law. They never abandon a charge, nor ignore an injustice. They cannot deny an appeal by the helpless. Keldanites will seek and destroy any who disturb the rest of the dead.

Keldan is closely allied with Dorn, and depends upon him for advice and guidance. He is the devoted protector and husband of Asta. He opposes and despises Volt, and hates Wylan for his crimes against Asta. He dislikes (and perhaps fears) Cara for her licentious and chaotic ways.

Organization

All clerics of Keldan are also knights and must belong to one of several holy orders. While some of these knightly orders are secular, their leadership consists entirely of clerics. Familiar ties and loyalties are superseded by obedience and duty to Keldan and one's knightly superiors. Clerics of Keldan who wish to marry must wed a Lady or Dame of Asta. Celibacy before marriage (and constancy afterwards) is demanded by the god.

The supreme temporal authority of the church is the *Highsword,* a cleric chosen by the god himself. A *Truesword* is a special knight who stands outside the regular hierarchy of the church and belongs to no one order. Also chosen by the god, a Truesword is answerable only to Keldan and the Highsword. Women may not be clerics of Keldan, although they may join cloistered orders as nuns. Female knights are extremely rare and frowned upon, but may join the Order of the Shield if they are virginal and swear an oath of celibacy.

Knights of Law – A closed (non-secular) order consisting entirely of cleric-knights. These knights supervise all other Keldanite orders, as well as monasteries and convents. They are responsible for the security of all churches and their fiefs.

Knights of the Land – Knights are appointed to this order by royal decree after having served at least ten years in another Keldanite order. They are responsible for the protection of the royal family and the capital.

Creation Myths of Bethany (Continued)

And so the Wars continued, age after age, and Asta's tears filled the oceans of the world.

Then Wylan in his anger whispered dreams into the ear of his father, and Darkness listened. And so they plotted foulness. Then fair Asta came into their hands, drawn by trickery and lies, and she brought with her the Sword of Keldan, for she thought to ransom her beloved's life.

Then even Volt's righteous anger paled beside the wrath of Keldan and the rage of Dorn. Even the earth mourned Asta's loss, and no new life came into the world. But alone Keldan's bright anger was no match for the coldness of the Dark One. Without the Sword, all was lost.

Dorn in his wisdom found another way.

And so began his hunt. Through long ages he sought through the Darkness, his cold flame lighting the way. Many perils, many tricks and traps did he overcome, many temptations did he face. But he persevered, though for a time he was counted among the lost.

But upon the coldest of nights, when all the light in the world was found in the stars that were the tears of Asta, did he return, bringing back the light of Lystran, leaving Wylan behind, bound in the darkness. And as the Sword left his hands, and was taken up by Keldan, bright flames remained to cloak Dorn, and from that day was he called the Wayfinder.

Then did Keldan stride forth triumphant, bringing Justice and Law once more into the world. The Dark One did Keldan sunder from the world with one swift blow and in Dorn's flames did the hosts of darkness perish. Cara danced through the shadows, always one step ahead of the bright blade.

Asta he rescued from the Dark One's foul halls, and set her in his own palace, where she has rested ever more by his hearth. And with her return, the world once more brought forth life, and thus man was born into the world.

But the world was forever tainted by the shadow of the Dark One, and ever do His children strive against the Light.

And so must we be ever wary, to drive out any taint of Darkness we may find within us, that Keldan might see us worthy of a place within his halls.

Continued on next page . . .

Knights of the Sword – A small secular order that accepts only members of noble blood. These knights often serve as leaders of the army, helping to protect the borders of Bethany.

Knights of the Shield – The largest Keldanite order, in which membership is won by right of arms. This is the only order which will accept a female knight, or one of illegitimate birth.

Guardian Knights of Vesma – A secular hospitaller order closely associated with the crofts of Asta. They also protect the Vale of Vesma, the birthplace of Keldan, Dorn and Asta.

Festivals

Swordcall – High Festival of Keldan, late in the fall of the year. It lasts six days, and is a favored time for initiations, oaths and knightings. During Swordcall, the Highsword goes through a series of fasts and purifications before disappearing to commune with the god, reporting on affairs of the church and receiving new directions.

Lumens – Early in the first month of the year, this is one of the most important festivals in Bethany. It celebrates the return of Asta and the Sword of Light. It is during this festival that all fires in Keldanite churches and strongholds are relit from the flame rekindled by the Keeper of Vesma (see p. 162) in the Vale of Vesma.

Garb

Clerics of Keldan wear white, symbolizing purity, innocence and the white-hot heat of metal being forged.

For practical wear (when they can be convinced to take off their padding and armor), Keldanites don simple tunics, belted at the waist. Fancier tunics might have the Sword of Keldan embroidered upon them. At all times they wear a small sword pendant in token of their vows. For the celebration of rituals all Keldanite priests – regardless of their order – wear a chasuble, alb and stole.

At High Festivals more elaborate garb is worn. A long cope, usually richly embroidered, is worn over standard ceremonial wear. A priest of Keldan never covers his head except at funeral services and during the Festival of Darkhunt.

Keldan nuns wear a long flowing garment called a *kris* and a veil of purest white. Over it they wear the *cowl,* another floor-length garment with sleeves long enough when let down (they are worn folded back) that they just touch the ground, and wide enough that they touch the knees when the hands are folded upon the breast. Beneath the veil a *wimple* is worn to constrain the hair, which is cropped short to avoid fuss.

Charge of Chivalry

A cleric-knight of Keldan has a double responsibility. He must always live according to both the Rule of his Order and the *Charge of Chivalry*:

"Thou art never to do outrageously, nor murder, and to always flee treason. Likewise thou art by no means to be cruel and to always do succor to ladies, damosels and gentlewomen."

"Take no battles in a wrongful quarrel, for no law nor the world's goods."

"Thou shalt be for all ladies, though thy own lady thou shalt honor above all ladies, and ever be courteous and never refuse mercy to him that asketh mercy, for a knight that is courteous and kind and gentle hath favor in every place."

Creation Myths of Bethany (Continued)

The Tale of Wylan

Now do not think that Wylan was a dark god, no. He shared his secret knowledge as was needed, and amused the other gods with his mysteries and puzzles. But none's delight could compare with the joy of Asta the Kindler when she beheld Wylan's gifts to her.

But Asta had another suitor, strong Keldan the Swordgod. His strength at arms and noble ways were no match for Wylan's gifts and did not win the Kindler's favor. Many times did Keldan seek Wylan's heart, to reave it from him so that Wylan might never win Asta's love. But Wylan was wise, and sought the aid of his sister, Cara the Shadowdancer, and together they eluded Keldan, tangling the Swordgod in the bindings of his own laws.

Asta, fearing for her beloved Wylan, took Keldan's Sword of Light, and fled, hiding the Sword deep within the shadows of the Night. And so for a great time there was peace among the gods, and Asta dwelt with Wylan in the shadows and from their love sprang the stars.

And then Dorn Armsman found the Sword of Light, and wrapped in his cold flames fled with it to Keldan's halls. Then did the hosts of Keldan war with Wylan and the Darkness was cut by the Sword. Stolen was Asta the Kindler, and chained upon the hearth in Keldan's own halls was she.

And Wylan was cast into the heart of the Darkness by Dorn, and wrapped in icy flames, to sleep until the end of time . . .

Long ages passed, then, until the coming of man. And as man surrendered his essence each night into Wylan's realm, so did the Sleeping God gain strength. Still the flames of Dorn bound him in eternal sleep, but nothing can bind the dreams of man.

So into the dark realm of Wylan came children: Sovar and Silar, the twin Lords of Dreams and Prophecy, and beauteous Marya, the Handmaid who guides and welcomes all into the dreamtime.

"Thou must keep thy word to all and not be feeble of good belief and faith. Right must be defended against might and the distressed must be protected."

"Know good from evil and the vainglory of the world, because great pride and bombast make great sorrow. Should anyone require of ye any quest that is not to thy shame or the shame of thy Order, thou shouldst fulfill the desire as thy duties permit."

"Thou shouldst not fail in these things: charity and truth."

"No knight shall win honor but if he be of honor and of good living and loveth Keldan and dreadeth Keldan, and else he getteth no honor here, be he ever so hardy."

"Do not, nor say not, anything that will dishonor in any way the Rule of thy Order. For only by a stainless and honorable life shall Keldan be truly served."

"Therefore be a good knight and if ye be of prowess and worthiness ye shall grow strong in the Light of Keldan."

Dorn Wayfinder

The secondborn of Daisha by the Lord of Light, Dorn is the Seer, the Councillor, the Finder of Ways. His spheres of influence are wisdom, judgment, strategy and knowledge. His symbol is the eternal flame, and his colors dark scarlet and gold. His clerics always wear some item of scarlet and at their initiation receive a ring of red gold.

Dorn's physical form is that of a flame-haired man with eyes of amber fire. He is seen in a variety of different garb, depending on whether he is acting as armsman, judge, or seer, though in all forms he wears crimson and gold.

Dorn is a thoughtful and practical god, often sacrificing his integrity for the betterment of the whole. He is generally benevolent, though as judge his rulings are absolutely impartial. He keeps a very close eye upon the world, and will, at times of duress, appear before individual followers. He has a secretive and mysterious nature. His weaknesses are an insatiable curiosity, and a belief that the end justifies the means.

The tenets of Dorn are simple: never prejudge, observe before considering and consider before acting. All actions should be restrained. One reacts to a problem or threat in a just and equal way. Yet this works both ways, and Dornites seldom restrain themselves from fighting fire with fire.

Dorn is a loyal liegeman and advisor to Keldan, offering practical advice. He is friendly with Asta, his clerics often teaching the children in her charge. Dorn dislikes Volt's unreasoning violence, and opposes him wherever he may. He competes with Wylan for hidden knowledge and is quite friendly with Cara, despite Keldan's disapproval.

Gods of Bethany

The people of Bethany worship a pantheon of gods, who are described in detail in the main text (see *The Gods of Bethany*, pp. 156-166).

All gods of Bethany are of limited influence. Their power and worship does not extend outside the lands of Bethany, nor beyond the realms which form the basis for their power. They all have humanoid forms and personalities, and are said to live in a realm separate from the mortal world. Those who die in the service of a god will usually enter this realm and aid the god in whatever capacity he requires. The interrelationships of the deities and their particular aspects and natures are described in the main text (see pp. 157-166).

Gods of Bethany can be affected by each other's actions, but cannot be killed through any mortal means. They depend upon their followers for influence in the "real" world, but will retain their archetypal powers whether they are actively worshiped or not.

Clerics of Keldan

There are three ranks of clerics within the Church of Keldan. The first (5-point Clerical Investment) includes all who dedicate themselves to the church. In order to be invested as a cleric, the applicant must be male and a knight of the realm.

The second rank consists of those who are inducted into the Knights of Law (10-point Clerical Investment). The cleric will be assigned an order, monastery, convent or church to supervise and defend. Only clerics who have distinguished themselves in service, bravery and valor will be appointed to this order. All such appointments are made at the discretion of the Highsword.

The third and final rank is that of Highsword (15-point Clerical Investment). There is only ever one Highsword, chosen by the mandate of Keldan himself.

Trueswords are not clerics in the classical sense, but they are the recipients of divine visions and have the ability to do Divine Interventions.

Continued on next page . . .

Organization

The church of Dorn is egalitarian, willing to accept anyone who has the wit and skill to pass its testing. Competence and experience, rather than rank of birth, determine one's place within the church.

The supreme temporal authority is called *the Flame of Dorn*. This person is a somewhat mysterious figure who leaves name and rank behind when accepting the mantle of Dorn. The Flame is always someone highly skilled in both magic and warfare.

There are three branches within the Church of Dorn.

Led by the *Armiger,* the Armsmen deal with the more martial problems the church might encounter. Those of a purely martial bent enter the Order of the Knights of the Flame. Those Armsmen of a more intellectual bent often become advisers and strategists.

The Acolytes, led by the *Magister,* are those Dornites who tend toward magery or secrecy. They usually travel and work alone, often in some sort of quiet disguise. The Acolytes wander the land, watching for problems and gathering information for the Advocates and their archives.

Advocates, led by the *Archivist,* deal with the interpretation of the law, history, tradition and teaching. It is the Advocates who run the Curia and monasteries of the church. No court or Lord in the land, not even the King, will pass judgment without the presence of an Advocate of Dorn. The Advocates also have a knightly order – the Knights of the Cup (also called the Chalciers). This Order is concerned with teaching and missionary work, having both cleric-knights and cleric-teachers.

Festivals

Highstar – High Festival of Dorn, early in the year about a month after Lumens. Oaths and initiations within the church take place at this time. Apprenticeships are also begun at this time throughout Bethany.

Darkhunt – this commemorates the beginning of Dorn's search for the Sword of Light. Held upon the winter's solstice, it is a time for serious reflection and thought. Rituals in memory of the dead are held at this time.

Garb

Dornites favor the color red, symbolizing blood and life and representing fire from the heavens.

Wayfinders of Dorn wear ceremonial garb in the Keldanite style, but in Dorn's colors. Acolytes of Dorn, however, have a definite fondness for secular garb and often wear it whenever ritual vestments are not required for church services. On formal religious occasions (such as rituals) both Acolytes and Advocates of Dorn wear a *cassock alb*. This is a more narrowly cut and tailored garment with a higher collar and a wide stiff belt, closing down one side from the shoulder to the floor. A wider stole is worn with this garment. The cassock alb is always scarlet in color and may be embroidered with flame patterns in varying shades of red and gold.

At High Festivals the Acolytes and Advocates of Dorn replace the cassock alb with the older-styled dalmatic and tunicle. Both of these vestments are simple T-shaped garments with slightly flaring skirts. A thin golden stole is also worn. All Dornite clerics veil themselves at High Festivals.

Clerics of Keldan (Continued)

Magics

Keldan is an active god who appears frequently to his chosen. He disapproves strongly of magic, however, so his clerics have few spells, most of which are defensive in nature. All clerics of Keldan undergo a Power Investiture as a part of their initial clerical initiation, permitting them to learn those spells which Keldan allows. Most use their swords for their Sacred Vessels (see p. 105).

Keldan clerics may learn the following spells: Armor, Bless, Consecrate, Detect Magic, Divination, Final Rest, Flash, Iron Arm.

Lead Worship, Light, Magic Resistance, Missile Shield, Oath, Sense Danger, Sense Spirit, Shield, Turn Zombie and Watchdog.

Clerics who belong to the Knights of Law may additionally learn the following spells: Continual Light, Dispel Magic, Drain Mana, Excommunicate, Exorcism, and a variation of Pentagram in the shape of a cross.

Keldan Consecrate spells will drain the mana from whatever object or area they are cast upon. Individuals with Magical Aptitude will have their fatigue reduced to zero. For this to work on magical items and people, the spell must be cast in its ceremonial form, with enough energy spent to equal twice that being drained. Areas of High or Very High Sanctity for Keldan are no-mana areas.

Knights

Knights of Keldan must prove their knowledge of the laws of Keldan and their ability to conduct themselves well in social situations as well as prowess of arms. They are trained in Dance, Heraldry, History, Law, and Savoir-Faire, as well as combat of arms. Most are excellent riders.

Asta the Kindler

The thirdborn of Daisha by the Lord of Light, Asta is the Kindler, the Lifegiver and Healer. Her spheres are mercy, light, the hearth, children, healing and fertility. Her symbols are the flint, the wheat sheaf and the chalice. Asta's physical form is of a pretty, dark-skinned woman with brown hair and eyes, wearing golden-brown and green robes. She is usually depicted carrying a variety of things, her symbols always among them.

Asta is an unfailingly kind and benevolent deity. She has a nearly limitless supply of mercy. She shares the forthright and lawful nature of her husband, Keldan, but is much more forgiving. Asta keeps a close, but beneficent eye upon her followers. Her weaknesses are her attraction toward her half-brother, Wylan, and a tendency toward overgenerosity.

Hospitality, mercy and charity are the main tenets of the church. Her clerics must bless and heal any who ask, and protect, comfort and cherish all children and mothers. Those who follow Asta strive to be selfless, kind and gentle.

Asta's clerics conceal their hair beneath a linen coif and dress in simple robes of golden-brown and green.

Asta loves her husband Keldan, but feels constrained at times by his protectiveness. She is friendly with Dorn, whose clerics teach the children she shelters. She opposes Volt, and pities him. Wylan draws her, yet she fears him. Cara she treats as a scandalous younger sister.

Organization

Only women may be clerics of Asta. The main concern of the church is charity and healing, and they establish *crofts* where they see need for them. A croft is a cross between a hostel, a soup-kitchen and an orphanage. Often these crofts are built near Dornite Curia.

Clerics of Dorn

There are three ranks of clerics within the Church of Dorn, organized into three orders. Initiates of Dorn (5-point Clerical Investment) must join one of the three orders – Acolyte, Advocate, or Armsman. They must be sponsored by a member of the order, and pass a test (see *Initiation Rite of Dorn*, p. 165) appropriate for their order.

The Magister, Archivist and Armiger are the leaders of the three orders, and hold the second of the three ranks (10-point Clerical Investment). These positions are appointed by the Flame of Dorn, and are responsible for administering their particular orders.

The Flame (15-point Clerical Investment) is the supreme head of the Church of Dorn, and is selected by the leaders of the three orders on the word of Dorn. All clerics within the church are considered eligible for the position. There is only ever one Flame.

Magic

Unlike his dour brother, Dorn accepts magic as a tool which can be put to good use. In addition to a wide range of clerical spells, those with magical talent are welcomed into the Church, usually as Acolytes. Indeed, the Church of Dorn is the repository of most of the magical teachings and knowledge in Bethany (though magical spells and knowledge are completely separate from clerical spells; see sidebar, p. 101). All clerics receive a Power Investiture as part of their initiation ceremony, symbolized by a red-gold ring given to them by the god.

Acolytes

Acolytes may learn the following clerical spells: Analyze Magic, Ancient History, Aura, Conceal Magic, Consecrate, Counterspell, Create Fire, Desecrate, Detect Magic, Dispel Magic, Divination, Essential Flame, Extinguish Fire, Far-Hearing, Flame Jet, Flaming Missiles, Flaming Weapon, Gift of Letters, Gift of Tongues, History, Hush, Identify Spell, Ignite Fire, Mage Sight, Pathfinder, Phantom Flame, Scribe, Scryguard, Scrywall, See Secrets, Seeker, Sense Foes, Shape Fire, Spell Shield, Trace, Truthsayer, Ward and Wizard Eye. They may also learn any first-rank Keldan or Asta spell in its ceremonial form.

Continued on next page . . .

Novices of the church use the title "Lady." These women do the work necessary to run the crofts – gardening, cooking, beer-making, weaving and so on. A Lady of Asta may travel from croft to croft, serving where she is needed. A few travel out into the world, accompanied by a Dornite Chalcier.

Crofts are run by senior clerics, called "Dames." A Dame must wed a Keldan knight upon her investiture. A Dame's knight is responsible for the defense of the croft. A Lady is free to wed anyone of good birth and nature, on approval of her clerical superiors. Dames are very concerned with the welfare of the Ladies in their charge and attempt to find good marriages for them. Most crofts have only one Dame, although the larger crofts (also called croftholds) have several under the authority of the Dame Mother.

The senior authority of the church is the Keeper of Vesma. She runs the crofthold in the Vale of Vesma, and is responsible for tending the eternal flame which burns upon the hearth there.

Festivals

There are many festivals of Asta, who is especially beloved by the peasants and farmers of Bethany. Children are brought to Asta just after their birth to be named and blessed.

Heathar – celebrated at the spring equinox by feasts and dancing after a Lady of Asta blesses the newly-planted fields and young animals.

Springfire – primarily a country festival and a favored time for betrothals and courting. Lovers leap across the bonfires that burn throughout the night.

Loavan – The first loaves of the harvest are eaten at these feasts. In the cities, chefs work overtime creating elaborate pastry creations.

Harvestfall – celebrated at the autumn equinox, this festival is of great importance. Clerics of Asta are kept busy blessing barns, homes and silos in preparation for the coming winter.

Garb

Those who serve Asta wear golden-brown and green, for these colors represent the earth and green is the color of life and birth.

Priestesses of Asta prefer simple and modest garments, regardless of the pageantry of the ceremony. They wear a short (ankle-length) tunic over a floor-length, tight-sleeved tunicle. Both garments are tightly belted – sometimes a wide apron-like garment is worn over all. Their hair is tightly braided out of the way and covered by a simple *coif*. On formal occasions the casual coif is replaced by a circlet and veil over a loosely-draped wimple.

Volt the Avenger

The firstborn of Daisha by the Dark Hunter, Volt is the Avenger, the Reaver and Temper's Flame. His spheres are courage, just retribution, strength, challenge, perseverance and revenge. His symbols are the axe and the thunderbolt. His colors are blood-red and black. Worship of Volt is forbidden by the Church of Keldan.

Volt's physical form is that of a tanned, dark-haired man with black eyes, wearing a blood-red tunic and wielding the axe and thunderbolt which are his trademarks.

Clerics of Dorn (Continued)

Acolytes vary greatly in personal abilities, but they are always curious, always questioning the world around them. They will tend to specialize in a few particular fields of professional and scientific skills, along with Detect Lies, Diplomacy, Disguise, Fast-Talk, Savoir-Faire, Scrounging, Stealth, Streetwise and Teaching. All are literate, and most have some training in combat skills.

Advocates

Advocates may learn the following clerical spells: Ancient History, Aura, Compel Truth, Consecrate, Detect Magic, Dispel Magic, and Divination, Excommunicate, Gift of Letters, Gift of Tongues, History, Oath, Scribe, See Secrets, Spell Shield and Truthsayer.

Advocates serve as the judges and the librarians. They are the keepers of knowledge and the arbiters of Keldan's Law. They are all literate, and are taught Heraldry, History, Law, Research, Teaching and Theology as a matter of course. Most also carry on research projects of their own on the side.

Armsmen

Armsmen may learn the following clerical spells: Armor, Aura, Banish, Counterspell, Create Fire, Detect Magic, Dispel Magic, Divination, Flame Jet, Flaming Missiles, Flaming Weapon, Ignite Fire, Missile Shield, Nightingale, Reverse Missiles, Scryguard, Scrywall, Sense Danger, Sense Spirit, Shape Fire, Shield, Spell Shield, Truthsayer, Turn Zombie, Watchdog. They may also learn any first-rank Keldan spell in its ceremonial form.

Armsmen serve Bethany as strategists and tacticians. Often they are the brains behind Keldan's might. They learn all areas of combat – mounted, infantry and artillery – equally, and are taught Strategy and Tactics along with Diplomacy, Heraldry, Law and Leadership.

Volt is a harsh, stubborn and unforgiving deity, never forgetting a slight, and never denying a challenge. He has a forthright and lawful nature, but his laws vary somewhat from those Keldan follows. He keeps a diligent watch upon his followers. His weaknesses are his lust for vengeance, and his hatred for weakness of any kind.

Those who follow Volt let no slight go unpunished. They fear nothing, and never deny a challenge or cry surrender. No cost is too great if it ensures success and vengeance.

Volt has no allies among the gods. He despises Keldan, thinking him a coward who protects weak fools. He hates Dorn's calm reasoning, envying his skill at arms, and considers Asta to be a meddling bitch. He has no use at all for Wylan's deceptions. He lusts after Cara and longs to someday teach her a lesson.

Organization

Only men may be clerics of Volt. There is no central organization of followers, only the simplest of hierarchies based upon strength and prowess. Those who would become clerics of Volt must first find another cleric willing to train them. Training another is a courageous act since clerics advance by challenging and killing their superiors. Many who follow Volt hire themselves out as mercenaries in bitter disputes, often favoring the losing side as a challenge.

Festivals

Darkstorm – occurs shortly after Swordcall. This is the only time that Volt's disorganized followers gather together to feast and fight. Ceremonies remembering the dead and settling advancements and feuds are common at this time. This festival is held in isolated locations since the Church of Keldan bans worship of Volt.

Garb

Clerics of Volt have little patience for frivolity and so have no formal garb. They favor dark reds in their daily dress, however, symbolizing blood, the fire of vengeance and the destruction of war.

Wylan the Sleeping God

The secondborn of Daisha by the Dark Hunter, Wylan is the Sleeping God, the Magiker, the Dreamweaver. His spheres are magic, the night, sleep, prophecy and dreams. His colors are black and midnight blue. The spindle, the skein and sand are his symbols.

Clerics of Asta

There are three ranks of clerics in the Church of Asta. The first, the novices (5-point Clerical Investment), are known as Ladies. They have just joined the church and are assigned to work with Dames within a croft.

The second rank (10-point Clerical Investment) is that of Dame. A Dame is one who leads a croft, or is recognized to hold certain rank within the church. Dames must marry a Keldan Knight upon elevation to this station, and are generally given a croft of their own to oversee.

The third rank (15-point Clerical Investment) is the Keeper of Vesma, the senior authority in the church.

Magic

Asta's clerics specialize in magics which aid other people. They are invested with the power of the goddess during their initiation rite.

Ladies may learn the following spells: Awaken, Bless Plants, Bless, Consecrate, Heal Plant, Lend Health, Minor Healing, Preserve Food, Purify Food, Purify Water, Share Strength and Test Food.

Dames may learn the following spells: Cure Disease, Divination, Lend Strength, Light, Major Healing, Neutralize Poison, Sense Life and Sterilize.

Duties and Responsibilities

Asta's clerics are charged with the well-being of the citizenry of Bethany. They heal the sick and wounded, feed the poor, and run orphanages for the unfortunate. They are taught Accounting, Administration, Animal Handling, Diagnosis, First Aid, Physician, and any craft skill.

Followers of Volt

Like his sister Cara, Volt has no formal, organized religion or clerics. His followers are few, but they are always fanatical. Bloodlust and Berserk are required disadvantages. They dedicate their lives to avenging Volt's name, and may perform Divine Interventions if their actions have pleased the god.

Long ago, Wylan lived in the world with the other gods. His quarrels with Keldan (and his theft of the Sword of Light) resulted in his magical imprisonment by Dorn in the void. But Dorn could only capture Wylan; he could not remove his power. Wylan's power changed his prison into the realm of dreams and now his influence reaches once more into mortal lands. Since his imprisonment by Dorn, Wylan has divided his power and manifests through his dream-children – *Sovar,* the Dreamlord, *Silar,* the Lord of Prophecy, and *Marya,* the Handmaid who welcomes all into the dreamtime. Worship of Wylan is forbidden by the Church of Keldan.

Wylan's physical form is that of a tall, slender, dark-haired, dark-eyed man, wearing midnight-blue robes embroidered with mystical symbols. All of his dream-children manifest in similar forms.

Wylan is a clever, curious deity with a random, mysterious nature. He never answers directly what he can make a riddle, and always pushes the edge to see what he can get away with. Unlike his siblings, he never appears directly before his followers, but rather through his dream-children. His weaknesses are his utter hatred of Dorn, along with his eternal fascination for puzzles, and his insatiable curiosity.

Those who follow Wylan never take an inch when they can take a mile, nor do they pass up an opportunity to twist the truth into a puzzle. It is best to be wary of what is asked of Wylan, for he might deliver it. Beauty is in the eye of the beholder, and what is seen is often not what it seems to be.

Wylan opposes Keldan, taking his laws and bending them until they scream. He utterly hates Dorn as a result of his imprisonment. Wylan loves Asta and dreams of the chance to seduce her away from Keldan. He dislikes Volt's brashness, but finds him useful and easy to manipulate. He is fond of Cara, finding her amusing and refreshing.

Clerics of Wylan

There are only two levels of clergy in the scattered groups which still pay homage to the Sleeping God. The junior clerics, or Students (5-point Clerical Investment), spend much of their time penetrating the many veils of mystery surrounding their deity. They are put through many tests and are always in competition with one another. Applicants must gain the sponsorship of a senior cleric within the order whose wisdom they seek. Most become Dreamweavers.

Those with enough talent, skill and initiative will become senior clerics, or Masters (10-point Clerical Investment). Any Student may seek this rank by proving himself worthy in the eyes of his Master. The penalty for failure is almost always death.

Magic

While he sleeps, Wylan is unable to manifest powers upon the mortal plane. Thus his servants choose only those with innate magical talent as Students. Many of the mysteries involve the learning of magical rites thought to be invocations of the deity's power – in reality they are little more than the casting of magical spells. Some small number of Masters have realized this, but maintain the charade in the interests of the church.

Dreamweavers

Dreamweavers specialize in subtle personal and political manipulations. They are often drawn from the nobility of Bethany, and most are considered to be loyal followers of Keldan.

Dreamweavers specialize in Illusion, Knowledge, Meta and Mind Control magics. Each will have slightly different specialties within the greater scope. Their spells are always associated with symbolic rituals, and the greater spells are carefully hoarded by those who have managed to learn them.

Social skills are important to Dreamweavers, particularly Acting, Diplomacy, Fast-Talk, Leadership, Politics and Savoir-Faire. They are generally also quite knowledgeable in Law and History.

Seers

Seers specialize in prophetic magics, particularly Divinations. Little is known of them. It is possible that they may even have shamanistic abilities (see *Shamanism,* pp. 116 and 128) which provide their visions and allow them access to the fears and dreams of those around them.

Continued on next page . . .

Organization

Anyone with magical aptitude may become a cleric of Wylan. Each cleric must choose which aspect suits them best – most follow Sovar. Senior clerics are called *Dreamweavers*. Each gathers a coterie of students and lesser clerics about them to aid in his plots. Clerics of Wylan delight in discovering secret information and manipulating political situations. They specialize in informational, illusionary and mind magics. There is no supreme authority in the church; rather each Dreamweaver strives to outdo the others and gain the god's favor. The prime concern of a cleric of Wylan – besides stirring up trouble – is discovering a means to free Wylan from his captive sleep.

Clerics of Silar – also called Seers – are rare and spend much of their time in a trance state. Each Dreamweaver tries to recruit a seer to aid him, for their prophecies are an invaluable asset.

Clerics of Marya are recluses who specialize in enchantments and illusions. Unlike the Dreamweavers, they are unconcerned with the politics and the affairs of others, living their lives in their own private worlds. Many believe that Marya's servants are not truly sane.

Festivals

Yearnight – High Festival of Wylan, when the old year ends and the new begins. At this time the god's power is greatest and the dreams of men are most susceptible to his clerics' influence. This festival is celebrated in secret by the faithful. Those who do not worship Wylan either ignore the significance of this day, or spend it behind locked doors.

Lunar – half a year from Yearnight, it provides an opportunity for the Dreamweavers to gather and plan for their god's awakening. Rites of initiation are also held. In much of Bethany the true meaning of this four-day festival is lost – instead, it is called *Fool's Fair* and is a time of tricks and gaming.

Garb

Those who serve Wylan dress primarily in secular garb except at their High Festival, when they wear many layers of elaborately-worked garments, in graduated shades of black and gray. These dark colors symbolize the night and sleep.

Cara Gildenheart

The thirdborn of Daisha by the Dark Hunter, Cara Gildenheart is the Temptress, the Siren and the Fabler. Her spheres are luck, artifice, intrigue, wealth, vice and temptation. Her colors are all the shades of the rainbow and her symbols are coins, jewels, dice, the cymbal and the dance. Worship of Cara is discouraged by the Church of Keldan.

Cara's physical form is that of a petite black-haired woman with mismatched eyes, wearing the brilliant clothing of her followers, always decorated with dangling jewelry of various sorts. She is often seen dancing, or holding the dice that are her symbol.

Cara is a mischievous, licentious deity, with a taste for fun and frivolity. Her attention is generally benevolent, though often self-serving. She requires nothing of her followers but that they enjoy life and play the "game." She is meddlesome by nature, and often appears to those who strike her fancy. She is very chaotic and mysterious. Her weaknesses are a love of danger and a marked preference for pretty things

Clerics of Wylan (Continued)

Marya

Marya's followers stay away from society, practicing their arts in remote villages and hidden monasteries dedicated to Wylan. They generally have an overwhelming reason or desire to escape from society.

Marya's clerics specialize in Illusion and Enchantment magics. Quite often Dreamweavers will seek to draw them into their service, coveting the items they create.

Followers of Cara Gildenheart

Cara has no formal, organized religion or clerics. She is a willful, capricious goddess who will often interfere in the lives of her favorite followers. The GM might want to make use of *Miraculous Magic* to handle this (see pp. 113-115), or leave it very freeform. As a patron, Cara has a very high Frequency of Appearance, though she is likely to interpret requests for aid in whimsical ways.

Initiation Rite of Dorn

Dressed in the simple frock, its bleached plainness hidden beneath her cloak, the initiate stands before a rough-hewn wooden door. As the first warming rays of the dawning sun spread across cobbles, the initiate takes hold of the great brass knocker upon the plain wooden door, and knocks.

Once. Twice. Thrice.

Silence stretches on after the third knock, bare echoes soon swallowed by the thick wood of the door. Then, when it almost seems that none will answer and she will be turned away, the door opens.

The priest stands before the initiate, the liturgical chant echoing between them.

"Who seeks . . ."

". . . Finds."

"Who watches . . ."

". . . Sees."

"Who asks . . ."

". . . Learns."

"Who knows . . ."

". . . Teaches."

"Who stands with knowledge, armed with wit . . ."

". . . Shall never fall."

Continued on next page . . .

Initiation Rite of Dorn (Continued)

The priest stands back and allows the initiate to enter, bringing her to the very center of the shrine, a place she has never before been.

"We gather here, within the seat of knowledge, to welcome another who seeks the congress of Dorn."

"Step forward, daughter."

As the initiate steps closer, a ring of cool fire springs into being around her, bright flames flickering at the hem of her gown, licking at her calves.

Fear and worry swells within her, and with it the flames grow, warming dangerously, linen darkening in its heat.

All around her stand in silence, watching, as she speaks the pre-taught words.

"Do not fear, for fear is the death of thought. It is the enemy. Fear twists and perverts, breeds resentment and discontent, fathers anger.

"What is understood, cannot be feared, for everything acts according to its nature.

"Watch, consider and learn. For with knowledge comes understanding and control. Remember restraint, for control and balance empower us.

"And with knowledge, all things are possible.

"We are the fire that burns away the darkness. We are the fire that sunders.

"Yet fire by its nature, unrestrained, unchained . . . destroys.

"Restraint in all things . . .

"We are those who harness the spirit of flame . . .

"We are those who meet challenge, and answer it with its own kind . . .

"We are the fires of Dorn, that shall ever burn . . ."

About her, the flames flicker, falling back the merest degree. Joyously her will embraces the flames that flare about her, accepting them . . . touching and touched.

The flames flicker, until their light is but the merest ring upon the floor about her, shining bright red-gold that burns her eyes. Yet she sees, a pure and blinding light illuminating, empowering, comforting, a fiery touch upon her very soul . . .

Then . . . the light is gone, the flames fading away, though the warmth still lingers through her. And at her feet, a plain ring of blood-red gold, marking her acceptance into the service of Dorn.

The tenets of Gildenheart are these: Never betray a trust or a secret – unless you want to. Life is but a game. Life is the dance. Resist nothing and dare all.

Cara Gildenheart is amused by Keldan and enjoys teasing him. She is friendly with Dorn and Asta, but Volt disgusts her and she often baits him. She is friendly with Wylan and weaves her own plots through his. She opposes law and constraint in all things. She is an extremely active goddess and spends much of her time disguised among her followers.

Organization

Cara will accept anyone who pleases her. She has no clerics as such – her followers needs no one else to intercede for them. Those who amuse or delight her she gifts with luck, wealth, knowledge or whatever else might strike her fancy at the moment.

Festivals

While Cara is disliked by the established church of Keldan, her festivals are far too popular to be suppressed, especially in rural areas.

Leis – also called *Loversmeet,* this is the first of Cara's festivals, a time for secret meetings and wooings. It takes place just before Merrymeet.

Merrymeet – a few weeks before Springfire, Merrymeet is a four-day festival of dancing, feasting and contests.

Heartsong – This takes place at midsummer and is a favored time for betrothals and weddings, even among the nobility.

Garb

Those who serve Cara favor bright clothes in all colors of the rainbow and lots of scarves and jewelry. They have no formal garb.

APPENDIX

Checklist for Religion Creation

Religions are complicated entities. The design of a religion must delineate many factors. Everything from the nature of the divinity worshiped, to the social influence, the rituals, the symbols and the eventual cultural effects should be considered. The following outline serves as a checklist of the issues and questions which must be raised in the development of a religion.

Origin Myth/Cosmology

The world (pp. 7-16)
The deity (pp. 9-11)
Origin of life (pp. 16-21)

Status/Relation to Culture

Social standing (pp. 51, 52-53)
Relationship with state (pp. 51-53)
Relationships with other prominent religions (p. 53)

History of Development

Origin of the religion (pp. 53-55)
Development over time (pp. 56-62)
Holy wars (p. 53)
Schisms (pp. 62-64)

Symbols

Appearance and dress (p. 67, 85-86)
Churches and temples (p. 68)
Sacred Items (pp. 68, 80-86)

Dogma/Scriptures/Laws (pp. 46, 48-49, 52)

Common Rituals

Birth (p. 72)
Initiation (p. 73)
Marriage (p.73)
Funeral (p. 73)
Others (pp. 74-75)

Holy Times/Holy Places (pp. 79-80)

Festivals (pp. 71-72)
Shrines (pp. 68, 77-78)
Pilgrimage (pp. 78-79)

Hierarchy/Organization of Clerics

Recruitment (pp. 50-51)
Advancement (pp. 49-50)
Special Orders (p. 50)

Clerical Abilities (pp. 96-97, 100-125)

Checklist for Deity Creation

Deities can also be quite complex. Whether considering the addition of one god or multiple pantheons, avoid problems by taking into account the following factors when designing. Note that not everything that people believe about a god is *necessarily* true!

Deity/Philosophy

Origins (pp. 23-24)
Nature and purpose (pp. 13-16)
Spheres of influence (pp. 24, 25-27, 104)
Attributes (pp. 24-34)
Physical forms (pp. 27, 25-29)
Residence (pp. 28-29)
Allies and enemies (pp. 34-37)
Worship (pp. 38-41)
Divine servants (pp. 40-41, 43-44)

Symbols

Graphic Shapes (pp. 66-70)
Colors (p. 87)
Animals (pp. 25-29, 67-68)
Sacred Items (pp. 68, 80-86)

Holy Times/Holy Places

Festivals (pp. 30, 33)
Shrines (pp. 28, 102, 103, 107)
Holy Days/Days of Weakness (p. 103)

Divine Magic

Spells (pp. 100-104, 108-125)
Divine Intervention/Divine Favor (pp. 93, 113, 114, 118)
Divination (pp. 16, 109-111, 115-116, 123)

BIBLIOGRAPHY

NON-FICTION BOOKS

Dictionaries

Cooper, J.C., *The Aquarian Dictionary of Festivals* (Aquarian Press, 1990).

Cotterell, Arthur, *A Dictionary of World Mythology* (Oxford Press University, 1986).

Crim, Keith (ed.), *The Perennial Dictionary of World Religions* (Harper & Row, 1989).

Eliade, Mircea and Ioan P. Couliano with Hillary S. Wiesner, *The Eliade Guide to World Religions* (HarperSanFrancisco, 1991).

Evans, Ivor H. (ed.), *Brewer's Dictionary of Phrase and Fable* (Fitzhenry & Whiteside, 1989).

Farmer, David Hugh, *The Oxford Dictionary of Saints* (Oxford University Press, 1987).

Leach, Maria (ed.) and Jerome Fried (ed.), *Funk & Wagnall's Standard Dictionary of Folklore, Mythology, and Legend* (Harper & Row, 1984).

Lurker, Manfred, *Dictionary of Gods and Goddesses, Devils and Demons* (Routledge & Kegan Paul,1987).

Monaghan, Patricia, *The Book of Goddesses and Heroines* (Llewellyn, 1990).

Opie, Iona (ed.) and Moira Tatem (ed.), *A Dictionary of Superstitions* (Oxford University Press, 1989).

Walker, Barbara G., *The Woman's Encyclopedia of Myths and Secrets* (Harper & Row, 1983).

Walker, Barbara G., *The Woman's Dictionary of Symbols and Sacred Objects* (Harper & Row, 1988).

General Studies

Adams, Doug (ed.) and Diane Apostolos-Cappadona (ed.), *Dance as Religious Studies* (Crossroad, 1990).

Bancroft, Anne, *Origins of the Sacred* (Penguin, 1987).

Campbell, Joseph, *The Masks of God: Primitive Mythology* (Penguin, 1969).

Campbell, Joseph, *Transformations of Myth Through Time* (Perennial, 1990).

Campbell, Joseph, with Bill Moyers, *The Power of Myth* (Doubleday, 1988).

Eliade, Mircea (tr. Willard R. Trask), *A History of Religious Ideas* (University of Chicago Press, 1978).

Eliade, Mircea (tr. Willard R. Trask), *Shamanism — Archaic Techniques of Ecstasy* (Princeton/Bollingen, 1974).

Fields, Rick, *The Code of the Warrior in History, Myth and Everyday Life* (HarperPerennial, 1991).

Goodrich, Norma Lorre, *Priestesses* (HarperPerennial, 1990).

Henderson, Joseph L. and Maud Oakes, *The Wisdom of the Serpent: The Myths of Death, Rebirth and Resurrection* (Princeton University Press, 1990).

Morris, Brian, *Anthropological Studies of Religion — An Introductory Text* (Cambridge University Press, 1987).

Norman, Dorothy, *The Hero — Myth/Image/Symbol* (Anchor Books, 1990).

Parrinder, Geoffrey (ed.), *World Religions From Ancient History to the Present* (Hamlyn/Newnes, 1985).

Stewart, R.J., *Prophecy* (Element Books, 1990).

Von Franz, Marie-Louise, *Patterns of Creativity Mirrored in Creation Myths* (Spring Publications, 1986).

Eastern and Asian

Agency for Cultural Affairs, *Japanese Religion — A Survey* (Kodansha International, 1981).

Campbell, Joseph, *The Masks of God: Oriental Mythology* (Penguin, 1976).

Danielou, Alain, *The Myths and Gods of India* (Inner Traditions, 1985)

Hopkins, Thomas J., *The Hindu Religious Tradition* (Wadsworth, 1971).

Kinsley, David, *Hindu Goddesses — Visions of the Divine Feminine in the Hindu Religious Tradition* (University of California Press, 1988).

Koller, John M., *Oriental Philosophies* (Scribner, 1970).

Lao Tzu (tr. Victor H. Mair), *Tao Te Ching — The Classic Book of Integrity and The Way* (Bantam, 1990).

Ross, Nancy Wilson, *Three Ways of Asian Wisdom* (Simon & Shuster, 1966).

Wing-Tsit Chan (tr.), *A Source Book in Chinese Philosophy* (Princeton University Press, 1969).

Western

Baldwin, Marshall W., *The Mediaeval Church* (Cornell University Press, 1968).

Bulfinch, Thomas, *Myths of Greece and Rome* (Penguin, 1979).

Campbell, Joseph, *The Masks of God: Occidental Mythology* (Penguin, 1976).
Clebsch, William A., *Christianity in European History* (Oxford University Press, 1979).
Farah, Caesar, *Islam* (Barron's, 1987).
Finkelstein, Louis (ed.), *The Jews: Their History* (Schocken Books, 1974).
Finkelstein, Louis (ed.), *The Jews: Their Religion and Culture* (Schocken Books, 1973).
Kraemer, Ross S. (ed.), *Meanads, Martyrs, Matrons, Monastics — A Sourcebook on Women's Religions in the Greco-Roman World* (Fortress Press, 1988).
McManners, John (ed.), *Oxford Illustrated History of Christianity* (Oxford University Press, 1990).
White Jr., Lynn, *Medieval Religion and Technology* (University of California Press, 1986).

Other

Bierhorst, John, *The Mythology of North America* (Quill William Morrow, 1985).
Budapest, Zsuzsanna, *The Holy Book of Women's Mysteries* (Wingbow Press, 1989). (Wiccan)
Carr-Gomm, Philip, *The Druid Tradition* (Element Books, 1991).
Frazer, J.G., *The Golden Bough: A Study in Magic and Religion* (Papermac, 1987).
Matthews, Caitlin, *The Celtic Tradition* (Element Books, 1989).
Matthews, John, *The Celtic Shaman* (Element Books, 1991).
Mooney, James, *The Ghost-Dance Religion and Wounded Knee* (Dover, 1973).
Nichols, Ross, *The Book of Druidry* (Aquarian/Thorsons, 1990).
Shafer, Byron E. (ed.), *Religion in Ancient Egypt* (Cornell University Press, 1991).
Schele, Linda and David Freidel, *A Forest of Kings: The Untold Story of the Ancient Maya* (Quill William Morrow, 1990).
Starhawk, *Spiral Dance — A Rebirth of the Ancient Religion of the Great Goddess* (Harper & Row, 1989).
Tyson, Donald, *Rune Magic* (Llewllyn, 1989).

Specific Mythologies

Addiss, Stephen (ed.), *Japanese Ghosts and Demons* (Spencer Museum, 1985).
Berndt, Ronald M. and Catherine H., *The Speaking Land — Myth and Story in Aboriginal Australia* (Penguin, 1989).
Bosley, Keith (tr.), *The Kalevala* (Oxford University Press, 1989). (translation of the Finnish epic)
Branston, Brian, *Gods and Heroes from Viking Mythology* (Schocken, 1982).
Burland, Cottie, *North American Indian Mythology* (Peter Bedrick Books, 1991).
Dalley, Stephanie (tr.), *Myths from Mesopotamia* (Oxford University Press, 1989).
Evans, Cheryl and Anne Millard, *Usborne Illustrated Guide to Norse Myths and Legends* (Usborne, 1986).
Gantz, Jeffrey (tr.), *Early Irish Myths and Sagas* (Penguin, 1981).
Gantz, Jeffrey (tr.), *The Mabinogion* (Penguin, 1976). (translation of the Welsh epic)
Graves, Robert and Raphael Patai, *Hebrew Myths: The Book of Genesis* (Arena, 1989).
Husain, Shahrukh, *Demons, Gods and Holy Men from Indian Myths and Legends* (Douglas & McIntyre, 1987).
MacCana, Proinsais, *Celtic Mythology* (Hamlyn, 1973).
McAlpine, Helen and William, *Japanese Tales and Legends* (Oxford University Press, 1958).
Narayan, R.K., *Gods, Demons, and Others* (Bantam, 1986). (Collection of information from the Hindu mythos)
Piggott, Juliet, *Japanese Mythology* (Hamlyn, 1969).
Roberts, Moss (ed. and tr.), *Chinese Fairy Tales and Fantasies* (Pantheon Books, 1979).
Ross, Anne and Don Robins, *Life and Death of a Druid Prince — The Story of an Archeological Sensation* (Rider, 1989).
Simpson, Jacqueline (ed. and tr.), *Scandinavian Folktales* (Penguin, 1988).
Tyler, Royall (ed. and tr.), *Japanese Tales* (Pantheon Books, 1987).
Waters, Frank, *The Book of the Hopi* (Viking Penguin, 1963).

Historical Fantasy

Forde, R. A., *Wisewoman* (NEL Hodder & Stoughton, 1988). Christian/Celtic conflict.

Tarr, Judith, *Alamut* (Doubleday, 1989). Crusades, religious conflict, magic.

Tarr, Judith, *Ars Magic* (Bantam Spectra, 1989). Intra-church conflict, magic.

Tarr, Judith, *The Dagger and the Cross* (Doubleday, 1991). Crusades, religious conflict, magic.

Alternative Historical Fantasy

Ball, Margaret, *Changeweaver* (Baen, 1993). Pseudo-Indian magical earth-religion.

Ball, Margaret, *Flameweaver* (Baen, 1991). Pseudo-Indian magical earth-religion.

Baudino, Gael, *Strands of Starlight* (Roc Penguin, 1989). Church vs. magic.

Bradley, Marion Zimmer, *Mists of Avalon* (Knopf, 1982). Christian/Celtic cultural and religious conflict, magic.

Carl, Lillian Steward, *Sabazel* (Ace, 1985). Warring cultures/religions, avatars.

Carl, Lillian Steward, *Shadow Dancers* (Ace, 1987). Warring religions, gods and avatars.

Carl, Lillian Steward, *The Winter King* (Ace, 1986). Warring cultures and religions.

Kurtz, Katherine, *The Deryni series* (Del Rey, 1970-1993). Religious magic, church vs. state, church vs. magic.

Kurtz, Katherine, *Knights of the Blood* (Roc Penguin, 1993). Cursed knights, church vs. magic.

Kurtz, Katherine, *Lammas Night* (Ballantine, 1983). World War II, magic vs. technology, good vs. evil.

Fantasy

Eddings, David, *The Elenium series* (Del Rey, 1989-1991). Questing knightly orders; church vs. magic.

Hodgell, P. C., *God Stalk* (Berkley, 1982). Polytheism, inter-church conflict.

Huff, Tanya, *Child of the Grove* (DAW, 1988). Interfering gods, divine magic.

Huff, Tanya, *The Last Wizard* (DAW, 1989). Divine magic, apotheosis.

Lee, Tanith, *Tales from the Flat Earth* (DAW, 1978-1987). Meddling gods and demons.

Leiber, Fritz, *Fafhrd and the Gray Mouser series* (Ace, 1970-1979). Meddling gods, divine champions, magic.

Lovecraft, H. P., *The Shunned House* (1928), *The Shadow Over Innsmouth* (1936), *The Outsider and Others* (1939), *Beyond the Wall of Sleep* (1943), *The Dunwich Horror* (1945), *The Shuttered Room* (1959), *The Dark Brotherhood* (1966). Lovecraft is responsible for the Cthulhu cycle. Gods from beyond, destructive forces, and things-we-were-not-meant-to-know.

Moon, Elizabeth, *The Paksenarrion series* (Baen, 1988-1989). Inter-church conflict, good vs. evil, divine magic, holy knights.

Moorcock, Michael, *Eternal Champion series* (various publishers, 1967-present). Law vs. chaos, divine magic, avatars, meddling gods, fated champions.

Paxson, Diana L., *The Westria series* (Pocket/TOR 1982-1990). Magical earth religions.

Reichert, Mickey Zucker, *The Last of the Renshai series* (DAW, 1992-1994). Norse mythos, fated champions, meddling gods, divine magic, demigods.

Sagara, Michelle, *Books of the Sundered series* (Del Rey, 1991-1994). Divine magic, light vs. dark, fated champions, inter-church conflict.

Severance, Carol, *Island Warrior series* (Ballantine, 1992-1993). Divine magic, avatars, cultic conflicts.

Smith, Julie Dean, *Caithan Crusade series*(Del Rey, 1990-1992). Church vs. magic.

Yolen, Jane, *Sister Light, Sister Dark* (TOR, 1988). Prophecy and exegesis, religious conflict, change over time.

Urban Fantasy

Hambly, Barbara, *The Darwarth Trilogy* (Del Rey, 1982-1983). Church vs. magic; church vs. state.

Hambly, Barbara, *The Silent Tower* (Del Rey, 1986). Church vs. magic vs. technology.

Hambly, Barbara, *The Silicon Mage* (Del Rey, 1988). Church vs. magic vs. technology.

Hambly, Barbara, *The Suncross Trilogy* (Del Rey, 1991-1992) Church vs. magic, church vs. state, magic vs. technology.

Huff, Tanya, *Gate of Darkness, Circle of Light* (DAW, 1989). Light vs. dark, avatars.

Kurtz, Katherine, and Deborah Harris, *The Adept series* (Ace, 1991-1993). Secret religious/magical orders.

Lackey, Mercedes, *Diane Tregarde series* (DAW, 1989-1991). Neopaganism, magic.

Paxson, Diana L., *Brisingamen* (Berkley, 1984). Divine magic, Norse mythos, neopaganism.

Science Fiction

Atwood, Margaret, *The Handmaid's Tale* (Bantam Seal, 1985). Orwellian theocracy.

Cherryh, C. J., *Wave Without a Shore* (DAW, 1981). Existentialism.

Cherryh, C. J., ed., *Merovingen Nights series* (DAW, 1987-1989). Political-religious factions on another planet.

Gentle, Mary, *Golden Witchbreed* (Arrow, 1983). Religious culture clash, church vs. tech.

Heinlein, Robert A., *The Day After Tomorrow* (Signet, 1949). Constructed religions.

Herbert, Frank, *The Dune series* (Berkley, 1965-1976). Religion vs. technology, church vs. 8.25state. Messianic movement.

Kingsbury, Donald, *Courtship Rite* (Pocket, 1982). Intra-church and cultural conflict.

Lichtenberg/Lorran, *Sime/Gen series* (DAW, 1978-1986). Post-holocaust society, mutants, merged and fractured religions.

Vinge, Joan, *The Snow Queen* (Dell, 1980). Constructed religion, church vs. state.

Game Products

Barker, M.A.R., ***Empire of the Petal Throne*** (TSR). Wonderfully detailed world of Tekumel, with intricate religions.

Laws, Robin D., ***GURPS Fantasy II — The Mad Lands*** (Steve Jackson Games, 1992). Weird maltheism — the gods are evil, or simply chaotic, and are avoided, *not* worshipped.

Schroeck, Robert M., ***GURPS Werewolf: The Apocalypse*** (Steve Jackson Games, 1993). Rich use of symbol and ceremony.

Filmography

This is a very subjective list. Undoubtedly, some of your favorites have been omitted. All but one or two of these movies are available on video.

Agnes of God (1985). Mystery set in a convent, interesting because of the clash between Jane Fonda's ultra-rational psychiatrist and Anne Bancroft as the Mother Superior defending the faith.

Angel Heart (1987). Mysterious Robert De Niro launches two-bit detective Mickey Rourke at the beginning of a twisted "deal-with-the-devil" plot.

Black Robe (?). Jesuit attempts to convert natives of 17th-century Canada. Lots of culture clash; very historically accurate.

Clash of the Titans (1981). Greek mythology brought to life, with nifty effects from Ray Harryhausen. Not very true to the classics, but good inspiration for a campaign where the gods meddle in mortals' daily affairs.

The Greatest Story Ever Told (1965). The story of Christ, with Max von Sydow in the title role (he later played the Devil in *Needful Things*, proof of the ultimate in acting range). Length varies with edition.

Jesus Christ Superstar (1973). Webber-Rice rock opera brought to the screen, with a few very odd visuals (why is Judas being chased by a tank?).

Jesus of Montreal (1989) Modern-day Passion-play interpretation with lots of different viewpoints; historical and archeological references are very accurate. Not available on video.

The Last Temptation of Christ (1988). Many protesters hated this adaptation of a Greek novel because it presented a Christ who had doubts about his mission.

Leap of Faith (1992). Overlooked great film, with Steve Martin as a con man masquerading as a faith healer. Interesting insights into the nature (and power) of faith.

Life of Brian (1979). This movie — possibly Monty Python's best — offended lots of folks, most of whom hadn't seen it. Incredibly funny, and much more of a political satire than any sort of blasphemy.

Name of the Rose (1986). Sean Connery struggles with lots of religious infighting in this medieval murder mystery.

Oh, God! (1977). George Burns is the Big Guy Himself; John Denver is the meek grocer chosen to be his modern-day prophet. Much better than it had any right to be.

The Rapture (1993). Mimi Rogers is amazing as a woman who fills her empty life with fundamentalism, only to fail the test on the Last Day. Watch for a cameo from the Four Horsemen of the Apocalypse.

The Seventh Sign (1988). Pregnant Demi Moore believes the Apocalypse is at hand, and that her boarder wants her baby for end-of-the-world plot.

The Ten Commandments (1956). Cecil B. DeMille's epic story of Moses and the Exodus from Egypt. Worth watching for the parting of the Red Sea alone.

The Wicker Man (1973). Edward Woodward is perfect as a pious Scottish police sergeant investigating a disappearance on a small island. The evidence of paganism shocks him more and more. Look for the 103-minute version.

Wings of Desire (1988). Two angels wander around West Berlin and muse on what it would like to be human

GLOSSARY

adherent: a follower, believer or worshiper.

afterlife: the state of existence after death.

agnosticism: belief that the divine is unknowable.

alms: food, clothes, money and so on given to the poor.

androgynous: having both male and female nature.

animism: belief that all reality is inhabited by souls and spirits.

anoint: to put oil on to consecrate; usually part of a ceremony.

antiphon: a song or chant that is sung in response to another.

apocalypse: a prophecy or divine revelation; particularly concerning the end of the world.

apotheosis: the elevation of a person or principle to divine honor; deification.

ascetism: self-denial as a means of spiritual discipline.

astrology: divination based upon the positions of the stars and planets.

astronomy: a science concerning the properties of celestial bodies.

atheism: disbelief in the existence of the divine.

belief: a conviction that certain things are true; trust or confidence; see also *faith*.

benevolence: kindliness; a tendency to do good.

berdache: a transvestite male North American Indian, who assumed the dress, role and status of a woman and was accepted as a woman; often thought to possess spiritual powers.

bless: to ask divine favor for; to consecrate; to grant; to glorify; to protect.

cadence: rhythmic sequence or flow of sounds in language.

canon: regulation or dogma as decreed by church council.

celebrant: one who performs rites, rituals or ceremonies.

celestial: relating to the sky, heavens or divinity.

celibate: abstaining from sexual intercourse.

ceremony: a formal act prescribed by tradition, ritual and protocol; a gathering of clerics and worshipers for religious purpose, often including the casting of a clerical spell.

chant: a repetitive liturgical melody.

chaotic: unpredictable, irregular, confused.

chastity: the state of being innocent of sexual intercourse; virginal.

cleric: an ordained individual who serves a form of divinity or belief.

code: a system of rules for expected behavior.

commune: to partake in a common rite or ritual; to experience the divine in the company of others.

conscience: individual and personal sense of morality and ethics.

consciousness: power of self-knowledge; state of self-awareness.

consecrate: to make or declare holy or blessed; to dedicate an object or area to the divine; to focus the deity's power within an object or area.

cosmology: the structure and nature of the universe, or a system of belief concerning it.

covenant: contract, promise or agreement

creation myth: stories and beliefs relating to the act of creation.

cult: a religious or quasi-religious sect, frequently living communally, led by a charismatic person with unorthodox or extreme views.

curia: the administrative body of a church, such as the Roman Catholic Church, made up of various courts, officials, departments, etc., under the authority of the head of the church.

demigod: semi-divine, immortal spiritual being.

desecrate: to violate the sanctity of a person, place or object.

destiny: an externally influenced, predetermined course of future events.

divination: the art or practice of determining future events.

divine: relating to gods or deities.

divine intervention: a direct manifestation of the deity's power or person.

doctrine: principles and laws stating fundamental beliefs and policies.

dogma: a doctrine accepted to be a divinely revealed truth.

dualism: a theory that reality consists of two irreducible elements.

ecstasy: a state of being beyond reason and self-control.

enlightenment: a state of illumination, insight and realization.

entropy: disorder and change leading to an ultimate state of inertness.

equinox: the time of the year when night and day are of equal length.

eulogy: a commendatory formal statement or set oration.

excommunicate: to cast out and separate from the community.

expiate: to atone for sin or offense, usually by suffering punishment.

fade: a deity's loss of divine power within the world, usually due to lack of followers.

faith: allegiance, duty, belief and trust in a principle or divine being.

fanaticism: excessive enthusiasm and intense unquestioning devotion.

fast: to abstain or eat sparingly from some foods.

fate: an inevitable and often adverse outcome or condition.

festival: a time of celebration marked by special observances.

ghost dance: 19th-century North American Indian ceremony connected with a messianic movement.

glossolalia: the ecstatic emission of (usually) unintelligible sounds, which some view as manifesting a deep religious experience.

hallow: sanctify; consecrate; to make holy; to honor as sacred.

haze: to harass, ridicule or criticize.

heresy: adherence to belief or opinion contrary to church dogma.

heretic: a dissenter from official and authorized belief.

holy war: a war waged by religious partisans to propagate or defend their faith.

incense: material used to create a fragrant smell when burned.

indulgence: partial or total release from divine temporal punishment still due for a sin that has been forgiven.

intercession: prayer, petition or entreaty in favor of another.

invest: to endow with qualities, attributes, etc.; to install in office; to furnish with power, privilege or authority.

Judgment Day: the end of the world, accompanied by the deity's final accounting of people's souls.

karma: concept that a one's acts hold spiritual consequences.

kismet: Arabic concept of fate or destiny.

kiss of peace: handshake, embrace, etc., to show mutual love, union, peace, usually given during a service.

knell: slow sounding of a bell; often a symbol of death.

kosher: fit to eat according to Jewish dietary laws.

laity, lay: ordinary people, as contrasted with clergy.

laud: praise; worship at dawn; morning prayer.

libation: ritual pouring out of wine, oil or other liquid, on the ground, an altar or elsewhere.

liturgy: collection of prescribed forms for public worship.

maltheism: the worship of a self-proclaimed evil deity.

meditation: to calm and focus one's thoughts.

medium: an individual who acts as a channel of communication with the spirit world.

mendicant: one who begs for alms; a member of a religious order who holds no personal or community property and lives mostly on alms.

messianic: centering around a person expected to save or liberate a country or a people.

metaphysics: philosophical study concerning the real nature of things.

miracle: an extraordinary event caused by divine intervention.

missionary: a person undertaking a religious mission to carry the faith into new lands and recruit new believers.

monasticism: a discipline of faith involving seclusion and ascetism.

monotheism: the belief and worship of a single god.

motif: a thematic element, influence or stimulus.

mysticism: experience of mystical union with ultimate or divine reality.

neophyte: a beginner, novice, new convert.

nirvana: state of complete enlightenment; the attainment of complete freedom from all worldly concerns.

novice: a person on probation with a religious order before taking vows; a beginner, apprentice, neophyte.

oracle: a prophetic response given by a representative of a deity in answer to specific inquiry, thought to be divine in origin.

oracular: relating to an oracle or prophecy.

ordeal: a means to determine guilt through trial or pain.

ordain: to invest or appoint officially to a position of religious authority.

pantheon: a group of associated deities.

penance: an act of self-abasement, mortification or punishment.

pilgrimage: a journey to a shrine or other sacred or special place.

plane: a realm of existence removed from the earth, often inhabited by spirits or deities.

polytheism: the belief and worship of more than one god.

priest: a cleric whose duties revolve around the welfare of the faithful.

prophecy: a prediction or divinely inspired declaration.

proselytism: the act of encouraging conversion to a faith or belief.

psychopomp: an escort of the soul and the dead.

purgatory: a place (or time) after death for a soul to be purified before continuing its journey to its reward.

querent: one who asks or questions, especially one who consults an astrologer or other diviner.

reincarnation: rebirth in new bodies or forms of life.

relic: object of sacred reverence; portion or fragment of a holy object or person.

religion: a system of beliefs, causes and principles held to by faith.

reliquary: a repository for relics.

ritual: the established form for a ceremony.

sacred: holy, entitled to reverence and respect.

sacrifice: an offering.

sanctity: saintliness; holiness; the measure of the deity's power in a given locale.

scarification: the act or process of creating marks and scars.

schism: the act or result of dividing a church into factions.

scriptures: holy, sacred or revered writings.

secular: relating to worldly or temporal concerns, nonclerical.

seer: a person of extraordinary moral and spiritual insight.

shaman: a person able to break through and contact other planes and spirits.

shrine: a holy place or receptacle.

soul: the animating essence of life, also called spirit.

taboo: holy, forbidden, or set apart.

tenet: a principle, belief or doctrine.

testament: a tangible proof or tribute, a witnessed account.

theocracy: a state or people ruled by a deity or a priestly class claiming divine authority.

totem: animal, plant or crafted object symbolizing a person or people; a tribe's guardian or ancestral spirit.

tutelary: relating to a guardian or guardianship.

unbeliever: a person who does not accept a, or a particular, religious belief.

unholy: not hallowed or consecrated; profane or impious.

veneration: worship and reverence.

vestment: religious and ceremonial clothing.

vigil: a period of testing, watching or surveillance.

visionary: able or likely to see visions.

vocation: a summons or strong inclination, a divine call to religious life.

ylem: in some cosmologies, the primordial material from which all elements supposedly derived.

INDEX

Printed in Great Britain
by Amazon

52076750R00099